Shade
Gardening

The TIME LIFE
Complete Gardener

Shade
Gardening

By the Editors of Time-Life Books
ALEXANDRIA, VIRGINIA

The Consultant

Robert S. Hebb is a horticultural consultant, garden designer, author, and frequent lecturer on gardening. He received a diploma of horticulture from the Royal Botanic Gardens in Kew, then became assistant horticulturist for Harvard University's Arnold Arboretum, where he wrote the pioneering book *Low Maintenance Perennials*. Hebb has been director of horticulture for the Mary Flagler Cary Arboretum of the New York Botanical Garden and executive director of the Lewis Ginter Botanical Garden in Richmond, Virginia. The recipient of the Massachusetts Horticultural Society Silver Medal for leadership in American horticulture, Hebb is the author of numerous works on low-maintenance gardening and oversees several estate gardens in the Richmond area.

Library of Congress Cataloging in Publication Data
Shade gardening / by the editors of Time-Life Books.
p. cm.—(The Time-Life complete gardener)
Includes bibliographical references (p.) and index.
ISBN 0-7835-4107-4
1. Gardening in the shade. I. Time-Life Books. II. Series
SB434.7.S46 1995   635.9'54—dc20   95-35804   CIP
First printing. Printed in U.S.A.
Published simultaneously in Canada.
School and library distribution by Time-Life Education, P.O. Box 85026, Richmond, Virginia 23285-5026.

This volume is one of a series of comprehensive gardening books that cover garden design, choosing plants for the garden, planting and propagating, and planting diagrams.

Time-Life Books is a division of **TIME LIFE INC.**

PRESIDENT and CEO: John M. Fahey Jr.

TIME-LIFE BOOKS

Managing Editor: Roberta Conlan

Director of Design: Michael Hentges
Editorial Production Manager: Ellen Robling
Director of Operations: Eileen Bradley
Director of Photography and Research:
John Conrad Weiser
Senior Editors: Russell B. Adams Jr., Janet Cave,
Lee Hassig, Robert Somerville, Henry Woodhead
Library: Louise D. Forstall

PRESIDENT: John D. Hall

Vice President, Director of New Product Development:
Neil Kagan
Associate Director, New Product Development:
Quentin S. McAndrew
Marketing Director: James Gillespie
Vice President, Book Production: Marjann Caldwell
Production Manager: Marlene Zack
Quality Assurance Manager: Miriam Newton

THE TIME-LIFE COMPLETE GARDENER

Editorial Staff for *Shade Gardening*

SERIES EDITOR: Janet Cave
Deputy Editors: Sarah Brash, Jane Jordan
Administrative Editor: Roxie France-Nuriddin
Art Director: Alan Pitts
Picture Editor: Jane Jordan
Text Editor: Paul Mathless
Associate Editors/Research-Writing: Katya Sharpe,
Mary-Sherman Willis
Technical Art Assistant: Sue Pratt
Senior Copyeditors: Anne Farr (principal),
Colette Stockum
Picture Coordinator: David Herod
Editorial Assistant: Donna Fountain
Special Contributors: Susan Gregory Thomas
(research); Vilasini Balakrishnan, Susan S. Blair,
Catriona Tudor Erler, Marie Hofer, Jocelyn Lindsay
(research-writing); Marge duMond, Marfé Ferguson-
Delano (editing); John Drummond (art); Lina B. Burton
(index).

Correspondents: Christine Hinze (London), Christina
Lieberman (New York). Valuable assistance was also
provided by Liz Brown (New York).

Cover: *Foliage predominates in this Oregon garden. Golden Taxus baccata 'Repandens Aurea' shares space beneath a maple tree with yellowish green Vancouveria hexandra, silvery-leaved Lamium maculatum 'Silbergroschen', and Hosta 'Gold Standard'.*
End papers: *A clump of big-leaved Ligularia dentata 'Desdemona' anchors this shady Northwest retreat, where a wide variety of foliage provides interest as well as color. Feathery spikes of astilbe, Geranium palmatum (background), and Meconopsis betonicifolia (foreground) brighten the scene.* **Title page:** *In Virginia, the heart-shaped blooms of Dicentra eximia dangle above blue-green leaves in the shelter of an Osage-orange tree.*

CONTENTS

Chapter One
GARDENING IN THE SHADE   6
The Nature of Shade   8
The Shade Garden Room   12
Shade near the House   14
Shade in the Garden's Middle Reaches   18
Gardening in a Shady Woodland   20

Chapter Two
FOLIAGE—NUMBER ONE IN THE SHADE   24
Crafting a Garden Design with Foliage Plants   26
Trees for the Shade Garden   28
Shrubs for Shady Designs   31
Designing with Herbaceous Plants   34
Ground Covers for Shady Spots   40

Gallery
SATISFACTION IN THE SHADE   43
A Guide to the Gardens   54

Chapter Three
LETTING YOUR SHADE GARDEN FLOWER   58
A Riot of Color   60
Planting for Year-Round Color   64
Adding Flowers to Shade   68

Chapter Four
PLANTING AND CARING FOR YOUR GARDEN   72
Putting in a Shade Garden   74
Maintaining a Shade Garden   79
Pruning   82

Reference
Answers to Common Questions   86
Troubleshooting Guide   92
Plant Selection Guide   96
Zone Map/Guide to Plant Names   102
Encyclopedia of Plants   104
Acknowledgments and Picture Credits   152
Bibliography   153
Index   154

CHAPTER ONE

Gardening in the Shade

Shade falls on just about every property at some time, and a large amount of it can leave a gardener feeling unlucky. But don't despair. The virtues of shade far outweigh the few restrictions it imposes.

Whether it is cast by trees or by the walls of a house, shade can make a garden into a refreshing place—a haven from heat and harsh sunlight. Shaded spots need not be dark, dank places. Even a patch that sees only short periods of sun, or perhaps no direct sun at all, can still collect enough light to grow sun-loving plants, such as the pale blue delphinium nestled among violets, columbines, and enormous foxgloves in the partial shade of the California garden at right.

In this book you will find out how to use shade to best advantage, both for its practical benefits and as a design element. You will learn ways of analyzing the light conditions on your property and, if need be, altering them. And you will discover the large array of plants from which to create a sublimely gratifying shade garden.

A. *Chrysanthemum parthenium (Tanacetum parthenium) (5)*
B. *Impatiens spp. (18)*
C. *Digitalis purpurea 'Foxy' (24)*
D. *Campanula poscharskyana (8)*
E. *Viola odorata (20)*
F. *Aquilegia atropurpurea (15)*
G. *Thalictrum simplex (5)*
H. *Delphinium sp. (1)*

The key lists each plant type and the number of plants needed to replicate the garden shown opposite. The letters and numbers above refer to the type of plant and the number sited in an area.

The Nature of Shade

Whether you live on a small city plot that is hemmed in by fences and neighboring houses or on a suburban property where saplings planted decades ago have matured into sizable trees, you must, as a gardener, come to terms with shade. The best way to start is to understand the practical benefits it offers.

Shade can be a gardener's best ally in hot climates. Not only does it provide a cool retreat from the sun; it also, by moderating extremes of heat, broadens the range of plants you can grow. The temperature under a tree, for example, may be 15° cooler than out in the sun.

To survive in the South, all but the toughest plants need some relief from the intense summer heat. For example, the delicate petals of *Clematis lanuginosa* 'Nelly Moser' can fade from a dark pink to a bleached-out tinge of color if they are not protected from strong sunlight. And although plants tend to bear fewer flowers in the shade than they would if they were growing in full sun, the blossoms will last longer. Even sun-loving annuals such as *Cleome* (spider plant) will have longer-lasting blooms when they are grown in partial shade.

Not just flower petals but also foliage may need the protection of shade. For example, the frosty blue leaves of *Hosta* 'Krossa Regal' (plantain lily) may turn brown in the direct sun of the South. *Cimicifuga* (bugbane) exposed to sun can collapse and wither away, even if the plant has been given plenty of water.

Another tantalizing benefit of shade is that no matter where you live, shade cuts down on maintenance chores. First, a shady garden needs less water. In the cool shelter of a tree or wall, moisture evaporates from the soil more slowly and needs replenishing less often.

Pruning becomes less of a chore as well. Plants that have evolved in the low light of the forest tend to grow more slowly and need less cutting back than sun lovers. If you choose plants that are conditioned to shade and grow them in adequate soil with ample space around each one, you should be able to leave them undisturbed for many years.

A shade garden will also have less of a struggle with certain pests—aphids, mites, and scale—although you may have to anticipate other pests and diseases that are partial to shade plants *(Troubleshooting Guide, pages 92-95)*.

Shade Foliage and Flowers

In addition to lightening a gardener's chores, shade also confers design benefits—in the types of plants you can grow and in the impact of shade itself on garden design.

Shade-tolerant species are among the most unusual and beautiful of all garden plants, producing leaves and flowers in a vast range of sizes, textures, and colors. In shade, you can grow the spectacular *Gunnera manicata* (giant rhubarb), with leaves that are sometimes as wide as 6 feet, and the minuscule *Soleirolia soleirolii* (baby's-tears), which carpets the ground with shiny green leaves that are as small as the nail on your little finger. You can also choose from an array of leaf textures and shapes ranging from the lacy brocades of ferns, astilbes, corydalis, and *Dicentra* (bleeding heart) to the broad masses of *Ligularia* (leopard plant), *Rodgersia*, hydrangea, and *Mahonia* (Oregon grape).

Much of the color in a shade garden will come from foliage, especially from variegated leaves. Varieties of hosta, *Pulmonaria* (lungwort), *Hedera* (ivy), *Elaeagnus* (oleaster), *Ilex* (holly), *Ajuga* (bugleweed), *Euonymus* (spindle tree), *Vinca* (periwinkle), and *Lamium* (dead nettle) are striped, speckled, or blotched with cream or white. Caladium, the ultimate shade foliage plant, is splashed with tones of cream, pink, purple, orange-red, or scarlet.

In addition to the marvels of shade foliage, you will also find a delightful assortment of flowers that are completely at home in shade. Some of the earliest-blooming plants in the garden do best when they are out of direct sunlight: perennials such as *Helleborus* (hellebore), lungwort, *Primula* (primrose), *Galanthus* (snowdrop), and *Scilla* (squill); the flowering shrubs *Hamamelis* (witch hazel), rhododendron, and *Corylopsis* (winter hazel); and the small trees *Cornus* (dogwood) and *Cercis* (redbud).

In the diffused light of shade, flower colors appear more saturated. Whites and pale yellows shine against the dark background of a shady spot and do not look faded, as they might in full sun. Yet strong contrasts among colors are toned down. Orange with blue, or yellow with purple, which might be eye-popping in strong light, become mellow in shade.

A FLOWERY OASIS AT WOOD'S EDGE
This Virginia garden sited between a sun-streaked lawn and a dappled woodland shows how plants with varying light requirements can be neighbors. Parts of the garden get enough light for such sun lovers as Achillea 'Moonshine', ornamental onion, Yucca filamentosa, variegated maiden grass, and roses. These coexist happily with such shade stalwarts as Hosta 'Gold Standard', ligularia, hardy geranium, and hellebore, planted to the left of the bed.

Analyzing Shade

To incorporate shade into a coherent garden design, you must first know what type of shade you have. You must understand the varied ways it manifests itself and how to track the shade footprint as it sweeps across your property from hour to hour and from season to season.

Shade comes mainly from two sources: structures and plants. A third, more ephemeral, shade maker is the atmosphere—clouds, fog, and even pollution, which can filter out substantial sunlight. This last source of shade is the reason cities generally receive less sun than dry, windy, and high-altitude areas.

Evaluating the light that reaches your plants is an inexact science. The common measures are duration and intensity, both of which vary by time of day, season, and latitude—the position of your garden relative to the equator *(pages 10-11)*.

Duration, however changeable it may be, can nonetheless be gauged through diligent observation. Intensity, on the other hand, requires a bit more thought. Sunlight is least intense in the morning, for three reasons: The sun is low in the sky; the earth is cool from the hours without sun; and the humidity near the ground is high, scattering some of the light.

The sun is at its most intense at noon because that is when its rays travel almost straight down through the atmosphere with minimal deflection or dispersion and shadows are at their shortest. By afternoon, although the angle of the sun's rays is once again becoming acute, the sun remains intense because the day's heat has evaporated most of the moisture from the ground surface.

Categories of Shade

A useful way to make sense of these complexities is to organize shade into general types based on a combination of duration and intensity:

- **Partial shade.** This is the sunniest shade, in which an area receives up to 6 hours of direct sun, including 4 or more hours in the morning, but lies in shadow the rest of the day. Many plants listed as requiring full shade will tolerate partial shade if the soil is kept moist, especially in cooler climates. And many sun plants will adapt well to partial shade. Note, however, that if 4 or more of those 6 hours of sun occur in the afternoon instead of the morning, the area is considered to be in full sun.

- **Filtered or dappled shade.** The sun's light is screened through the open foliage of high-branched trees or through latticework structures. It shines in shifting patterns all day, thus striking with diminished intensity. Most plants will thrive in dappled shade, though sun lovers might produce fewer flowers than they would in full sun.

- **Full shade.** Direct sunlight never reaches an area in full shade. Some full shade may be deep and dense, and few plants will survive there. But an area in full shade can also experience considerable ambient or reflected light and sky shine. These conditions often occur on the north side of a building, fence, hedge, or tree. Shade-tolerant plants will grow in this kind of full shade if they have enough air circulation and moisture. By contrast, if trees are spaced too close together or include species with dense roots on or just below the surface, the soil will have little water or nutrients for other plants. This so-called dry shade condition is the worst kind of full shade for gardeners.

Planning a Shade Garden

As straightforward as these categories seem, probably no environmental condition on a property is as hard to quantify as shade. It not only shifts through the day and year but also deepens and spreads as trees mature and suddenly disappears when a tree dies or is removed. So give yourself as much time as possible to study the shade on your property through its many manifestations before doing anything irrevocable to change it. Look at the garden in winter, when it is least shaded, and in summer, when plants are in full leaf. Map out where the sunlight falls through the day and through the year. Look for indicators, such as the presence of moss, that might point out shadows in places where you simply never noticed them.

Tracking Shade Patterns

The sun will arc over your property not only from east to west each day but also from a position starting low to the south in spring, moving higher overhead in summer, then low to the south again in fall. Thus the shadows cast by major shade makers on or around your land will shift continually throughout the year.

The length and location of these shadows will also depend on your position relative to the equator. Because of the earth's curve, the farther north you are, the more slanted will be the sun's rays reaching you, and the longer the shadows.

The illustration at right shows shade patterns at different times of the day in spring and fall. Summer shadows are shown opposite.

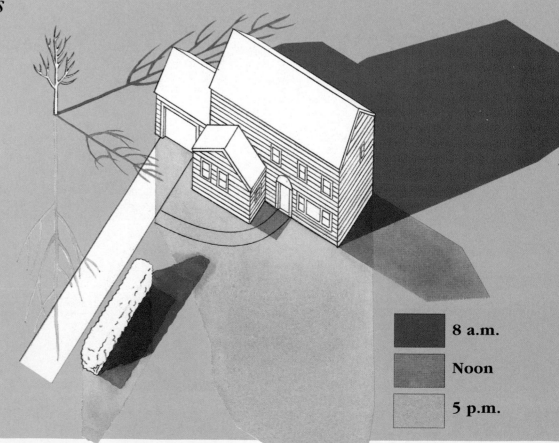

▓	**8 a.m.**
▒	**Noon**
░	**5 p.m.**

If there are any high walls or large trees that substantially block out light, consider making changes. You could paint a dark wall a pale color to reflect more light, or prune large trees to thin out the leafy canopy *(pages 84-85)*. A more drastic step is to remove a tree. Plan this action carefully, however—tree removal can be costly and is, of course, permanent. Keep your best shade trees, especially those with deep roots and small leaves that don't block sun and rain. Those preferred for moderate climates are oak *(Quercus)*, Kentucky yellowwood *(Cladrastis lutea)*, and black tupelo *(Nyssa sylvatica)*; olive *(Olea)* and loblolly pine *(Pinus taeda)* are desirable in warm climates; and bald cypress *(Taxodium distichum)* works well in boggy soil.

The bane of the shade garden is shallow-rooted trees with dense leaf canopies that rob underlying plants not only of light but also of moisture and nourishment. The greediest types are beech *(Fagus)*, elm *(Ulmus)*, and the particularly troublesome Norway, sugar, and silver maples *(Acer platanoides, A. saccharum,* and *A. saccharinum,* respectively)*. Remove elms and silver maples and arrive at a modus vivendi with the others by making a raised bed around the tree *(page 77)* or, as a last resort, by trimming the roots *(page 75)*. Note, however, that trimmed tree roots may reinvade in a single season. In this case, a container garden at the base of the tree may be the best alternative.

Recognizing Shade Lovers

Shade plants have evolved to compete effectively *for the limited light of a woodland or rain forest. Generally, their leaves, like those of this Hosta 'Frances Williams', are large, dark, and flat, enabling them to absorb the maximum possible light for photosynthesis. The surfaces also shed rainwater easily, which helps them resist disease. Shade plants conserve energy by producing fewer flowers and fruit.*

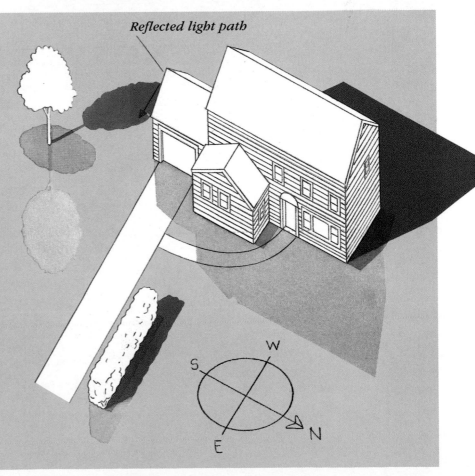

Reflected light path

In spring and fall (left), shadows are long. *Both the house and the hedge on this property—located at latitude 38°N, which stretches from Washington, D.C., to San Francisco—throw a small patch of all-day shade along their northern side year round. But during these seasons, much larger shadows begin in the west in early morning (green shadows), shorten considerably at noon (red shadows), and lengthen to the east in the afternoon (blue shadows). With the sun low in the sky to the south at these times, the northern side of the house and the hedge stay chilly. The soil and the plants residing in their shadows are thus protected from cycles of freezing and thawing.*

The same property in summer (right) receives far more sunlight, *as the shadows shrink closer to house and hedge. Full shade still exists along the northern wall and on the north side of the hedge, where morning, noon, and afternoon shadows overlap. But south-facing vertical surfaces bear the brunt of unrelieved sunshine throughout the day and reflect it back to the ground. Thus the shade under the tree, though full, is quite bright. In the morning and afternoon, the sun's rays, striking at a slant, cast longer shadows than at noon. But with surface moisture dissipated by the afternoon, the sun burns hotter, and plants getting a western exposure need extra water.*

The Shade Garden Room

Shade, by its very nature, infuses a given space with attenuated light, thus producing a sharp contrast with the sunlit spaces around it. For this reason we are able to think of shade as creating "rooms" in a garden.

The architecture of a shade room consists of plants or structures such as trees or tall shrubs, walls, or fences forming vertical planes, or "walls," and woody or herbaceous plants of varying heights forming horizontal layers. The framework of the room begins generally with a ceiling or canopy of tall trees overlying a tier of smaller understory trees. This structure is followed by furnishings of successively shorter shrubs and herbaceous plants and is finished with a plush carpet of ground covers.

The Highest Tier

At the topmost level, the leafy canopy and network of branches of tall shade trees establish the mood of the garden room. A dense, low-hanging canopy will produce a dark, somber space with cool, damp air. By contrast, a high canopy of arched branches can feel like the vaulted ceiling of a cathedral.

You can raise the canopy by limbing up the branches of tall trees *(pages 84-85)*. With further pruning you can open up the canopy to allow glimpses of sky and shafts of light to penetrate. The cheerfully dappled pattern of light and shade that results will not only add visual interest but will also give you more leeway for installing a variety of plants.

Shade created by vertical elements—the walls of the room—can be trickier to manipulate. While buildings and brick or stone walls are more or less permanent and unchangeable, you can wield some influence over such vertical shade makers as fences and the barriers formed by rows of tree trunks or shrubs. Masses of greenery can be made lighter and more open with pruning; tall hedges can be lowered to let in light. Even a solid fence, if it has an oppressively dark effect, can be remodeled to let some light pass through, or it can be replaced with a trellis.

Vines and climbing plants are the curtains and draperies of the shade room, serving as backdrops or screens. Many vines, such as clematis and jasmine, will keep to a moderate height

and flower in partial shade. Others, such as climbing roses, are sun lovers that can start in shade but will clamber to the highest point to find the light they need.

Furnishing the Middle Layer

Smaller understory trees and shrubs act as the heavy furniture of the shade room. They occupy the midstory, their profiles and spatial interrelations establishing the interior layout.

On this level, too, you can have an effect, manipulating existing plantings to alter the overall floor plan and light patterns of the room. You can, for example, arborize a shrub, carefully pruning it to create a diminutive tree that will shelter perennials and other ground-level plants *(page*

SHAPE AND TEXTURE DEFINE A GARDEN ROOM
In the partial shade of this garden near Lake Oswego, Illinois, a striking column of Irish yew and other dense understory shrubs and trees establish walls around tiered clusters of bird's-nest spruce.

19). You can also transplant established shrubs to other locations. The great diversity among shade-tolerant plants gives you the opportunity to use new plantings to design your garden room to meet your precise wishes for color and texture *(pages 14-17)*.

Covering the Ground

The floor of your garden room should be cushioned with vegetation or mulch to make it easier to walk on, to halt erosion, or simply to alleviate the monotony of bare earth. Very low growing ground covers such as *Asarum* (wild ginger), ajuga, periwinkle, and *Mazus* can all be used to serve this purpose, providing color and texture and acting as a living mulch around other plants. And, of course, a lawn that has been developed from well-chosen turf-grass varieties can flourish in partial shade and provide a durable walking surface *(pages 19 and 40-41)*.

But there is yet another choice. Given the right growing conditions, you can install an unusual and attractive moss lawn. Mossy expanses like the one shown below thrive in shade, provided the climate is cool and the soil is moist and acid. Moss presents a velvety, slightly springy surface, and some species are capable of withstanding moderate foot traffic. An expanse of shady ground can be covered with several varieties of moss, adding visual interest to the scene with changing textures and multiple shades of green. And a moss lawn requires little maintenance once it is established *(box, page 78)*.

If you have trouble growing even moss, cover the ground with a wood-nugget or gravel mulch. It will keep plant roots cool and moist, suppress weeds, and keep mud from splashing on plant leaves during a rain.

DAPPLED SHADOWS ON A MOSS LAWN
Cool, moist shade beneath tall oaks is ideal for growing moss and other understory plants in this New Jersey garden. Gravel accentuates the shape of the island beds, and a tiny birdbath reflects a glimmer of light.

Shade near the House

Shade gives definition to a property, making it possible to discern three distinct areas, or zones, each with unique characteristics. An inner zone, the area immediately around the house, will have periods of shade on its east and west sides and permanent shadow on its north side. A middle zone will probably be an open space devoted to lawn and perhaps broken up by shade trees or small ornamental trees. The outer zone, on the perimeter of the property, is likely to have large shade-casting trees and shrubs.

The inner zone serves as a transitional space between the house and the rest of the property. From within the house, this is the part of the garden you can see best and the part that frames your views to the farther reaches of the property. For most homeowners it is also the most heavily used part of the garden, a place to put a table and chairs for outdoor relaxation, dining, and entertaining. When paved with flagstone or brick, it becomes an extension of the house itself, another room.

Shade in the Inner Zone

Shade in the inner zone will come from the house but may be increased by nearby trees planted for that purpose. Oaks, fast-growing maples, *Acer pseudoplatanus* (sycamore maple), *Aesculus hippocastanum* (horse chestnut), and *Liriodendron tulipifera* (tulip tree) can offer relief from a sweltering summer sun. In winter, they shed their leaves to allow the sun to warm the house.

But inner-zone trees can become a problem if they grow to the point that the shade they create is cold and dank, or if their large branches closely overhang the house, preventing the roof from drying out after a rain. In addition, oaks, maples, and sycamores can fill your gutters and blanket your patio with thick, heavy leaves.

If you plan to retain your mature shade trees, hire an arborist to assess their structural integrity, secure the heavy branches with cables if need be, and thin the branches out—an operation that should be repeated every 4 to 5 years to keep the trees healthy, manageable, and shapely.

Alternatively, you can replace the large trees with smaller understory trees such as dogwood, redbud, magnolia, and flowering cherry, which provide dappled shade and may be more in scale with the space near the house.

Evergreen trees and shrubs give more consistent shade than do deciduous shade makers. Aside from holly, try *Ligustrum* (privet), pittosporum, or the hollylike *Osmanthus* (devilwood). For dappled shade, look for medium-sized conifers that have an open or umbrella-shaped habit, such as *Pinus parviflora* (Japanese white pine), *P. rigida* (pitch pine), or, in Zone 9, *P. pinea* (umbrella pine).

Another source of shade for the house itself is the vines and climbers you can train up its walls. These decorative plants, such as *Parthenocissus*

A SHADY HIDEAWAY ON A SUMMER DAY
Azaleas, caladiums, and a climbing hydrangea line a shady passageway between two houses in Richmond, Virginia. This space—just wide enough for a hammock—is irresistible on a blinding, sweltering midsummer afternoon.

quinquefolia (Virginia creeper), climbing hydrangea, and Boston ivy, can clothe the side of a house completely and insulate it from the sun's heat.

Shade Structures

If the inner zone of your garden does not possess a leafy canopy of tree branches, you can build a shade structure onto or near the house. The cheapest and least elaborate of these would be an awning stretched over a light framework of wooden or metal poles anchored to the ground. A canvas covering, opaque and waterproof, would create a dense, dry shade but could be rolled out of the way when desired. So-called shade cloth, available at hardware stores, is like a heavy mosquito netting and will give you filtered light and some protection from the rain. Or if you prefer something a bit more substantial, consider woven bamboo matting to cover the frame: This inexpensive removable roofing material casts an attractive mottled shade.

Another option is to grow vines across an over-head trellis or arbor. Wisteria will dangle lovely scented blooms in spring, and grapevines produce ripened fruit at the end of summer. Both vines are deciduous and allow the sun to filter through in the winter. In hot climates, evergreen vines work best. Try bougainvillea, fragrant *Clematis armandii* (evergreen clematis), or *Gelsemium sempervirens* (yellow jessamine).

A more permanent shade-making structure is a lath house. This is a freestanding or attached shed of vertical supports and ceiling panels built from 2- or 3-inch-wide wooden slats spaced an inch or so apart. The slats are oriented north to south so that the shadows move with the sun. Unlike a trellis or an arbor, a lath house is designed to make dappled shade by itself, without help from covering vines. However, it may serve as a trellis as well.

Shade in the City Garden

Instead of needing to create shade near the house, city dwellers must cope with an inner zone that is plunged in gloom and dampness. The problem is

A MOON GATE FRAMING A GARDEN VIEW
Seen through a gate opening, the vista down the length of this narrow shade garden in Washington, D.C., is broken up by trees, shrubs, and even a granite boulder, giving the impression of a large space full of inviting nooks and crannies. A brick path winds sinuously toward the rear and out of sight. Sunlight filters through the foliage of a large dogwood and casts dappled shade over small Japanese maples, azaleas, ferns, hostas, and variegated liriope.

15

compounded if yours is a small plot surrounded by large, light-blocking buildings or towering trees on your neighbors' property. In the case of the trees, you may be able to negotiate some judicious pruning with an obliging neighbor—though it won't solve the problem of encroaching roots.

Many city gardens suffer from poor soil and ventilation as well as from deep shade, making normal gardening virtually impossible. A practical solution here is to pave over the site, creating a terrace or courtyard decorated with container plants.

Fill pots and planters with shade-friendly annuals and perennials. You can also grow small shrubs in pots, such as yew and evergreen holly for their berries and *Pieris* (andromeda) and rhododendron for their flowers. Even small trees will grow in large planters or tubs, and in partial shade they will bloom. Try early- and late-blooming magnolias, spring-flowering cherry, and *Malus sylvestris* (crab apple).

Baskets of flowers hanging under a porch roof or from tree branches add a touch of welcome color. Try small-flowered bedding begonias, packed to overflowing in a basket, or the luscious tuberous begonias that naturally cascade over the edge

of your patio, for instance. The outer zone may be nothing more than a hedge that screens the sight of your neighbor's window, or a vine-covered fence or wall. By consciously creating areas of sun and shade, however, you can give definition to your small garden and create the illusion of greater space.

For example, you can blur the boundary line of the garden by planting small trees and shrubs that block your view of its edges and give the suggestion of an outer-zone planting. Fill in the back edge of your property with small understory trees such as dogwood or Japanese maple, and then underplant them with shrubs and a few perennials and ground covers.

Another technique for increasing the apparent size of a garden is to break up the view. Create a winding passageway through the garden that narrows and widens at certain points. Site some plants to move the eye toward the passageway's center: Low-growing and medium-sized shrubs will narrow the area and make visual barriers to the view beyond. At other points, widen the passageway to create a niche. Here, taller trees or a trellis arched across the pathway will frame the view.

One of these niches in an out-of-the-way corner can become a private retreat. Put in a bench where you can relax and get a new perspective on your garden. The plantings along a winding path leading to this retreat can create a great deal of interest and atmosphere—a suggestion of a forest, say, with an arrangement of ferns and woodland plants, interspersed in brighter areas with exotics such as a clump of *Agapanthus* (African lily).

Several design fundamentals apply to working in a small space. First, keep your plants in scale with the space and with each other. In a small garden, that means that the trees should be relatively small—not more than about 30 feet tall. Because space constraints may keep you from ever moving far enough away from a tree to appreciate it as a whole, consider its parts. Choose a tree for its decorative bark, its interesting profile or foliage, or its blooms. Better still, pick one that combines several of these characteristics. Remember that you have to live with it all year, not just for the 10 days or so that it might be in bloom. The more features it combines, the greater its value.

Finally, consider a few simple optical tricks: Vertical lines emphasize the narrowness of a space, so look for broad-headed trees and spreading shrubs to provide a horizontal accent. Fine-textured foliage will seem farther away than large, coarse leaves, visually enlarging a space. And cool colors—blues, violets, and greens—make a space look larger than warm colors do.

IN THE SHADE OF A MIGHTY TREE
Splashed with sap from the high branches of an 80-year-old spruce, the big blue-green leaves of Hosta sieboldiana 'Elegans' form part of an informal bed of shade-loving plants—violas, pink impatiens, and variegated Solomon's-seal—in the inner zone of this Maryland garden.

of a pot. Or mix in a pot pink-bloomed, bronze-leaved New Guinea impatiens with red 'Roy Hartley' tuberous begonias and the pink-and-purple flowers of *Fuchsia* 'Gruss aus dem Bodenthal'.

Capitalizing on a Small Space

With a small plot of land, your concept of the zones of your property must be compressed. The middle zone may be just a pool of light at the end

Shade in the Garden's Middle Reaches

A property's middle zone is the relatively sunlit, open area separating the more markedly shady inner and outer zones. It is the likeliest place for a lawn, but you may wish to accent the space with a scattering of trees, bringing cooling shade closer to the house and smoothing the transition toward denser woodland on your property's margin.

The light collected by the middle zone makes it a logical place to install a herbaceous bed or border. Any shade cast over the site only heightens your opportunity to experiment with the overall character of your planting.

Shade in Beds and Borders

It is generally true that the character of a plot of herbaceous plants grown in shade will be different from that of one grown in full sun. In shade, foliage comes more to the fore. In fact, the foliage of shade plants tends to be more interesting than that of sun-loving plants. Foremost among them are the hostas, in numerous hues of gold, silver, blue, and green, as well as colorful ferns like *Athyrium nipponicum* (painted lady fern). Some flowering plants are appreciated as much for their distinctive foliage as for their lovely blooms. For example, the lacy leaves of dicentra, astilbe, and columbine echo the ferns' graceful foliage. And mossy saxifrage, speckled pulmonaria, and scallop-edged alumroot are appealing candidates for the front of a border.

If flowers are your main goal, the flowering plants described above will perform well in partial shade. Others will bloom freely with no direct sun at all, including numerous annuals and biennials—wax begonia, impatiens, *Browallia* (bush violet), ageratum, nicotiana, foxglove, and forget-me-not, to name a few. Scores of perennials bloom in low light, including primrose and violet in full shade and daylily, bugleweed, and spring-blooming bulbs in partial shade. And even shade-

A SUNNY LAWN IN THE GARDEN'S MIDDLE ZONE
A bright patch of lawn in the midst of this Pennsylvania garden provides a refreshing change of pace from the dark green of its shade borders. The tight, rounded forms of the box bushes encircling the sundial in the foreground contrast with the open, tiered branches of the Kousa dogwood and Japanese maple in the distance.

Any planting under a tree or shrub must take into account competition from the larger plant's root system and the umbrella effect of its leaf canopy in the rain. But well-chosen companions can coexist happily. Here, a large *Rhododendron barbatum* has been pruned back to several large stems and underplanted with *Helleborus orientalis.* The rhododendron protects the hellebore from scorching sun, while the hellebore keeps the ground cool and moist.

Not all pairings work as well. Some trees suffocate small plants with their large fallen leaves. Others, like the eucalyptus and black walnut, drop leaves that are harmful to plants below and have roots that secrete toxins into the soil. In these situations, consider container plantings.

tolerant ornamental grasses such as *Briza* (quaking grass) and *Pennisetum* (fountain grass) have decorative flower heads.

A border in your garden's middle zone may lie partly in sun and partly in shade. For example, the back of the plot might be shaded by a north-facing wall, while the flowers farther forward stand clear of the shadow. If you have mapped your garden's sun and shade patterns, you can plan accordingly. Use the encyclopedia *(pages 104-151)* and the Plant Selection Guide *(pages 96-101)* to help you choose plants that are right for your light conditions and that fit in with your garden-design ideas.

Yet you needn't go strictly by the book in selecting shade plants. Some perennials listed for full sun, for example, can do fine with less light, especially in hot climates. But avoid plants with a tall habit, as they are likely to grow even taller in low light and might flop as they lean to the light. And remember that many flower heads, particularly daffodil, tend to face the strongest light and may turn away from your view if sited wrong.

The Shady Lawn

Many gardeners today are reducing the size of their lawns, preferring to plant other kinds of ground covers that take less time, water, and work to maintain. But a pool of velvety green grass in an open spot in your yard still might be irresistible.

Turf grass is a practical ground cover in a clearing set aside for play or relaxation. It is soft and resilient to walk on, and many turf-grass species can tolerate considerable traffic. A smooth green sward also contrasts nicely with the textural intricacies of surrounding flower beds and borders.

Most turf-grass varieties are sun loving. With care, however, you can have a fine lawn even in full shade if the indirect light is bright. The trick is to select lawn seed that does well in shade. For moderate temperatures, use a mixture made up predominantly of *Festuca rubra* (red fescue) and *F. r.* var. *commutata* (Chewings fescue). In hot climates, *Paspalum notatum* (Bahia grass) and *Eremochloa ophiuroides* (centipede grass) are best for shade. See pages 40-41 for more on selecting seed for a shade lawn.

Turf grass does not compete well with shallow-rooted trees, which rob the surface soil of water and nutrients. In these conditions, till the soil well and enrich it with topsoil or compost before sowing your grass seed, and sow at twice the recommended rate to give your lawn a good start. Give the grass extra water and fertilizer, and mow the lawn frequently, keeping it short to promote the growth of wide, stout grass blades; in shade, grass becomes thin and straggly if allowed to grow long.

Gardening in a Shady Woodland

To successfully turn a woodland into a garden, your hand must be light enough not to disturb a carefully established natural balance, yet firm enough to build on the aesthetics of nature. You should try to create a beautiful setting and an ecologically stable habitat in which pests and plant-care requirements are kept to a manageable level.

Wherever you have a collection of trees, you can plant a woodland garden. The most extensive plantings will be at the farthest reaches of your property, in the outer zone, where cultivation gives way to wildness. If you have no such area, create one by planting a grove of small, fast-growing understory trees in company with large, slower-growing shade trees. The small trees will provide enough cover for woodland plants and will survive in the shade when the larger trees mature. Silver bell *(Halesia),* dogwood, and Carolina cherry laurel *(Prunus caroliniana)* are excellent choices.

If your woodland is already in place, you must first decide where to locate your garden. The sunniest part of a wood is its perimeter. Or you may want to go into the deeper shade, selectively removing a tree here, pruning a branch there, and laying a winding path to make a woodland walk.

The area of transition between open lawn and woodland, or the space in a forest where a tree has fallen and created a small clearing, can sustain both sun- and shade-loving plants. Partly sheltered by trees, plants in a transitional space will be exposed to moderate degrees of both sun and shade. Here is where most flowering trees are found—low-growing species such as hawthorn, cherry, *Amelanchier* (serviceberry), witch hazel, dogwood, redbud, sumac, magnolia, camellia, and the "escaped" specimens of domestic fruit trees called wildings.

Stocking Your Woodland Garden

When shopping for woodland plants, choose native, unhybridized species when possible. Species rhododendrons and azaleas, for example, look more at home in a naturalized setting, and are less demanding, than their hybrid cousins. *Rhododendron viscosum* (swamp azalea), which grows from Maine to the Carolinas and as far west as Mississippi and the Great Smokies, can survive in soggy ground and has deliciously scented blossoms.

SPRING FLOWERS AT WOODLAND'S MARGIN
This colony of celandine poppies has spread around the feet of maples and a pair of hemlocks at the edge of a Pennsylvania hardwood forest. In moist woods like these, the poppies may bloom a second time in fall.

A RESTFUL PATHSIDE STOPPING PLACE
A mossy stone bench surrounded by Trillium ovatum (coast trillium) and T. sessile (toadshade) and overhung with blossoms of a Rhododendron yakusimanum 'Ken Janek' provides a spot to sit and contemplate this woodland walk in Oregon.

Plants for Dry Woods

SHRUBS

Aucuba japonica
(spotted laurel)
Gaultheria shallon
(salal)
***Ligustrum* spp.**
(privet)
***Mahonia* spp.**
(Oregon grape)
Myrica californica
(California wax myrtle)
Pittosporum tobira
(Japanese pittosporum)
Taxus canadensis
(Canada yew)

PERENNIALS

Brunnera macrophylla
(Siberian bugloss)
Chrysogonum virginianum
(goldenstar)
Euphorbia amygdaloides
(wood spurge)
Geranium maculatum
(wild geranium)
***Hemerocallis* spp.**
(daylily)
***Hosta* 'Frances Williams'**
(plantain lily)

FERNS

Athyrium filix-femina
(lady fern)
***Polystichum
acrostichoides***
(Christmas fern)

GROUND COVERS

***Ajuga* spp.**
(bugleweed)
Epimedium
(bishop's hat)
Euonymus fortunei
(winter creeper)
***Lamium maculatum*
'Beacon Silver'**
(spotted dead nettle)

*Note: The abbreviation "spp."
stands for the plural of
"species"; where used in lists
it means that many, but not
all, of the species in a genus
meet the criterion of the list.*

At ground level, spring-blooming plants start the season off, growing in full sun under a latticework of bare tree limbs. Naturalized bulbs like daffodils, species tulips, squill, and crocus, planted in wide swaths in the grass along the woodland margin, will reappear year after year, spreading into the woods. Once the foliage canopy has filled in for summer, shade-tolerant natives like *Lilium canadense* (Canada lily) and *L. philadelphicum* (wood lily) come into bloom.

Other spring flowers to try are such natives as columbine, dicentra, *Thalictrum* (meadow rue), Solomon's-seal, and *Tiarella* (foamflower). Mix these with some of the many native ferns, such as the maidenhair *(Adiantum)*, lady *(Athyrium filix-femina)*, hay-scented *(Dennstaedtia punctilobula)*, shield *(Dryopteris)*, and chain *(Woodwardia)* ferns *(pages 36-37)*.

As dependable and appropriate as native plants are, a woodland verge can accommodate exotics as well. Spice up the garden with plants imported from the flower bed—perennials like astilbe, hosta, hellebore, and *Rheum palmatum* (ornamental rhubarb); annuals like shimmery *Lunaria* (money plant), self-sowing forget-me-not, and fragrant nicotiana; and bright ground covers like lamium, *Ajuga reptans* 'Multicoloris', or, in warm regions, *Fittonia,* with its small yellow flowers, and the evergreen *Aspidistra* (cast-iron plant).

Remember to include some evergreen shrubs and trees to give the garden shape in winter, when deciduous trees are bare. Reliable performers include Oregon grape, daphne, holly, and hemlock.

Preparing the Site

As you plot your woodland garden, spend time observing how the wild vegetation on the site grows. In spring, at the height of summer, and in fall, catalog the plants and note how the light reaches them. Preserve some of the area's wild growth in a remote corner of the woodland as a source of food and shelter for wildlife, but clear out noxious or destructive plants like *Rhus radicans* (poison ivy), *Vitis labrusca* (fox grape), and *Convolvulus arvensis* (field bindweed).

If the shade is too dense, hire an arborist to help you take out trees and prune branches to create small clearings. For an additional fee, a professional will also take away the cut wood or provide you with a log splitter to make firewood. Rent an industrial-grade wood chipper to convert medium-sized branches and twigs into mulch. Branches pruned in winter, being bare, make cleaner, longer-lasting mulch.

Designing with Nature

The design of your woodland garden should be a collaboration between you and nature, which has created the conditions that exist in your woods.

Such an open-minded approach on your part will not only ensure the survival of your plants but will also produce a more pleasingly natural result.

After taking into account the shade conditions, determine the quality of your soil and choose suitable plants. Woodland soil, at its surface, is made up of decomposing leaves, which render it acidic. Plants that have evolved in the woods have developed a taste for this kind of soil and should do well with a light fertilizer and a generous covering of leaf mulch. Soil that is sandy and fast draining can be conditioned by adding leaf mold or humus, as can clayey and waterlogged earth.

Soil nutrients in a woodland setting are probably less of a problem than is aridity. In an environment where the soil is densely packed with thirsty roots and the area overhung with a canopy of rain-blocking leaves, soil can be surprisingly dry in the summer. You could install an irrigation system to water your woodland garden, but a more practical approach is to choose drought-tolerant plants.

Plotting a Woodland Path

A path enables you to get close to your woodland garden without trampling on the plants or getting your feet muddy. It should meander along inviting curves and be flanked with interesting plants, as in this Maine garden bursting with *Primula japonica* (Japanese primrose) and columbine.

For two people to walk abreast, a path should be 4 feet wide—or, at any rate, wide enough for a garden cart to pass. To keep weeds down, smother them with thick layers of newspaper, which will eventually decay to a mulch. Then cover the paper with materials natural to the woods. Woodchips from recycled tree cuttings are long-lasting. Pine needles make a silky, springy walking surface but can be slippery on an incline.

Achieving the Desired Look

Woodland plants do best, and also look most natural, when they are arranged in colonies or clusters. This applies to a stand of *Mertensia virginica* (Virginia bluebells) or *Podophyllum peltatum* (May apple) at ground level as much as to a group of hollies or a grove of hemlock. And since nature is constantly replenishing itself, saplings will grow alongside mature trees. To reinforce the natural look of your woodland shade garden, intersperse young plants among the older ones.

Large shrubs and trees can fill the interior of a woodland garden and cut off views to the woodland edge, giving an illusion of greater space. Place scented azaleas or witch hazel along the path, to sweeten the air and hide where the path is going.

A Rock Garden in the Woods

If you have a rock outcrop in your woods, use it as a focal point to provide texture, color, and a visual anchor for your garden. Rocks can act as a foil for small woodland plants that might get lost amid lush growth. A cluster of jewel-like *Primula vialii* (Littons primrose) or the dainty native *Aquilegia canadensis* (wild columbine) paired with delicate *Adiantum pedatum* (northern maidenhair fern) will stand out beautifully against a large granite or limestone rock.

Newly exposed rocks will lose their raw look and acquire the patina of age as moss and lichens build up on them in the shade. If your rock has a level or slightly concave top, cap it with a layer of transplanted moss installed atop an inch or two of soil. Keep the moss out of direct sun and water it well through the first summer to get it established.

A slope in the woods is a good place to establish a woodland rock garden, especially if you can lay a path up the slope to permit viewing of the plants up close. Grow smaller ferns and hostas, the hardy *Shortia,* natives such as violets, *Gaultheria,* and *Mitchella repens* (partridgeberry), and such ground-hugging plants as *Cornus canadensis* (bunchberry), wild ginger, and saxifrage. Be sure to cover the ground around the plants with a layer of leaf mulch to build up the soil and keep it moist and cool.

A CLEARING IN DAPPLED SPRING SHADE
The widening of a pathway provides a sunny resting place among the trees of this shaded woodland garden in New Jersey. Close enough to the house for outdoor eating or for sitting in the evening, and paved with local flagstone to make a terrace, this retreat can be a destination in its own right or a stopping place before venturing deeper into the woods.

CHAPTER TWO

Foliage—Number One in the Shade

Foliage takes primacy over flowers in the shade garden, creating the visual framework of the garden and sometimes serving as the featured attraction as well. The rich variety among shade-tolerant foliage plants provides wide scope for design. Look to plants with variegated leaves whose bright hues—myriad shades of green plus many other colors—rival those of flowers. Consider tropical-looking beauties hardy to subzero temperatures; plants with large, lobed leaves and those with fine, delicate foliage; shrubs with small, compact shapes; and those with sprawling habits. In the Maryland shade garden at right, for example, two Atlas cedars trained into an arch and wrapped in an Akebia quinata vine frame the entrance to a bower. Carex (sedge), painted lady fern, and dwarf spruce ring the fountain to create a cool, lush setting.

On the following pages you'll find a dazzling menu of such plants and suggestions for marrying them to compose a shady retreat that subtly exploits every nuance of color and line.

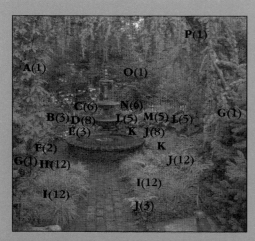

The key lists each plant type and the number of plants needed to replicate the garden shown opposite. The letters and numbers above refer to the type of plant and the number sited in an area.

A. *Akebia quinata* 'Alba' (1)
B. *Polystichum acrostichoides* (3)
C. *Kirengeshoma palmata* (6)
D. *Rohdea japonica* (8)
E. *Carex morrowii* 'Goldband' (3)
F. *Astilbe japonica* (2)
G. *Picea abies* 'Maxwellii' (2)
H. *Viola x wittrockiana* (12)
I. *Carex morrowii* 'Variegata' (24)
J. *Athyrium nipponicum* 'Pictum' (23)
K. *Saxifraga stolonifera* (many)
L. *Hosta sieboldiana* 'Elegans' (10)
M. *Hosta undulata* (5)
N. *Polygonatum odoratum var. thunbergii* (6)
O. *Taxus cuspidata* 'Capitata' (1)
P. *Cedrus atlantica* 'Glauca' (1)

Crafting a Garden Design with Foliage Plants

Just as a flowering garden changes from month to month and from season to season as plants bloom and fade, a shady foliage garden also presents a series of new faces over time. Spring-blooming bulbs, growing in the sunlight that filters through the bare branches of deciduous trees, can give way to winter-dormant perennials known for their appealing foliage, such as hostas, astilbes, ferns, and daylilies. The fresh leaves of these plants will conceal those of the spent bulbs and will remain attractive throughout the summer.

Keeping company with the perennials can be a mixture of evergreen and deciduous shrubs. To form a tapestry that will engage the eye through the growing season and beyond, combine shrubs that have contrasting leaf colors and textures. Vivid fall color is assured if you choose shrubs such as *Amelanchier canadensis* (shadblow serv-iceberry), a large plant that turns brilliant orange-red; *Aronia* (chokeberry), showing red in fall; or *Hamamelis mollis* (Chinese witch hazel), *H. vernalis* (American witch hazel), or *H. virginiana* (common witch hazel), with yellow autumn color.

In cold climates, evergreens enhance the shade garden's winter appeal. Yew, boxwood, rhododendron, *Pieris,* and holly are among the many shrubs that remain green year round. In addition, a number of perennial foliage plants manage to survive above ground during the winter. Some, such as *Polystichum setiferum* (soft shield fern) and *P. lonchitis* (northern holly fern), become large enough to assume the design role of a small shrub.

To alleviate bare ground during the winter months, plant evergreen ground covers such as *Ajuga* (bugleweed), pachysandra, *Mazus reptans,* and *Heuchera* (alumroot).

Combining Foliage Plants

Once you've decided which foliage plants to include in your shade garden, your next step is to fit them into a harmonious design. As you plan your garden's layout, take time to consider each plant's form, texture, and color. If you will be including flowering plants in the design *(pages 68-71),* plan for them as well.

The form, or shape, of a plant is often its most noticeable feature. When small plants have distinctive forms, mixing them together higgledy-piggledy can create a discordant design. To unify a composition, group three or more of one type of plant together and arrange clusters of perennials in naturalistic drifts that flow through the garden. If you are planting a shady border, occasionally repeat the pattern of plants to create a visual rhythm. The exception to planting in groups occurs when you want to use one dramatic plant as a specimen.

Sometimes a plant whose greatest virtue seems to be its ability to complement others in a harmonious grouping can also make a powerful statement when mass-planted on its own. *Polygonatum biflorum* (small Solomon's-seal), for example, is delightful combined in a woodland garden with *Trillium* (wake-robin), *Smilacina* (false Solomon's-seal), ferns, and *Mertensia virginica* (Virginia bluebells). Yet when it is mass-planted, its arching stems form a display that is downright impressive. Likewise, a mass planting of a hosta cultivar with a low-growing habit can prove a dramatic variation on a ground cover.

Marrying Foliage Textures and Colors

Juxtaposing plants of different textures can create fascinating effects in your garden. For an intriguing composition, try mixing fine-leaved plants with those that have larger, coarser leaves. A broad-leaved hosta paired with a feathery fern, for example, or the straplike foliage of daylilies or *Liriope* (lilyturf) with the heart-shaped foliage of *Epimedium* (barrenwort) creates an appealing contrast.

Color adds yet another dimension to plant pairings. Use accents of gold, lime green, or bluish green to enrich a combination, or use gold or variegated leaves where you need a flash of light. For example, the yellow-green and bronze-purple varieties of the Japanese barberry shrub *(Berberis thunbergii)* create a vivid pairing in light shade, with the darker foliage seeming to recede behind the brighter leaves. In fact, you can visually enlarge a shady spot by placing dark or cool-colored foliage toward the back of the garden, where it will subtly blend into the shadows. If a cozier space is what you want, put brighter-colored foliage in the back; it will appear to leap forward, foreshortening the distance.

A SWEEP OF FINE FOLIAGE
Demonstrating how a shady border can depart from the traditional floral emphasis of a sunny one, this planting in Vancouver, British Columbia, features a pleasing mix of leafy perennials. The Solomon's-seal in back arches protectively over the hostas and maidenhair ferns in front, adding height and movement to the design.

Trees for the Shade Garden

In nearly every shade garden there are two types of trees—small, shade-tolerant trees, and large, shade-making trees. In the wild, shade-tolerant trees, especially those that flower, tend to grow on the fringes of forests, where they enjoy some sunlight and air circulation. Called understory trees because they grow under the protection of larger forest trees, they have a compact growth habit that makes them ideal for a city garden and a small suburban lot, as well as for a larger property that has a wooded area. Many understory trees briefly burst into flower in spring and produce fruit later in the season, but it is their widely varied forms and commanding displays of foliage that help shape the character of the shade garden.

Trees that grow comfortably in shade can serve many purposes in your garden plan. Use them to break the monotony of a horizontal line created by plants or by a wall or fence. Plant a single tree as a specimen, with room to spread and develop its own unique form. Or cluster some of the smaller shade dwellers, such as dogwood, *Acer palmatum* (Japanese maple), *Stewartia,* or *Cercis* (redbud), to create the sense of a woodland area scaled down to suburban size.

To create a lush effect with your overall shade-foliage planting, use a tree to enrich the composition of a grouping of shrubs and perennials. To add even greater visual interest, you might grow a shade-tolerant vine, such as the lacy-leaved *Akebia quinata* (five-leaf akebia), up the tree.

Trees as Design Highlights

Trees can also serve as design accents in the shade garden. Consider planting a pair of trees to mark the entrance to the garden or to frame a view. If you want a formal effect, choose a pair of yews or hollies and prune them into cones, or perhaps pillars topped with spheres. For a more informal look—and one that will require less trimming—choose trees of looser habit. Consider redbud, with its lush, heart-shaped foliage—'Forest Pansy'

COLORFUL TREES FOR SHADY SPOTS
The burgundy foliage of a Japanese maple contrasts in color and texture with the large-lobed, toothed leaves of Darmera peltata (umbrella plant) and the delicate yellow flowers of Mimulus guttatus (common monkey flower) in this Pacific Northwest garden.

has leaves that emerge reddish purple, then turn dark green—or *Halesia carolina* (Carolina silver bell), which is best known for its flowers but has bright green, finely toothed leaves that turn yellow in fall, as well as gray bark with off-white streaks.

In a narrow woodland garden, create a vista by planting an avenue of *Stewartia pseudocamellia* (Japanese stewartia), which takes a pyramidal to oval shape with foliage that turns red to dark purplish red in fall, or *Amelanchier laevis* (Allegheny serviceberry), which bears a mass of snowy white

28

Shade-Loving Trees

Acer pensylvanicum
(striped maple)
Cornus florida
(flowering dogwood)
Cornus mas
(cornelian cherry)
Cornus nuttallii
(Pacific dogwood)
Halesia
(silver bell)
Ilex
(holly)
Illicium anisatum
(Japanese anise tree)
Magnolia fraseri
(ear-leaved umbrella tree)
Prunus caroliniana
(Carolina cherry laurel)
Stewartia monadelpha
(tall stewartia)
Stewartia ovata
(mountain stewartia)
Styrax japonicus
(Japanese snowbell)
Styrax obassia
(fragrant snowbell)
Taxus
(yew)
Tsuga
(hemlock)

blooms against purplish green leaves in spring. Cover a straight path between the trees with hardwood-bark nuggets and place a bench, birdbath, or some other feature at the end as a focal point.

You can bring this idea to the front of the house, as well, to enjoy a driveway or walkway lined with trees. Choose small-scale shade-tolerant species that have a relatively compact habit and plant them in rows. *Hamamelis mollis* (Chinese witch hazel) is a good choice, as is a dogwood species, *Cornus mas* (cornelian cherry), which bursts into a froth of yellow blossoms in late winter to early spring in Zones 5 to 8. A line of matched trees is also an attractive way to define your property boundary.

Training Plants for Special Effects

Almost any tree or shrub can be induced to grow flat against a fence, wall, or trellis as an espalier *(page 76)*. The technique is particularly useful for softening the visual impact of a large expanse of bare wall, especially in a spot where shade may be problematic, such as the north side of the house. Depending on your taste, you can create a lacy,

TIPS FROM THE PROS

How to Buy the Right Tree

Although you may be tempted to splurge on the largest tree available, you are better off spending less money on a younger, smaller tree. The more mature a tree, the more vulnerable it is to transplant shock; a larger tree will need several years just to reestablish its root system. In many cases, young trees planted at the same time as more mature ones will catch up to their elders in just a few years.

Buy from reputable nurseries only, and insist on a guarantee. Always examine the roots of the tree. If its roots are bare, make sure they are moist and plump, with no sign of rot. If the tree is container grown,

check that the roots haven't begun to kink or spiral around the inner wall of the pot. Unless you can unwind the roots before you plant the tree, the root-bound problem will persist, ultimately weakening or even killing the tree.

Also inspect the tree's trunk for signs of distress. Flattened, split, or dull-colored bark indicates sunscald, a condition that leaves the tree vulnerable to borer infestation *(page 86)*. Reject any tree that shows signs of insects or disease. Finally, bear in mind the ultimate size of your tree when you plan where to put it. Allow enough room for it to spread its canopy in a graceful, natural form.

free-form pattern of branches or you can train the tree to grow in one of the many stylized espalier designs. These include the cordon, where side branches are trained to grow in horizontal rows; the palmette, where parallel rows of branches are trained at a gentle upward angle, creating a shape resembling the leaf of a palmetto palm; and the Y-shape, where two lateral branches are trained upward at 45° angles. A row of trees planted at regular intervals and trained in a Y-shape so that their branches intersect will form a diamond pattern on the wall known as a Belgian fence.

Choosing Shade-Making Trees

If you live in a home that was recently constructed, leaving the lot bereft of trees, or if your property simply could use more shade, you may want to plant taller, sun-loving species as well as understory trees. The ideal shade tree is the oak. Oaks have deep roots that allow room for underplanting and high branches that permit early-morning and late-afternoon sun—as well as rain—to reach the plants below. Other good shade makers include *Cladrastis lutea* (Kentucky yellowwood) and *Nyssa sylvatica* (black tupelo), which have small leaves or leaflets that produce a dappled shade. In warm, dry climates, look to *Olea europaea* (common olive); in moist soils, consider *Taxodium distichum* (bald cypress), *Magnolia acuminata* (cucumber tree), *M. fraseri* (ear-leaved umbrella tree), or *M. tripetala* (umbrella magnolia).

Steer clear of troublesome trees such as the sycamore or paulownia, which have large leaves that block sunlight and rain. Likewise, avoid trees such as the horse chestnut, which drops a profusion of large leaves in autumn, smothering the ground. Trees that grow aggressive networks of shallow roots will cause planting problems, as will trees such as *Acer saccharinum* (silver maple) and eucalyptus, which exude toxins.

PLANTING IN PAIRS FOR EFFECT
Framed by pruned boxwood hedges, a pair of Chinese witch hazel trees lend balance to this formal garden in Portland, Oregon. Witch hazel thrives in light shade, and the Chinese species, Hamamelis mollis, can be grown as a large shrub or small tree. Its leaves turn golden in fall, and fragrant golden yellow flowers appear in winter.

Shrubs for Shady Designs

Shrubs are invaluable for giving the garden structure and form as well as color and textural interest. Large-leaved shrubs provide a dramatic but coarse texture; small-leaved shrubs, a more refined appearance. The surface of the leaves—glossy or matte—also affects how they look in the landscape, especially in shade. Glossy leaves glint in dappled sunlight; those with a matte finish are more subdued. And whereas dark green foliage makes a beautiful background to other plantings, colored foliage jumps out as an accent.

Many shrubs can be arborized—shaped into what is called a standard, a topiary form that resembles a miniature tree—by pruning off the lower branches. In tiny gardens, a large standard may serve as a small tree. A standard shrub also allows growing space beneath its branches for perennials, annuals, and ground covers that prefer shade.

Shade-tolerant shrubs can be found to fill nearly every design need, and many of them can perform more than one job. Shrubs that make excellent hedges, for example, can also do duty as privacy screens or windbreaks. Some of these same shrubs are also ideal for masking the foundation of your home, for softening its corners, or for adding another layer of green to your garden.

Shrubs for Hedges

For generations, the classic hedges for shady locations have been yew, boxwood, and the small-leaved *Ilex crenata* (Japanese holly). While these are still reliable favorites, growing boxwood has become problematic. It is prone to attack by a pest called the leaf miner and, in the South, to a mite affliction known as boxwood decline. While many people still use box successfully, you can avoid these problems by substituting Japanese holly, which resembles box, or one of a number of other shrubs appropriate for hedges.

For a sturdy hedge in partial shade that will grow to about 8 feet tall, look to *Abelia* x *grandiflora* (glossy abelia). Frost hardy in Zones 6 to 9, this shrub's bronze-colored new growth matures to a glossy dark green, setting off its abundant small tubular flowers. White with a tinge of pink, the fragrant blooms cover the branches from midsummer to midautumn. Purple or copper-colored sepals remain once the flowers have dropped, extending the season of interest into late fall. Particu-

larly worthy of note is the cultivar 'Francis Mason'.

A number of other excellent hedge shrubs also flower in shade—azaleas, for example, or rhododendrons. Allow them to grow in their natural, billowy form, and enjoy a wall of flowers during the blooming season. *Camellia,* too, has hedge potential. It can be clipped into a formal style or allowed to grow naturally. Take care not to plant annuals or perennials too near either camellias or azaleas, however, or you'll disturb their shallow roots.

Other fine hedging shrubs include *Berberis julianae* (wintergreen barberry) and *B. verruculosa* (warty barberry), which are both dense-growing evergreens hardy to Zone 5. They also grow thorns, making them useful as barriers. The leaves

A SHADE SHRUB FOR ALL SEASONS
A graceful evergreen, Mahonia (Oregon grape) tolerates even dense shade, such as that occurring under the pine trees in this Maryland garden. Here the mahonia serves as a transition between the woods behind it and the mass planting of astilbes and 'August Moon' hostas in the foreground.

azalea, holly, *Pieris,* and viburnum. Since these shrubs will be competing with the trees for root room, nutrients, and water, prepare a wide, deep hole for each shrub and backfill it with rich soil to give the plant a head start. Fertilize established shrubs early in the growing season to keep them healthy, and fertilize the trees separately at root-ball depth. Water deeply if conditions get dry. A generous layer of mulch around the shrub's roots will help retain moisture in the soil.

Hardworking Shrubs

Although trees are generally considered the best plants for creating screens or windbreaks, large shrubs can also do the job. You can use just the shrubs, or let them step in during the time it takes a line of trees to grow large enough for the task. Suitable fast-growing shrubs include photinia, *Lonicera maackii* forma *podocarpa* (Amur honeysuckle), *L. tatarica* (Tartarian honeysuckle), *Rhamnus frangula* 'Columnaris' (alder buckthorn), *Viburnum dentatum* (southern arrowwood), *V. lentago* (sheepberry), and *V. sieboldii* (Siebold viburnum).

A shade-tolerant bamboo such as *Sasa palmata* (palm-leaf bamboo) also makes an excellent screen. It is a rampant spreader, however, so don't plant it unless you have barriers in place to prevent its expansion or you are willing to commit yourself to curbing it diligently as it grows.

Slower-growing options for screens and windbreaks include boxwood, American witch hazel, privet, and *Thuja occidentalis* (eastern arborvitae). The advantage of these choices is that they generally are longer lived than fast-growing shrubs. Indeed, many old gardens on the East Coast contain boxwood and privet shrubs that are hundreds of years old.

If erosion is a problem on a shady bank, select shrubs that have roots or stolons that spread rapidly to grip and anchor the soil. Among the best choices are *Cornus alba* (Tartarian dogwood), *Diervilla sessilifolia* (southern bush honeysuckle), *Leucothoe fontanesiana* (drooping laurel), and *Myrica pensylvanica* (northern bayberry).

Foundation Plantings

The classic American solution to the problem of hiding the unsightly foundation of a house—and at the same time integrating the structure into the landscape—is to plant shrub camouflage. But unless you want to revamp your foundation plantings

A COLLAGE OF GREENS
The gold-dappled leaves of an aucuba enliven a planting at the base of a dark stone wall in this Pennsylvania garden. Along with a deep-hued Matteuccia (ostrich fern), the shrub provides a lush backdrop for a pleasing mix of herbaceous foliage plants, including glossy dark green barrenwort, pale Hosta 'Kabitan', and bleeding heart.

of the warty barberry, which has a more compact growth habit than the wintergreen, are white on the underside. If you don't mind a deciduous hedge, try *Hydrangea quercifolia* (oakleaf hydrangea). Its long-lasting white flowers and handsome, deeply lobed dark green leaves, which turn reddish in fall, make it a shrub for all seasons.

In mild climates—Zone 7 and south—*Photinia serrulata* (Chinese photinia) tolerates partial shade and grows very quickly into a hedge. The shrub is prized for its foliage, which is brilliant bronze-red when young; repeated pruning encourages new red shoots. *Ligustrum* (privet) is another valuable hedging shrub that accepts semi-shade. It is deciduous in cold regions, however.

A Second Layer of Shrubs

Some vigorous shade-loving shrubs are ideal for planting under fairly extensive groves of trees. Shrubs that are suited to this type of woodland setting include mountain laurel, rhododendron,

every few years, you'll need to take into account the ultimate size of shrubs you've chosen for this purpose. A common misstep is to place shrubs too close together in an effort to instantly achieve the look of a 5-year-old planting. Usually within a year or two the gardener finds that the shrubs have become overcrowded. Equally upsetting is the realization that the young shrub you planted in front of a window has quickly grown to block the view.

Keeping mature size and seasonal interest in mind, select a variety of shrubs to create an artful mix of shape, size, color, and texture. Any of the shrubs appropriate for hedges—azaleas, hydrangeas, hollies, and camellias among them—are suitable. Add a shrub with a variegated leaf, such as *Daphne odora* 'Aureomarginata', for another interesting dimension. To soften the corners of your house, plant hollies or camellias there.

In addition to good looks, many shade-tolerant shrubs have a pleasant fragrance. Plant *Buxus sempervirens* 'Suffruticosa' (common box), *Laurus nobilis* (true laurel), *Lindera benzoin* (spicebush), or bayberry near a window so you can enjoy the scent of their foliage indoors. Be prepared to prune the laurel and bayberry, however, to keep them small. And keep one thing in mind if you are growing azaleas or other plants that prefer acid soil: Over time, lime will leach out of the foundation walls into the soil. You will then have to reacidify the soil to keep the plants happy.

Leafy Vines for the Shade

Nothing adds atmosphere to a shade garden like a leafy vine, as evidenced by the ivy festoons and pillars on the wooden fence in the Richmond, Virginia, garden above. Twining up a tree or trellis, vines such as *Akebia quinata* (five-leaf akebia) or *Euonymus fortunei* (winter creeper) can give your garden the cool, lush look of a jungle retreat. If you have a patio with a trellis overhead, you can grow *Parthenocissus quinquefolia* (Virginia creeper) or, in Zone 10, *Tetrastigma voinieranum* (chestnut vine) in large containers and train them to roof your shady retreat.

For a shady wall or fence, consider clinging vines such as *Ficus pumila* (creeping fig), winter creeper, *Hydrangea anomala* var. *petiolaris* (climbing hydrangea), or *Parthenocissus tricuspidata* (Boston ivy). Ivy is a fast grower that thrives in deep shade as handily as in full sun, and is ideal for cloaking walls or chain-link fences. Bear in mind, however, that it spreads like wildfire and can damage mortar, so use it with care.

Designing with Herbaceous Plants

Although most shade-tolerant herbaceous plants are grown primarily for their bloom, many of them also have lovely foliage. And because such plants are generally shallow rooted, they are ideal for shade gardens, where competition with the roots of trees and shrubs is often intense.

Cimicifuga (bugbane) sends up beautiful plumelike flower spikes in summer, but its ferny foliage is equally attractive during the rest of the season. A tall plant that will tolerate partial shade, bugbane should be placed in the back of flower borders or on the fringes of woodlands. For the edge of a path or in a rock garden, consider *Corydalis lutea* (yellow corydalis), a low-growing, clumping plant with gray-green fernlike leaves. Its delicate yellow flowers will persist through most of the growing season if it is kept well watered.

Other flowering perennials with fine, feathery foliage include bleeding heart, astilbe, *Aruncus* (goatsbeard), and *Aquilegia* (columbine). For interesting contrast, try mixing them with the strappy leaves of shade-tolerant daylilies, the large heart-shaped leaves of *Begonia grandis* (hardy begonia), or the geranium-like foliage of *Alchemilla* (lady's-mantle).

If you're looking for a plant to light up a dark spot or act as an accent, combine variegated *Pulmonaria saccharata* (Bethlehem sage) with the deep purple leaves of *Heuchera micrantha* 'Palace Purple'. Another heuchera with striking foliage is *H. americana* 'Garnet' (rock geranium), which has a geranium-shaped leaf with apple green margins and deep purple veins.

The Wide World of Hostas

Hostas, also known as plantain lilies, are an astonishingly varied group of plants, the majority of which prefer shade. They grow in most of North America, although they are less successful in regions that don't get winter chill or are extremely arid. Because of the diversity of size, texture, and color in this genus, there is a hosta to meet almost any landscape requirement. Some grow only a few inches tall with petite leaves; others have large paddlelike leaves and grow to a substantial 36 inches tall and wide. *Hosta fortunei* 'Gold Standard', a chartreuse-leaved cultivar edged with dark green, makes clumps that grow to a width

of 5 feet or more. Foliage color among hostas ranges from bright yellow, gold, and creamy white, usually in the form of variegation, to the entire spectrum of greens and blues. Leaves can be long and thin, broad and round, oval, heart shaped, or pointed. Foliage textures vary as well, from smooth to deeply ribbed.

Hostas adapt to a variety of growing conditions; they thrive in both dry and wet locations. The yellow varieties tend to do best when their shade is no more than partial; those with blue foliage usually prefer more time in the shade. However, in each case you can experiment with the amount of light.

A DRAMATIC MASS PLANTING
Petasites japonicus var. giganteus 'Fuki' (giant butterbur) blankets a New Jersey border with leaves that can grow up to 4 feet in diameter.

THE DIVERSITY OF HOSTAS
Cultivars encircling a tree are (counterclockwise from top left) H. 'Kabitan', H. x tardiana 'Blue Wedgewood', H. 'Antioch', H. fortunei 'Francee', and H. sieboldiana 'Elegans'.

Mining Hosta's Assets

Put hostas to work in your shade garden. Edge a path or walkway with midsize cultivars such as *H.* 'So Sweet', which has green leaves with white margins and very fragrant flowers; 'Golden Tiara', with long heart-shaped green leaves edged in gold; or the cream-edged *H. undulata* 'Albo-marginata'.

Create a striking ground cover by mass-planting small hostas such as *H.* 'Kabitan', a narrow, gold-leaved variety, or *H.* 'Ginko Craig', a green-and-white beauty. Although hostas don't spread by means of runners like traditional ground covers, you can space the clumps so that the leaves overlap to completely cover the ground. For spring color, plant early-blooming daffodils between the hostas; the hosta foliage will appear just as the daffodils are fading.

Large hostas perform well as foundation plantings, in mixed-flower borders, or as specimen plants. Giants—as tall as 3 feet and 5 feet or more across—include the blue *H. fortunei* var. *hyacinthina; H. sieboldiana* 'Elegans', a blue-green cultivar; *H.* 'Sum and Substance', prized for its 2-foot-wide heart-shaped chartreuse leaves; and *H.* 'Blue Angel', which has striking heart-shaped, deeply ridged blue leaves.

Experiment with hostas and other plants to create exciting color and texture combinations. Plant a broad-leaved hosta such as *H. sieboldiana* 'Frances Williams' next to a feathery *Athyrium filix-femina* (lady fern). Or combine *H.* 'Gold Edger', a chartreuse-leaved cultivar, with a variegated ivy that picks up the same yellow-green color. Equally eye-catching is a collection of different hostas that echo and accent one another's colors and forms. Don't be afraid of trial and error. Hostas are sturdy, and you can move them around without much damage if they don't marry happily.

Ferns: Prehistoric Wonders

Ferns are another group of adaptable and intriguing shade performers. There are ferns suited to just about any garden condition, from full sun to deep shade, from wet conditions to dry, and from alkaline to acidic soil. The less fussy ones will put up with whatever situation they are given. *Thelypteris noveboracensis* (New York fern), for example, prefers damp, acidic soil and light shade but will tolerate fairly dry conditions, neutral soil, and medium shade.

The diversity of ferns provides the shade gardener with a wealth of choices. There are creepers that make excellent—although sometimes invasive—ground covers. *Dennstaedtia punctilobula*

(hay-scented fern), for example, will quickly fill a space with its 30-inch-tall fronds. It tolerates wet or dry conditions and deep shade. Other good ground covers include *Gymnocarpium dryopteris* (oak fern), *Polypodium aureum* (rabbit's-foot fern), and *Polypodium glycyrrhiza* (licorice fern).

Designing with Ferns

To create a soft, lacy effect in your garden, choose a genus with dainty foliage, such as one of the many maidenhair ferns. Depending on the species, these ferns form dense clumps ranging in height from 8 to 20 inches. One of the best is the hardy *Adiantum pedatum* (northern maidenhair). For a splash of color, add the purple-and-silver *Athyrium nipponicum* 'Pictum' (painted lady fern).

Ferns are particularly attractive around ponds and along streams, especially when they weep over the water, softening the shoreline and creating reflections. *Osmunda cinnamomea* (cinnamon fern) and *O. regalis* (royal fern), which tolerate deep shade, are ideal for such settings.

Ferns as Woodland Companion Plants

In woodland gardens, combine ferns with rhododendrons, azaleas, and delicate woodland flowers. Members of the genus *Dryopteris,* also known as fancy ferns, have finely cut rich green foliage that rises from a central crown; they mix admirably with trillium, bleeding heart, phlox, and primrose.

A diminutive woodlander, growing just 4 inches tall, is the oak fern. It looks charming mixed with *Linnaea borealis* (twinflower), *Claytonia virginica* (spring beauty), and *Dicentra cucullaria* (Dutchman's-breeches). When the Dutchman's-breeches foliage dies back in early summer, the fern can fill in the gap.

Because of their striking foliage and forms, ferns make excellent accents in a shady flower bed or border. Good candidates for this role include many *Dryopteris* species. And *Asplenium nidus* (bird's-nest fern) also does the trick with thin, leathery, tonguelike fronds that will grow an impressive 4 feet high in warm, humid conditions.

In cooler zones, *Matteuccia* (ostrich fern) is a good choice. With its erect feathery fronds that stand 3 feet tall and resemble a shuttlecock, this fern makes a dramatic display. Combine it with spring-flowering bulbs or woodland flowers, or let a clump of the ferns make a showing on their own. For evergreen ferns, try the flat, swordlike

FILIGREED PERFECTION IN THE WILD
A dependable shade performer, Athyrium filix-femina (lady fern) grows to a height of 3 feet and thrives in moist soil. The wild species, shown above in its springtime glory, often looks tired and tattered by summer's end; try one of its hybrids, such as A. f.-f. 'Victoriae', instead.

AN ARTFUL ARRANGEMENT OF FERNS
In this Seattle shade garden, northern maidenhair ferns (Adiantum pedatum)—also known as five-finger ferns—display their "fingers" against leathery spears of Asplenium scolopendrium (hart's-tongue fern). Overarching fronds of Polystichum munitum (western sword fern) add weight to the design.

A HERALD OF SPRING
Hairy leaf buds known as fiddle-heads mark the early appear-ance of Osmunda cinnamomea (cinnamon fern). As the season progresses, the fiddleheads grad-ually unfurl into fertile cinna-mon-colored fronds, later to be joined by sterile green fronds.

A MATCHING COLOR SCHEME
The dark olive shade of the broad, crinkled Heuchera (alumroot) leaves accentuates the dark ribs of Athyrium nipponicum 'Pictum' (painted lady fern) in the St. Louis, Missouri, shade garden at left. The fern's silvery fronds add streaks of light to the composition.

fronds of *Polystichum acrostichoides* (Christmas fern), which grow to a length of 24 inches, and the equally substantial *P. setiferum* (soft shield fern).

A Perfect Match: Ferns and Rocks

Tiny, shallow-rooted ferns are ideal for growing in rock gardens, on the earthen risers of garden steps, and even in the crevices of walls. In fact, the warmth radiated by a wall may create a micro-climate that enables you to grow a fern that is only borderline hardy in your zone. For such spots, try *Cystopteris fragilis* (fragile fern), which is much tougher than its name suggests; *Polypodium vir-ginianum* (rock polypody), which will grow hap-pily in just 2 inches of soil; the 6-inch-tall *Asple-nium trichomanes* (maidenhair spleenwort), or *A. scolopendrium* (hart's-tongue fern), with its crinkled, tongue-shaped fronds.

In a shady, moist rock garden, plant *A. rhizo-phyllum* [also classified as *Camptosorus rhizo-phyllus*] (walking fern). It especially appreciates limestone rocks. An intriguing miniature for Zone 10 is the spreading *Selaginella kraussiana* (mat spike moss), which grows only half an inch tall.

Caladiums

The brightly colored heart- or arrowhead-shaped leaves of caladiums come in a beautiful silvery white that is veined with dark green, or in striking mixtures of pink, green, and cream. Well suited to shrub and flower borders as well as containers, ca-ladiums grow in clumps about 12 inches tall and will thrive in either full or partial shade. They pre-fer evenly moist but well-drained soil, and their favorite weather condition is hot and humid; they are hardy perennials only to Zone 10. Cala-diums do produce flowers, but they are so un-distinguished that connoisseurs generally remove them, along with spent foliage, to encourage more leaf production. The broad, colorful leaves make caladiums a delightful foil next to any lacy green plant, including ferns, columbine, and astilbe. Use the silvery varieties in front of deep green plants such as yew; they will shimmer in contrast.

Coleus

Like caladium, coleus will grow as a perennial in very warm regions but in colder climes must be treated as an annual. Coleus flaunts a wide range

of foliage colors, including solids or mixtures of salmon, pink, red, maroon, chartreuse, yellow, and bronze. Dwarf varieties grow to about 6 inches tall, with leaves as small as an inch long; others may reach 36 inches, with leaves from 3 to 6 inches long. Leaf texture may be velvety to crinkled, with smooth, scalloped, or serrated edges.

Put the dwarf varieties to work in the front of a shady border. The larger coleuses look handsome combined with tall ferns, which help isolate the multiple bold colors. Because of the diversity of color and textures, coleus is an excellent plant to combine with other shade plants to create your own unique plant marriages. Try a pink-leaved coleus next to the deep purple foliage of *Heuchera micrantha* 'Palace Purple', or combine a red or maroon specimen with a blue hosta.

Coleus does best in indirect light or light shade. Pinch back the stems in early summer to encourage bushy growth, and remove the inconspicuous flower spikes that emerge throughout the summer. This will help the plant focus its energy on foliage production.

You can create an unusual specimen by training a potted coleus as a standard. Remove side growth to encourage the plant to grow a tall stem and to leaf out on top. The plants are easy to propagate from cuttings in either water or a rooting medium, so you can reproduce your present inventory—and even increase your supply—by taking cuttings in autumn and overwintering them indoors.

Woodland Foliage Plants

A woodland setting is a shade gardener's paradise, for this is the natural habitat for many of the shade-loving species. It presents a classic opportunity to create a foliage garden that is not only in tune with nature but also complements it by adding a measure of order and design. Many woodland plants have an exquisite but ephemeral bloom season; their foliage is the dominant feature for the rest of the growing season. Think in terms of massing and combining plants to produce a pleasing flow of foliage color and texture in the woods.

Some of the woodland plants, such as Virginia

Ornamental Grasses for Shade

Although the list of ornamental grasses for full shade is not long, you should be able to find something to meet your needs. One of the best is *Hakonechloa macra* 'Aureola' (golden variegated hakonechloa), shown above tucked in next to a hosta and beneath a blue spruce. Hardy in Zones 5 to 9, it grows in clumps 16 inches tall and 18 to 24 inches wide. Other grasses that do well in full shade include *Carex* (sedge) and *Deschampsia caespitosa* (tufted hair grass). For partial shade, try *Miscanthus sinensis* 'Variegatus' (eulalia) or *Chasmanthium latifolium* (northern sea oats). *Liriope* (lilyturf) works well along shady borders.

bluebells, bleeding heart, and Dutchman's-breeches, have pretty foliage and flowers in spring, but then die back in early summer. Combine them with plants such as columbine, ferns, hostas, and Solomon's-seal, which will fill in the bare spots created by the summer-dormant woodland plants.

For a fascinating foliage mix, combine *Trillium erectum* (purple trillium), with its whorl of three leaves on a 6- to 18-inch tall stem; *Tiarella cordifolia* (foamflower), which spreads over the ground by runners; *Sanguinaria* (bloodroot), another colonizing plant with rounded, shallow-

LEAVES TO RIVAL FLOWER PETALS
The mottled magenta-and-lime-green foliage of a St. Louis planting of Coleus 'Bellingrath Pink' assumes the role of a floral accent next to the lacy bluish green leaves of Pelargonium denticulatum (fern-leaf geranium).

lobed pale green leaves; *Viola* (violet); Solomon's-seal; and *Clintonia borealis* (corn lily), which grows clusters of oval leaves about 6 inches long.

Another attractive woodland composition is achieved by joining purple trillium with *Asarum canadense* (wild ginger), a ground cover with velvety heart-shaped medium green leaves, and *Aquilegia canadensis* (wild columbine). Equally admirable—and unusual—is *Podophyllum* (May apple). On each stem is one broad, deeply lobed leaf that opens each spring like an umbrella. The foliage carpets the ground until midsummer, when it withers and dies back. As an encore to the May apple, interplant *Galium odoratum* (sweet woodruff). It doesn't mind the deep shade under the May apples, and it will provide a pretty green cover when they are gone. For information on which woodland species will do best in your area, contact local botanical gardens, arboretums, nursery and garden centers, and local plant societies.

Ground Covers for Shady Spots

Shade-tolerant ground covers are great problem solvers. They work perfectly in spots that are too dark for grass to grow well, and in areas where you want a lush look but few chores. Ground covers also work to unify a large design by tying together different elements in the landscape. And they are perfect on hillsides or in gullies, which may have erosion problems or be difficult to mow.

When choosing a ground cover for a particular spot, consider upkeep. Those that grow in a loose network—such as the low-growing, spreading *Phlox divaricata* (wild sweet William) or *P. stolonifera* (creeping phlox)—will probably need periodic weeding. Those with a denser habit, such as hosta, lady's-mantle, and lady fern, will eventually grow thick enough to keep out all but the most persistent weeds. Useful and versatile as they are, however, most shade-tolerant ground covers cannot handle regular foot traffic. Periwinkle, *Mazus reptans,* ivy, and liriope will bounce back if walked on occasionally, and dichondra can take considerable wear. But most genera are less durable.

Covering Problem Spots

An excellent ground cover for dry, shady areas is *Bergenia crassifolia* (Siberian tea), a tropical-looking plant that spreads well even in poor soil and under shallow-rooted trees. Hardy to Zone 3, it has glossy evergreen leaves that grow up to 10 inches across. *Aegopodium podagraria* 'Variegatum' (bishop's-weed) is an aggressive spreader that is well suited to dry woods. Its blue-green leaves edged with cream brighten up shadowy spots.

In moist, rich soil, wild ginger spreads rapidly into a dense carpet. Foamflower likes the same sort of conditions, and after its blooms have faded, the maplelike leaves present a soft-textured mass of dark green. Another ground cover for cool, damp shade is *Tolmiea menziesii* (piggyback plant). A mat-forming perennial with foliage that resembles that of ivy, it is hardy where temperatures don't drop below zero. A lush ground cover for Zones 9 and 10 is *Soleirolia soleirolii* (baby's-

AN ISLAND OF SHADY GROUND COVERS
In this Easthampton, New York, garden, an island of moss thrives in a moist spot under a grove of maples. A patch of glossy periwinkle and a careful arrangement of ostrich ferns and weighty boulders contrast with the delicate moss in color, texture, and size, giving this naturalistic composition depth and serenity. In a small garden, this design could be recreated on a lesser scale using smaller stones.

TURF GRASS VARIETIES FOR SHADE

TYPE OF GRASS	ZONE	HABITAT PREFERENCE	SHADE TOLERANCE	RECOMMENDED VARIETIES
W A R M S E A S O N				
BAHIA GRASS (*Paspalum notatum*)	Zones 9 - 11	Broadly adapted	Partial	'Argentine', 'Pensacola'
CENTIPEDE GRASS (*Eremochloa ophiuroides*)	Zones 8 - 9	Infertile, sandy soils of coastal plains	High, open	common, 'Oaklawn', 'Tennessee Hardy', 'Centennial'
TALL FESCUE (*Festuca eliator*)	Zones 5 - 7	Broadly adapted	Partial	'Apache', 'Arid', 'Bonanza II', 'Duster', 'Mustang', 'Pixie', 'Rebel Jr.', 'SR8200', 'Tomahawk'
ST. AUGUSTINE GRASS (*Stenotaphrum secundatum*)	Zones 9 - 11	Well adapted to hot, humid conditions	High tolerance	common, 'Roselawn', 'Bitterblue', 'Floralawn', 'Floratine', 'Raleigh'
ZOYSIA (*Zoysia* species)	Zones 8 - 9	Less well adapted to Zone 9	Partial	'Belair'
C O O L S E A S O N				
FINE FESCUE (Chewings, *Festuca rubra* ssp. *commutata*; creeping red, *F. rubra* ssp. *rubra*; and Hard Fescue, *F. longifolia*)	Zones 1 - 6	Tolerant of poor soil and drought; may suffer summer dieback in Zone 6	Dry shade; fine fescue is the most shade-tolerant grass	'Aurora', 'Jamestown II', 'Reliant', 'Scaldis', 'Sparta', 'SR3100', 'SR5000', 'SR5100'
KENTUCKY BLUEGRASS (*Poa pratensis*)	Zones 1 - 6	Broadly adapted, but prefers good-quality neutral soil	Partial, especially in Zone 6	'A-34', Georgetown', 'Glade'
PERENNIAL RYEGRASS (*Lolium perenne*)	Zones 4 - 6	Best in mild coastal climates	Partial	'Advent', 'APM', 'Express', 'Fiesta II', 'Manhattan II', 'Palmer II', 'SR4000', 'SR4100', 'SR4200'

tears); watch it carefully, however, since it can be invasive. Other shade-tolerant ground covers that enjoy moist soil include lungwort and bunchberry, which does best in cool climates (Zones 3 to 5).

Lawns in the Shade

Although a few turf grasses will tolerate some shade, even these will thin out if they don't get enough sun. In addition, shady spots are more humid than sunny ones, generally have less air circulation, and experience longer-lasting early-morning dew. All these factors enhance the potential for lawn disease. Therefore, it is important to choose named cultivars that are bred for shade tolerance as well as for disease and pest resistance.

Once you've planted an appropriate turf grass you will likely still have to work at keeping it healthy. You may need to prune lower tree branches to bring in more light, and perhaps remove plants that obstruct air circulation. To expose as much of the blade surface as possible to the light, set your lawn mower's cutting height one-half to 1 inch higher than you would for grass growing in

sun. Water the lawn thoroughly but infrequently to encourage deep root growth, and when fertilizing, minimize nitrogen to slow top growth and maximize potassium to encourage healthy roots. Despite the best preventive measures, however, diseases such as leaf spot, powdery mildew, mold, or rust may appear. Applying fungicides is one option; if you choose it, use the least toxic type available and follow all package instructions.

Another solution to a problematic lawn is moss. Many people wage a battle against moss in lawns, but you may be wise to allow it to flourish. In really dense shade or where tree roots are shallow, however, opt for ground covers or mulch.

If you are starting a lawn from scratch, buy the best-quality seed you can find. Make sure the seed mix has a germination rate of at least 85 percent and no more than 0.5 percent weed seeds. The package label should also state "no noxious weeds"—referring to weeds that are very difficult to control in lawns. Finally, since annual grasses are not suitable for a permanent lawn, choose seed that has no more than 3 to 5 percent annual grass. For named varieties of good shade grasses, consult the chart opposite.

Shade-Loving Ground Covers

Ajuga
(bugleweed)
Arum italicum
(Italian arum)
Asarum
(wild ginger)
Epimedium
(barrenwort)
Euonymus fortunei
(winter creeper)
Gaultheria procumbens
(wintergreen)
Hakonechloa
(hakonechloa)
Hedera
(ivy)
Lamium
(dead nettle)
Liriope
(lilyturf)
Mazus reptans
(mazus)
Pachysandra
(pachysandra)
Phlox stolonifera
(creeping phlox)
Saxifraga
(saxifrage)
Tiarella
(false miterwort)
Vinca
(periwinkle)

Satisfaction in Shade

Above any other condition, shade asks a gardener to observe: to appreciate the flowering plants that fairly glow in the shadows, to delight in a leaf with ruffled edges, purple veining, or streaks of gold. In sun, too, such nuances matter, but they often play second fiddle to flower color. The intimacy of shade, the calm it creates, invite the closer look, beg the gardener to experiment in imaginative ways with foliage and flowers, textures and shapes, to compose a uniquely satisfying garden.

No matter what type of shade you have—partial, dappled, or full—you won't lack color. Both flowering plants and their foliage partners will shine, as evidenced by the gardens shown on the following pages. For a list of plants and a planting guide for each garden, see pages 54-57.

A SEA OF COLOR IN SHADE
A medley of shade-loving plants, their low-growing, rounded habits broken by spiky leaves and filigrees of flowers, receives morning sun and then dappled shade in this east-facing Oregon garden.

AN INTIMATE GARDEN NOOK

Clustered invitingly around a terra-cotta birdbath, nodding trumpets of Mertensia virginica (Virginia blue-bells) combine with the perky five-lobed blossoms of pink-and-white Primula kisoana (primrose) and frothy white Tiarella cordifolia ssp. collina (foamflower) to create a sense of intimacy and softness in this informal Minnesota garden. The textured foliage of ostrich ferns and the open habit of the star magnolia and daphne reinforce the mood while providing a deep green back-drop to the cool, colorful plantings.

HIGHLIGHTS OF YELLOW-GREEN FOLIAGE

Inspired by the use of yellow-green in English gardens, the owner of this California foliage border has successfully carried on the tradition with the help of two redwood trees, whose shade mimics the light of Eng-land's overcast or rainy days. Carex elata 'Bowles' Golden' (sedge) and Physocarpus opulifolius 'Luteus' (dwarf ninebark) get the partial sun they need to maintain their brilliant yellow-green hue, but remain pro-tected from the intense California sun. Golden echoes come from the Phlomis (Jerusalem sage) and the spiky center of the calla lily, with textural contrast supplied by the dark green ruffled leaves of the lily and the spires of foxglove.

A DAPPLED WOODLAND GARDEN

Bright yellow primroses line a timber stairway as it wends its way up a north-facing slope planted with pleasingly contrasting Phlox divaricata (wild blue phlox) and punctuated with red primroses, yellow daffodils, Aquilegia canadensis (wild columbine), and a variety of azaleas. Located under a high canopy of deciduous trees, this low-maintenance garden in Virginia gets 6 to 7 hours of dappled light daily.

A SURPRISING MIX OF SPRING COLORS

A cultivated Alabama garden merges into a picturesque woodland setting, surprising the eye with the unexpected color of pink-blossomed 'Paula Fay' peonies and yellow 'Narcissus' tree peonies in a shady area. Situated at the edge of the woods, these early-blooming perennials receive the direct sun they need to flower before the deciduous trees leaf out, but enough shade later to keep their blooms from fading too quickly. The garden has a southern exposure, but the canopy of trees filters the sun, causing a play of light and shadow over the ground that allows for a great diversity of plantings.

49

WARM COLORS IN COOL SHADE

The tropical feel of this stunning combination of perennials belies its Oregon roots. Backed by a stand of limbed-up poplar trees that block direct sunlight from the south and growing under a deodar cedar, these plants—including deep gold Trollius chinensis (globeflower), tall, rose-colored Primula secundiflora (sideflower primrose), and Meconopsis betonicifolia (Himalayan blue poppy)—are exposed to an open, northern sky, giving them a full day of bright, indirect light. The complex planting also includes many groupings of Primula Candelabra Hybrids.

A LUSH TERRACED WOODLAND BORDER

Swells of luxuriant foliage in every shade of green project the colors of rosy red Centranthus ruber (Jupiter's-beard), towering Digitalis purpurea (common foxglove), and a mixture of native columbines toward the opposite side of the path, where low-growing English ivy flows. Grown beneath a ceiling of giant bay trees, this California garden, with its informal stone bed and pathway, was artfully created more than a decade ago; allowed to naturalize and spread, it has achieved the look of a semiwild woodland.

A UNIQUE MOSS GARDEN

A river of fern moss (Thuidium delicatulum), interrupted by mounded deep green islands of haircap moss (Polytrichum communa), provides year-round cushiony green paths through this north-facing, gently sloped section of a property in Pennsylvania that makes a home for more than 20 moss species. Located under a canopy of deciduous trees, borders of easy-care dwarf evergreen shrubs, evergreen ground covers, and ferns are highlighted throughout the growing season by pockets of seasonal flowers such as dwarf Japanese iris, Phlox stolonifera (creeping phlox), and Lobelia cardinalis (cardinal flower), providing color from March through October. The gardener's aim was to achieve a naturally landscaped area that required little or no maintenance— and no grass to cut; the garden is now more than 30 years old.

A SEA OF COLOR IN SHADE
pages 42-43

A. *Astilbe x arendsii 'Fanal'* (1)
B. *Hydrangea macrophylla 'Mariesii Variegata'* (1)
C. *Acer palmatum 'Ukigumo'* (1)
D. *Hosta 'True Blue'* (1)
E. *Hosta 'Bold Edger'* (1)
F. *Heuchera americana* (1)
G. *Carex elata 'Aurea'* (4)
H. *Dryopteris dilatata 'Lepidota Cristata'* (3)
I. *Geranium pratense 'Striatum'* (1)
J. *Tsuga canadensis 'Jeddeloh'* (1)

K. *Ruta graveolens 'Curly Girl'* (3)
L. *Carex plantaginea* (1)
M. *Artemisia stellerana 'Silver Brocade'* (8)
N. *Geranium x cantabrigiense* (1)
O. *Hosta 'Allan P. McConnell'* (12)
P. *Astilbe simplicifolia 'Willy Buchanan'* (1)
Q. *Disporum sessile 'Variegatum'* (6)
R. *Corydalis flexuosa 'Blue Panda'* (2)

S. *Tsuga canadensis 'Humphrey Welch'* (1)
T. *Weigela florida 'Variegata'* (1)
U. *Alchemilla erythropoda* (5)
V. *Geranium cv.* (1)
W. *Acanthopanax sieboldianus 'Variegatus'* (1)
X. *Hosta 'Fragrant Bouquet'* (1)
Y. *Hydrangea quercifolia* (1)
Z. *Hosta 'Mildred Seaver'* (1)

AN INTIMATE GARDEN NOOK
page 44

A. *Dicentra spectabilis* (1)
B. *Daphne x burkwoodii 'Carol Mackie'* (1)
C. *Mertensia virginica* (6)
D. *Athyrium nipponicum*

'Pictum' (1)
E. *Primula kisoana* (3)
F. *Hosta decorata* (1)
G. *Tiarella cordifolia ssp. collina* (1)

H. *Epimedium x youngianum 'Niveum'* (1)
I. *Sanguinaria canadensis* (1)
J. *Matteuccia struthiopteris* (3)
K. *Magnolia stellata* (1)

HIGHLIGHTS OF YELLOW-GREEN FOLIAGE
pages 44-45

A. *Pyracantha coccinea* (1)
B. *Hemerocallis hybrid* (1)
C. *Choisya ternata 'Sundance'* (1)
D. *Filipendula rubra 'Venusta'* (3)
E. *Campanula persicifolia ssp. sessiliflora 'Highcliffe'* (3)
F. *Aquilegia hybrid* (2)

G. *Carex elata 'Bowles' Golden'* (4)
H. *Origanum vulgare 'Aureum'* (5)
I. *Euphorbia x martinii* (1)
J. *Zantedeschia aethiopica 'Hercules'* (1)
K. *Veronica sp.* (3)

L. *Physocarpus opulifolius 'Luteus'* (1)
M. *Digitalis purpurea* (1)
N. *Phlomis fruticosa* (1)
O. *Magnolia stellata 'Royal Star'* (1)
P. *Populus alba 'Richardii'* (1)
Q. *Digitalis purpurea 'Alba'* (15)

A DAPPLED WOODLAND GARDEN
pages 46-47

A. *Rhododendron 'Glacier'* (1)
B. *Phlox divaricata* (many)
C. *Narcissus 'Coral Ribbon'* (1)
D. *Phlox subulata* (1)
E. *Primula veris* (100)

F. *Primula elatior 'Gigantea Mischung'* (1)
G. *Narcissus 'Accent'* (many)
H. *Narcissus 'Tresamble'* (many)

I. *Aquilegia canadensis* (2)
J. *Rhododendron 'Gaiety'* (2)
K. *Rhododendron 'Aphrodite'* (2)

NOTE: The key lists each plant type and the total quantity needed to replicate the garden shown. The diagram's letters and numbers refer to the type of plant and the number sited in an area.

A SURPRISING MIX
OF SPRING COLORS
pages 48-49

A. *Magnolia grandiflora*
'Madison' (1)
B. *Paeonia lutea 'Narcissus'* (1)
C. *Paeonia 'Prairie Moon'* (1)
D. *Phlox divaricata*
ssp. laphamii (many)
E. *Paeonia 'Paula Fay'* (3)

F. *Lilium 'Sterling Star'* (2)
G. *Aquilegia hybrid* (1)
H. *Aquilegia alpina* (3)
I. *Dianthus barbatus*
'Newport Pink' (12)
J. *Iris xiphium 'Blue Ribbon'* (10)
K. *Iris spuria 'Wadi Zem Zem'* (1)

L. *Iris orientalis (I. ochroleuca)* (1)
M. *Rhododendron mucronatum*
hybrid (3)
N. *Rhododendron 'Fielder's*
White' (3)
O. *Iris tectorum 'Alba'* (1)
P. *Rhododendron cv.* (1)

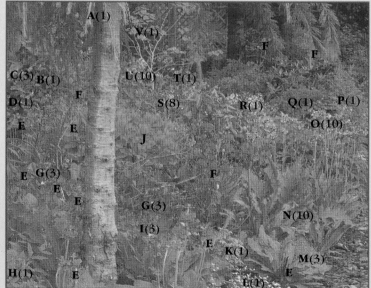

WARM COLORS
IN COOL SHADE
page 50

A. *Cedrus deodara* (1)
B. *Hydrangea aspera*
ssp. sargentiana (1)
C. *Polemonium caeruleum* (3)
D. *Cotinus coggygria 'Royal*
Purple' (1)
E. *Primula Section Proliferae*
(Candelabra) (many)
F. *Trollius chinensis* (many)
G. *Primula beesiana* (6)

H. *Fuchsia magellanica 'Jeanne'* (1)
I. *Primula chungensis* (3)
J. *Sedum x 'Autumn Joy'* (many)
K. *Acanthopanax sieboldianus*
'Variegatus' (1)
L. *Saxifraga moschata*
'Bob Hawkins' (1)
M. *Veronica prostrata*
'Trehane' (3)
N. *Meconopsis napaulensis* (10)

O. *Primula secundiflora* (10)
P. *Lonicera nitida 'Baggesen's*
Gold' (1)
Q. *Euphorbia polychroma* (1)
R. *Cymbalaria muralis 'Alba*
Compacta' (1)
S. *Primula sikkimensis* (8)
T. *Geranium palmatum* (1)
U. *Meconopsis betonicifolia* (10)
V. *Cercis chinensis 'Avondale'* (1)

A LUSH TERRACED
WOODLAND BORDER
pages 50-51

A. *Aquilegia hybrid* (several)
B. *Digitalis purpurea* (4)
C. *Astilbe x arendsii* (3)
D. *Tiarella cordifolia* (3)
E. *Centranthus ruber* (2)

F. *Dicentra spectabilis* (2)
G. *Hedera helix* (many)
H. *Aquilegia formosa* (3)
I. *Cornus florida* 'Cherokee
Sunset' (1)

A UNIQUE
MOSS GARDEN
pages 52-53

A. *Polystichum acrostichoides* (1)
B. *Lobelia cardinalis* (many)
C. *Scutellaria integrifolia* (2)
D. *Hosta sp.* (many)

E. *Iris gracilipes* (1)
F. *Polytrichum communa* (many)
G. *Thuidium delicatulum* (many)

H. *Gentiana scabra* (2)
I. *Chamaecyparis obtusa* 'Nana' (1)
J. *Phlox stolonifera* (many)

NOTE: The key lists each plant type and the total quantity needed to replicate the garden shown. The diagram's letters and numbers refer to the type of plant and the number sited in an area.

CHAPTER THREE

Letting Your Shade Garden Flower

Conventional gardening wisdom holds that a shady area is fine for foliage, but only a sunny plot can bring you abundant flowers throughout the seasons. Not so! More and more gardeners are finding that a shade garden can be much more than the green-clad poor relation of a sunny bed or border. The Virginia garden at right hints at the wide variety of plants that bloom opulently in the shade.

Growing flowers in low light can be a rewarding exercise in mastering challenges and maximizing possibilities, arousing a certain pride of achievement in the gardener. Some shady plots do indeed offer serious difficulties—soil that is boggy or hard and dry or suffused with tree roots, or space that is deep in shadow. But if you choose your plants wisely and make use of proper cultural techniques, detailed on the following pages, you can bring almost any shady spot into flower—even if the solution ends up being container plants placed strategically throughout the garden.

A. *Geranium maculatum (volunteer seedlings)*
B. *Tiarella cordifolia (15)*
C. *Phlox divaricata (volunteer seedlings)*
D. *Rhododendron 'Echo' (1)*
E. *Rhododendron 'Delaware Valley White' (1)*

The key lists each plant type and the number of plants needed to replicate the garden shown opposite. The letters and numbers above refer to the type of plant and the number sited in an area.

A Riot of Color: The Teeming Ranks of Shade-Flowering Plants

Shade plants were among the first flowering vegetation to appear on earth. Cousins of those primordial flowers flourish in shady gardens today in the form of rhododendron and magnolia species, and many other shade plants have since evolved in the shadows of taller neighbors. Nurseries now offer a steady stream of new shade-tolerant varieties.

Ornamental trees are the most prominent plants to display brilliant color in the shade. Many produce not only flowers but also colorful fruit. Dogwood *(Cornus)* trees, for example, bear flowerlike bracts in the spring and may display bright berries or tinted bark in the winter. *Stewartia* produces white flowers in summer and exhibits handsomely mottled bark throughout the winter.

Shrubs and Vines

At eye level come a host of shrubs that, like ornamental trees, bring sparkling color to the shade garden not only with flowers but also with berries in many hues. Rhododendron species—which include the azaleas—are mainstays for shady areas throughout much of North America. Their bloom times range from early spring into the summer, and flower colors run from white to deep purple. While most azaleas are deciduous shrubs, almost all other rhododendrons are evergreen, helping to maintain the garden's structure year round.

Hydrangea is another reliable shade shrub, with long-lasting summer blooms in white, pink, or blue. Soil chemistry governs color in some cultivars, with acid soil producing blue flowers and alkaline soil, pink. A climbing form, *H. anomala* var. *petiolaris,* winds along walls or around trees.

Less commonly grown, but handsome, shrubs for the shade garden include the evergreen *Mahonia* (Oregon grape), with cascades of yellow flowers in early spring and edible berries later. In late spring, *Gaultheria shallon* (salal) yields spikes of tiny white or pink flowers, followed by purple to black berries.

Strong performers for partial shade include *Chionanthus virginicus* (old-man's-beard), which produces fragrant white flowers in late spring, and mountain laurel *(Kalmia latifolia)*, which fares well in full shade but flowers best with some sun.

Most flowering vines are considered sun lovers, but a few, such as *Gelsemium sempervirens* 'Pride of Augusta', *Akebia quinata* (five-leaf akebia), and some species of clematis and *Lonicera* (honeysuckle), will bloom in partial shade, and some, such as *Aristolochia macrophylla* (Dutchman's-pipe) and x *Fatshedera lizei* (miracle plant) don't care for direct sun at all.

Herbaceous Bloomers

Shade-loving herbaceous perennials make up a long and colorful list *(encyclopedia, pages 104-151, and Plant Selection Guide, pages 96-101).* No perennial bed or border in shade need lack for variety and visual impact. But the story doesn't end there. Gardeners in the South can also use partially shaded sites to grow a large number of perennials that require full sun in northern zones. Indeed, no matter where you live, you may be able to stretch the ostensible cultural limits of perennial species and cultivars by observing the plants' characteristics, understanding their origins, and getting tips from other gardeners who have grown them.

Annuals, like flowering vines, are generally held to be sun plants, but many can bloom in dappled or partial shade. The beautiful, easy-care impatiens flowers freely in whites, pinks, reds, oranges, and a few blue-violets. Ageratum, a tidy little plant with blue, pink, or white flowers, tolerates partial shade and blooms for a long time without deadheading. Begonia flowers dependably from spring through to frost—or year round, in frost-free zones. Similarly, fuchsia blooms richly as an annual in hanging baskets in the shade, and hardy varieties survive the year in mild climates.

Wildflowers hold a special place in shade gardens: Shade-conditioned native plants can provide color and interest from earliest spring through late summer. Some, like jack-in-the-pulpit or dogtooth violet, grow, bloom, and disappear quickly. But others, including the dainty spray of Solomon's-seal, last for weeks, while a rare native, *Spigelia marilandica* (Indian pink), opens new blooms over a long period.

Bulbs are another good source of herbaceous flowers for the shade garden. About half of all bulb genera tolerate, prefer, or require a degree of shade. A few are comfortable even in full shade—for example, *Achimenes* (orchid pansy), *Arisaema*

COLOR FROM THE GROUND UP
The sprightly pale lavender blooms of the perennial Anemone nemorosa (wood anemone) spread a frothy carpet from which the compact forms of the evergreen Rhododendron yakusimanum emerge, bursting with bell-shaped pink flowers. Forming a backdrop to this cheerful Oregon garden is another, larger rhododendron and the pendulous brilliant yellow blossoms of a small Laburnum (bean tree).

(dragonroot), *Begonia* x *tuberhybrida* (tuberous begonia), dogtooth violet, *Hyacinthoides,* and *Ornithogalum nutans* (nodding star-of-Bethlehem).

Ground Covers

And finally, carpeting the shade-garden floor with blossoms are some of the most popular evergreen and deciduous ground covers, with flowers ranging from white to yellow to blue-purple. *Vinca* (periwinkle) sends evergreen strands across almost any soil and produces blossoms in white or violet, according to the cultivar. Heuchera displays beautifully veined foliage and red, pink, or greenish white flowers. And several types of *Epimedium* (bishop's hat), such as *E. perralderanum* and *E.* x *versicolor* 'Sulphureum', blanket the ground even in dry shade and produce lovely yellow blossoms.

Unique Traits of Shade Plants

Diverse though they are, flowering shade plants share many characteristics derived from the often difficult conditions in which they exist. Adapted to soil already congested by tree roots, for example, most shade-loving varieties are perforce shallow rooted. This makes planting them easy; even large rhododendrons have manageable rootballs.

Shade lovers are also highly sensitive to moisture levels in the soil. Many require a natural layer of leaf litter or an application of mulch to keep them from drying out. Paradoxically, this trait makes the shady flower garden a fairly low-maintenance proposition. In fall, you need remove only the heaviest drifts of fallen leaves from areas planted with flowering species, leaving in place a protective covering of leaf litter.

A SWIRL OF FLOWER COLORS SET OFF BY VIBRANT FOLIAGE
In the partial shade of this Pennsylvania cottage garden, a gold-tipped Chamaecyparis obtusa 'Crippsii' (Hinoki false cypress) and a white-blossomed viburnum anchor drifts of pale lavender-blue forget-me-not and snowy candytuft. Hybrid tulips provide splashes of pink.

Shade-flowering plants have a few other virtues that make life easier for the gardener. Many of them self-sow, meaning that if you don't tidy up too much, you'll get more seedlings to increase your stock of plants. And those plants pollinated by insects are shameless in their strategies to attract them. In shrubs such as *Chionanthus* (fringe tree), which blooms in spring, or those that flower in late winter, such as *Hamamelis* (witch hazel) and *Chimonanthus* (wintersweet), rich fragrance entices the pollinators. Color, too, plays a role. Foraging bees respond to blue and yellow above all other colors, and bright yellow is among the commonest flower colors in shade-blooming species. The vivid red of cardinal flower *(Lobelia cardinalis),* one of the few shade-blooming plants pollinated by birds, attracts hummingbirds to its languid blossoms.

The Effects of Color

Besides attracting pollinators, color contributes mightily to the mood of a garden. The glowing yellow of spring flowers warms us and draws us in; the heat of summer seems moderated by pastel flowers under trees, furthering the shade's actual cooling effect. Shadows tend to make colors look deeper and to heighten blue tones. White flowers can gain an assertive brightness in deep shade, an effect quite unlike that produced by the blending role they assume in sunny gardens.

In fact, the same blossom on a given plant may take on a color in shade that is markedly different from the one it wears in sun. And because shade softens contrasting flower colors, you can use bolder combinations than you might otherwise dare. Bear in mind, too, that a given flower color can strike different notes on different types of plants. A sprinkling of pink lily blooms is gentle and soothing, while the massed blossoms of one pink azalea can inflame an entire area.

A PARADE OF ALL-SEASON COLOR
Flowering dogwood glows in the dappled shade of spring in this St. Louis garden. The tree's fall foliage and bright berries will shine long after the bluebells and bleeding heart below it have retired.

TIPS FROM THE PROS
Choosing Flowers for Shade

Remember these tips when making your plant selections:

- Plants grow leggier in shade, so buy the bushiest, most compact specimens you can.
- Don't collect wildflowers from the wild. Learn what plants can be nursery propagated, and buy them only from sources certifying that the plants were propagated— not merely grown—in the nursery. Consult native-plant societies and local arboretums for suggestions about plants and other information.

- When buying plants that are marked shade-tolerant, pick varieties that bloom early, when deciduous trees still admit the light they need for their most active growth.
- If you like a certain sun-loving plant but have only shade, try it there. Many sun plants appreciate afternoon shade; others adjust to dappled shade, especially in the South. Sun plants that originated in cool areas are good candidates for growing in partial shade in the South.

Planting for Year-Round Color

With careful planning, it's possible for shade gardens in many North American hardiness zones to have flowers or fruit displaying color all through the year. Milder climates favor flowery displays, of course, but even in snow country, a shade garden can be bright through the cold months.

Your greatest allies are trees and shrubs, which not only may produce berries and display colorful bark but also will provide shelter for other plants. Massed plantings of trees and shrubs cut the force of drying winds, both winter and summer. Even leafless bushes make a noticeable windbreak.

Sizing Up Your Site

One secret to achieving a garden with color the year round is to make use of microclimates. These areas, created both by shade and by the effects of various physical features, can allow you to grow plants you might otherwise not consider.

The shady north wall of your house, for example, may be the perfect place to set an early-blooming shrub, shielding it from sun that might encourage it to flower a little too early for its own good. And the same cover that gives your plants shade—be it wall, fence, or tree—also provides some protection from battering by hard rain, hail, or wind. Rocks, too, provide protection, not only from desiccating wind but also from sunscald, a kind of damage that can occur to bark low on the west side of tree trunks exposed to intense afternoon sun in winter. And large rocks not only cast shade but also absorb and store heat, creating microclimates around them.

Similarly, an exposed slope that looks frigid might actually warm up faster on winter mornings than a naturally enclosed "frost pocket" at the bottom of the hill. And a water feature—a stream, or even a small lily pond—has at least a modest tempering effect on cold or heat, letting temperature-sensitive plants flourish near it.

Choosing the Plants

When deciding on flowering plants to add to your shade garden, keep in mind the ideal of a succession of bloom. A sequence of flowers seen through more than one season is far more interesting than a great show of bloom all at once, followed by long stretches of green only. Mixing plants that bloom at different times also lets you use flower colors to alter your garden's moods dramatically during the year.

Spring's Explosion of Color

Spring is the peak time for flowering for most shade-tolerant genera, just as it is for sun lovers. In a secluded corner under a white-flowering dogwood, for instance, a brilliant splash of tulips can open the gardening season with panache. As the tulips fade and their foliage becomes shabby, an early shade perennial like *Dicentra spectabilis* (common bleeding heart), with its arching lines of pink and white blossoms, can take over the area; for yellow blossoms, use *Corydalis lutea*.

Indeed, you can fill a bed with almost any color that suits you, including the blues, violets, and whites that so nicely light up a shaded area. Virginia bluebells or Siberian iris are good choices for

TULIPS AND PHLOX LEAD THE SPRING PARADE

Blooms of these two sun lovers adorn a wooded Alabama pathway in early spring, before the trees leaf out overhead. The blue Phlox divaricata (wild sweet William) will hide the dying tulip foliage later in the season, just as the blossom focus shifts to the massed azaleas at upper right and to other shade-loving species.

POOLS OF PINK AND LAVENDER BLOSSOMS

The rosy purple foliage of spring-blooming blue ajuga forms a ground-cover mat beneath the hostas at left in this northeastern shade garden. Hydrangea contrasts with the wall of evergreen trees behind, echoing the pink in the spring-blooming irises.

most areas. You can also set out tender annuals after the last frost date: Impatiens, begonias, and ageratums cover most of the color families, with yellows best represented by tuberous begonias.

Ground covers can adorn your open spaces with flowers in shades of yellow *(Mahonia repens)*, white *(Pachysandra terminalis)*, or blue *(Vinca major)*. *Akebia quinata*, with its racemes of dark purple blooms, yellow-blossomed *Gelsemium sempervirens* 'Pride of Augusta', and white climbing hydrangea are among the vines that flower early. And spring is also the season when the great majority of flowering shrubs and trees for shade produce their blooms *(chart, page 66)*.

Summer-Flowering Plants

Although the possibilities are not quite as broad as in spring, enough shade-loving perennials bloom in summer to allow you to plan for a wide range of colors—in fact, there is no spring color you cannot duplicate in your summer herbaceous shade bed or border. Possibilities for summer-flowering ground covers are fewer, but include white-blossomed *Ardisia japonica* (marlberry) and bright yellow *Hypericum calycinum* (creeping St.-John's-wort). For vines, choose *Aristo-*

lochia macrophylla, with purplish brown, yellow-throated flowers; bluish purple *Clematis* 'The President'; or *Jasminum officinale* 'Grandiflorum' (common white jasmine), whose blooms carry over into autumn.

Among shrubs, several hydrangea and kalmia cultivars, as well as white-blooming *Abelia* x *grandiflora* 'Prostrata', golden yellow *Hypericum* 'Hidcote', yellow-green *Laurus nobilis* (laurel), fragrant white sweet bay magnolia, and purple-and-orange *Stewartia ovata* var. *grandiflora* (mountain camellia) flower in summer. Summer-blossoming trees include *Stewartia pseudocamellia* (Japanese stewartia), with orange-and-white flowers, and *Styrax obassia* (fragrant snowbell), with flowers hanging in white racemes.

Autumn and Winter Bloomers

Fall-flowering herbaceous plants still offer a fair range of colors. If, for example, you add Japanese anemone to the mix of plants in your bed or border, you'll get late-summer flower heads in shades of red and pink that coordinate with the changing foliage of trees and shrubs. Some late-blooming hardy chrysanthemums tolerate light shade, too. Autumn crocus bulbs, concealed among tree

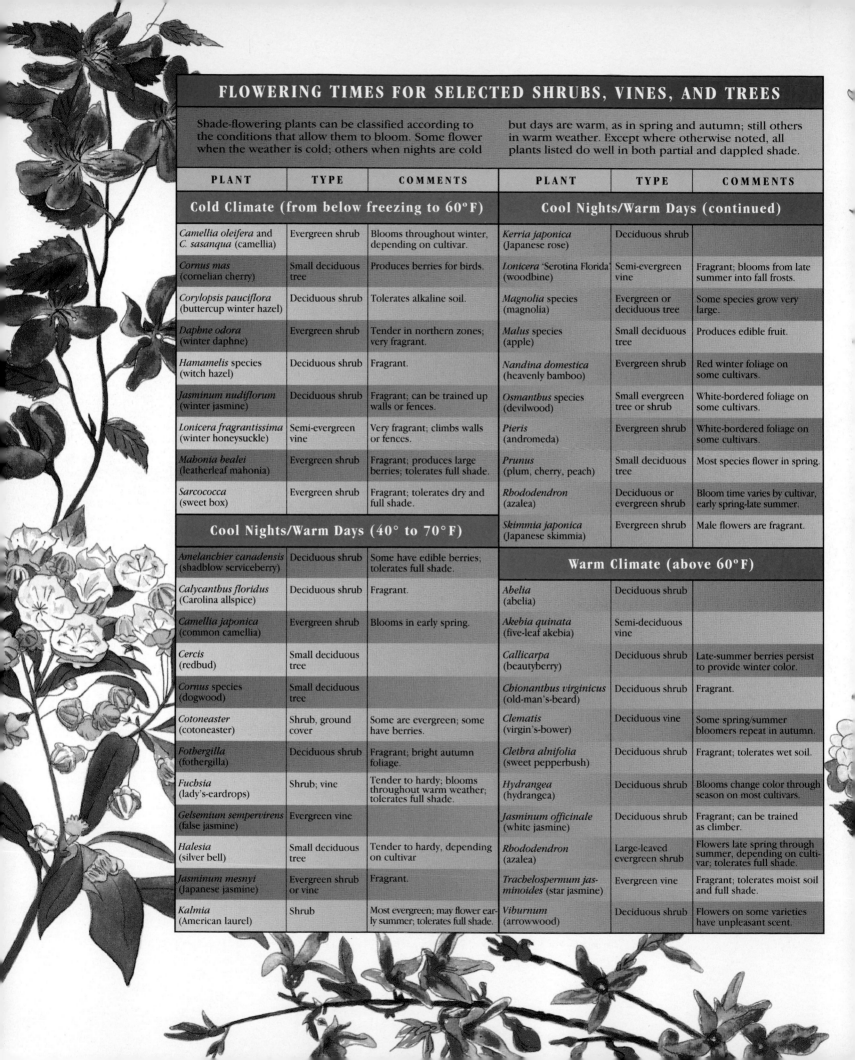

FLOWERING TIMES FOR SELECTED SHRUBS, VINES, AND TREES

Shade-flowering plants can be classified according to the conditions that allow them to bloom. Some flower when the weather is cold; others when nights are cold but days are warm, as in spring and autumn; still others in warm weather. Except where otherwise noted, all plants listed do well in both partial and dappled shade.

PLANT	TYPE	COMMENTS
Cold Climate (from below freezing to 60°F)		
Camellia oleifera and *C. sasanqua* (camellia)	Evergreen shrub	Blooms throughout winter, depending on cultivar.
Cornus mas (cornelian cherry)	Small deciduous tree	Produces berries for birds.
Corylopsis pauciflora (buttercup winter hazel)	Deciduous shrub	Tolerates alkaline soil.
Daphne odora (winter daphne)	Evergreen shrub	Tender in northern zones; very fragrant.
Hamamelis species (witch hazel)	Deciduous shrub	Fragrant.
Jasminum nudiflorum (winter jasmine)	Deciduous shrub	Fragrant; can be trained up walls or fences.
Lonicera fragrantissima (winter honeysuckle)	Semi-evergreen vine	Very fragrant; climbs walls or fences.
Mahonia bealei (leatherleaf mahonia)	Evergreen shrub	Fragrant; produces large berries; tolerates full shade.
Sarcococca (sweet box)	Evergreen shrub	Fragrant; tolerates dry and full shade.
Cool Nights/Warm Days (40° to 70°F)		
Amelanchier canadensis (shadblow serviceberry)	Deciduous shrub	Some have edible berries; tolerates full shade.
Calycanthus floridus (Carolina allspice)	Deciduous shrub	Fragrant.
Camellia japonica (common camellia)	Evergreen shrub	Blooms in early spring.
Cercis (redbud)	Small deciduous tree	
Cornus species (dogwood)	Small deciduous tree	
Cotoneaster (cotoneaster)	Shrub, ground cover	Some are evergreen; some have berries.
Fothergilla (fothergilla)	Deciduous shrub	Fragrant; bright autumn foliage.
Fuchsia (lady's-eardrops)	Shrub; vine	Tender to hardy; blooms throughout warm weather; tolerates full shade.
Gelsemium sempervirens (false jasmine)	Evergreen vine	
Halesia (silver bell)	Small deciduous tree	Tender to hardy, depending on cultivar
Jasminum mesnyi (Japanese jasmine)	Evergreen shrub or vine	Fragrant.
Kalmia (American laurel)	Shrub	Most evergreen; may flower early summer; tolerates full shade.

PLANT	TYPE	COMMENTS
Cool Nights/Warm Days (continued)		
Kerria japonica (Japanese rose)	Deciduous shrub	
Lonicera 'Serotina Florida' (woodbine)	Semi-evergreen vine	Fragrant; blooms from late summer into fall frosts.
Magnolia species (magnolia)	Evergreen or deciduous tree	Some species grow very large.
Malus species (apple)	Small deciduous tree	Produces edible fruit.
Nandina domestica (heavenly bamboo)	Evergreen shrub	Red winter foliage on some cultivars.
Osmanthus species (devilwood)	Small evergreen tree or shrub	White-bordered foliage on some cultivars.
Pieris (andromeda)	Evergreen shrub	White-bordered foliage on some cultivars.
Prunus (plum, cherry, peach)	Small deciduous tree	Most species flower in spring.
Rhododendron (azalea)	Deciduous or evergreen shrub	Bloom time varies by cultivar, early spring-late summer.
Skimmia japonica (Japanese skimmia)	Evergreen shrub	Male flowers are fragrant.
Warm Climate (above 60°F)		
Abelia (abelia)	Deciduous shrub	
Akebia quinata (five-leaf akebia)	Semi-deciduous vine	
Callicarpa (beautyberry)	Deciduous shrub	Late-summer berries persist to provide winter color.
Chionanthus virginicus (old-man's-beard)	Deciduous shrub	Fragrant.
Clematis (virgin's-bower)	Deciduous vine	Some spring/summer bloomers repeat in autumn.
Clethra alnifolia (sweet pepperbush)	Deciduous shrub	Fragrant; tolerates wet soil.
Hydrangea (hydrangea)	Deciduous shrub	Blooms change color through season on most cultivars.
Jasminum officinale (white jasmine)	Deciduous shrub	Fragrant; can be trained as climber.
Rhododendron (azalea)	Large-leaved evergreen shrub	Flowers late spring through summer, depending on cultivar; tolerates full shade.
Trachelospermum jasminoides (star jasmine)	Evergreen vine	Fragrant; tolerates moist soil and full shade.
Viburnum (arrowwood)	Deciduous shrub	Flowers on some varieties have unpleasant scent.

roots, send up lavish pink cups amid russet fallen leaves to startle and delight garden visitors.

In addition, you can expect a pretty spectrum of autumn blossom colors to emerge on the pale-green-flowered vine x *Fatshedera lizei;* shrubs such as lavender-pink *Camellia* 'Winter's Interlude', white *Fatsia japonica* (glossy-leaved paper plant), and white *Osmanthus heterophyllus* 'Variegatus' (holly olive); and the orange-flowered ornamental tree *Osmanthus fragrans* (sweet olive).

After a hiatus during the first part of winter, you can complete the year of shade perennials with late-winter-blooming plants such as white-flowering *Galanthus nivalis* 'Flore Pleno' (common snowdrop) and *Leucojum vernum* (spring snowflake), yellow *Eranthis hyemalis* (winter aconite), or purple *Viola odorata* 'Royal Robe' (sweet violet). The seed heads left standing on the Japanese anemones that flowered in late summer make a further contribution to the shade garden's winter look—they assume striking shapes when snow mounds on them.

A number of shrubs flower during this season, including *Camellia japonica* 'Berenice Boddy', with pink semidouble blooms; lavender *Daphne mezereum* (February daphne); rosy purple *D. odora* (winter daphne); reddish-brown-and-yellow *Hamamelis mollis* 'Goldcrest' (Chinese witch hazel); yellow to red *H. vernalis* (American witch hazel); yellow winter jasmine; and cream-colored *Sarcococca confusa* (sweet box).

Beyond Blooms

After their flowers are gone, some woody plants keep the color coming with berries, which come into their own as the leaves fall from deciduous shrubs and trees. On evergreen species, berries ripen to showy colors in autumn. Besides being decorative, many berries attract birds and other wildlife to your garden. Most of the berries are borne on shrubs—the fruits of the herbaceous perennial *Arum italicum* (Italian arum) and ornamental holly trees are exceptions. Reliable berry-growing shade species include red chokeberry, American holly, *I. verticillata* (winterberry), beautyberry, *Fatsia japonica, Gaultheria procumbens* (wintergreen), *G. shallon,* bayberry, heavenly bamboo, *Viburnum prunifolium* (black haw), and *V. dilatatum* (linden viburnum).

If you want to keep the berries on your bushes longer, put in cultivars that produce yellow or orange fruit; the birds go for the red ones first. Use the chart at left to help you choose shrubs that flower at different times.

A New Breed of Camellias for the Cold-Climate Shade Garden

Bearing glossy evergreen leaves and large, elegant flowers of white, pink, or red, shade-loving *Camellia* resembles rhododendron in its qualities and growing preferences. Both genera originated in mountain woodlands, which means they prefer shade and acid soil. Both often have shallow roots. Depending on species and cultivar, camellia blooms either in fall and early winter or in early to late spring. But unlike rhododendron, until lately it was too tender to grow in most of North America north of Zone 8. A breeding program begun at the National Arboretum in Washington, D.C., has developed crosses between a fall-blooming camellia, *C. oleifera*, from the People's Republic of China, and three other species, yielding plants hardy to -2°F. The encyclopedia *(pages 104-151)* names several good camellia cultivars.

Plant the new hardy camellias where they will be protected from winter winds and morning sun, setting the base of the stem slightly higher than the surrounding soil. Water thoroughly once a week through the first season. Maintain 2 to 4 inches of mulch around the plant to keep the soil moist and stable through periods of freezing and thawing.

Adding Flowers to Shade

Whether you are adding flowering species to an existing shade garden or are planning a new garden area, deciding which plants to put in requires some forethought. Impulse purchases at the local nursery can be fun, but may also result in a hodgepodge of plants. To create a garden that is visually exciting, you must think of it as a community of plants and choose its occupants according to how well they work together for the look you want. As you appraise plants that attract you, imagine them in the garden, in the company of existing plantings or of other potential plant choices.

Look for foliage shapes, textures, and colors that complement the leaves of nearby plants; choose flower colors that will mingle happily with those of neighboring blossoms. Make sure you have enough room for a new specimen at its mature size, so that it won't dominate the space and crowd out established plants. And remember, plants that tolerate both sun and shade tend to grow taller in shade.

Next, consider your soil, drainage, and light, and match your plants to your growing conditions. A plant may grow for you in the wrong situation, but it may or may not bloom there. Consult the encyclopedia *(pages 104-151)* and the Plant Selection Guide *(pages 96-101)* for cultural information on a variety of flowering plants.

Building the Garden Structure

When planning for the addition of flowers to a shady space, remember those horizontal layers and vertical planes that can mark a shade garden off into "rooms" filled with "furniture" *(pages 12-13)*. For instance, in a yard where high shade is cast by tall trees underplanted only with grass, you can develop a more interesting design by first setting in a middle layer of flowering shrubs. Then add favorite shade-loving perennials and annuals around and under the shrub framework. If your shade is cast mainly by tall, mature shrubs, or by a wall or fence, consider adding a flowering accent tree—say, a magnolia or dogwood—to break the horizontal line of the shade makers.

Above all, place plants so that they will appear to best advantage when in bloom. Oakleaf hydrangeas *(Hydrangea quercifolia),* for example, are showy enough to be effective at a distance, so you can put them in the depths of the garden. But you might want to set low-growing, delicate-bloomed wildflowers like trout lilies along the path to the front door or at the edge of the patio, where they can be easily seen and admired.

Solving Shade Problems

While some gardeners enjoy the wonderful growing conditions that prevail in bright shade, many others have to deal with truly daunting situations: areas choked with tree roots; dry, deep shade where the soil is poor and thin; soggy patches where the soil is poorly drained; a strip of dense, all-day shade in a city lot. Proper plant selection is the key to converting problem shade into beautiful garden vistas, but a few tricks of the trade may also help in your own difficult site.

If your shade garden is punctuated by trees with large, greedy roots, your choice of plants will be limited; most flowering shrubs and perennials languish in such conditions. You can try shallow-

rooted ground covers—among the best are *Epimedium alpinum,* which creates a blanket of gray-and-yellow blossoms with red spots; white-blooming *E. grandiflorum;* and yellow *E. pinnatum* var. *colchicum.* But the most prudent solution may be to surround the offending trees with container plants.

While they can be planted with everything from the tiniest flowers to shrubs and small trees, the most versatile containers are the ones you can move about—allowing you to vary the plants' effect or to give them more or less shade as the season progresses. Whatever their size, container plants will usually need more watering, feeding, and general care than the same plants set in the ground, so you may want to use them judiciously.

Match your containers first to the size and type of each plant. A shrub may need a half whiskey barrel, while a planting of impatiens will do fine in a 10-inch terra-cotta pot. Consider, too, your plants' growth habits—a sprawling fuchsia might look too casual in a formal stone urn but just right in a hanging rattan basket. Trailing species look best in hanging planters; tuberous begonias, with their large flowers in a wide range of colors, do particularly well in them. Swing the planters from the branches of shade-making trees or, with equally good effect, from walls, fences, or the sides of buildings. For a rugged, natural look, plant small woodland genera like *Viola* (violet) or shallow-rooted ones like *Ajuga* (bugleweed) in hollowed logs scavenged from the woods. Or hide pots in soil or mulch, or among ground-cover plants.

Plants are more directly exposed to cold in containers than in the earth, so either choose hardy species or plan to move those that are borderline frost-tender into a sheltered porch or greenhouse for the cold weather. Shade-flowering plants that do well in containers include *Acanthus mollis* (common bear's-breech), anemone, *Bergenia,* camellia, *Convallaria* (lily-of-the-valley), fatsia, fuchsia, hosta, impatiens, holly, mahonia, daffodil, *Nicotiana* (flowering tobacco), rhododendron, *Saxifraga* (saxifrage), *Pieris,* thunbergia, *Myosotis* (forget-me-not), skimmia, *Thalictrum* (meadow rue), *Viola,* and periwinkle.

Planting in Dry, Deep Shade or Hot Shade

Dry shade, another challenging garden habitat, can occur under a tree whose canopy of leaf cover is so dense that it acts like an umbrella, diverting most

clude ajuga, *Aquilegia canadensis* (wild columbine), epimedium, heuchera, Japanese anemone, *Pulmonaria* (lungwort), *Scilla*, *Tradescantia*, and *Vinca*. Shrubs that bloom in these conditions include *Sarcococca*, kalmia, *Myrica cerifera* (wax myrtle), and some viburnum cultivars.

In parts of the West, where dry shade is accompanied by high heat and low humidity, plants that do well include begonia, *Enkianthus*, epimedium, *Gaultheria*, hellebore, heuchera, *Hosta lancifolia* (narrow-leaved plantain lily), hydrangea, saxifrage, skimmia, and yucca.

Boggy Shade and Poorly Drained Soil

At the other end of the soil spectrum lies the problem of wet ground. Muddy patches that persist even in dry weather or areas where rainwater regularly pools reveal poor drainage and a boglike condition that is deadly to many plant species. Planting bog-tolerant species is an easy-care solution, one that is far simpler than trying to change soil drainage patterns.

Some of the many flowering shade dwellers that flourish in boggy soil are *Calycanthus floridus* (Carolina allspice), *Clethra alnifolia* (sweet pepperbush), *Hemerocallis* (daylily), forget-me-not, hosta, winterberry, impatiens, lobelia, sweet bay magnolia, bayberry, *Primula* (primrose), species irises, and *Rhododendron viscosum* (swamp azalea).

In moist but drained soil at the edge of a bog, try *Astilbe*, *Dicentra* (bleeding heart), *Ligularia* (leopard plant), and *Fothergilla;* just be sure their crowns are above the wet soil.

Planting in City-Lot Shade

City gardens often have challenging environments. Many lots are narrow, squeezed between buildings or fences that produce dense shade where few plants can grow. Painting walls, fences, and even paving stones a light color, so that they reflect available light, helps considerably. Even a 1 percent increase in ambient light can greatly increase plant growth and blooming.

Flowering vines such as climbing hydrangea (*Hydrangea anomala* var. *petiolaris*) or shade-tolerant varieties of clematis can turn those same walls and fences from liabilities to assets. You might train a shrub or small tree as an espalier against a wall, or let clematis climb along a fence *(page 76)*. Use small, open-structured trees to

REACHING SKYWARD IN THE SHADE
Making spectacular use of dappled vertical shade, this 30-year-old climbing hydrangea vine grows into the canopy of a large tulip poplar (Liriodendron tulipifera) in Delaware. The deciduous hydrangea blooms in mid-summer; later on, its elegant shape and exfoliating bark make a fine winter display.

rainfall to the soil outside its drip line. Few flowering shade plants thrive in dry, poor soil areas. Your best bet is to turn dry shade into moister shade.

Digging organic matter such as leaves, compost, or rotted manure into the soil will help. If direct soil amendment is too difficult, a 2- to 4-inch layer of organic mulch spread on the ground and under shrubs can begin the process. Renewed over several seasons, the mulch will enrich the soil and help hold what little water soaks in. You can also loop soaker hoses through the areas you want to plant. Cover them with a leaf-litter mulch and water slowly on a regular basis.

Flowering herbaceous plants for dry shade in-

showcase climbing plants as well, letting their flowers peep out among the branches.

Flowering shrubs, trees, and herbaceous plants can do much to reconfigure a narrow lot; use them, in combination with foliage plants, as focal points and accents to lead the eye through the garden. And if your garden, because of a narrow, channel-like shape, suffers from a wind-tunnel effect, a well-placed row of a shrub such as Chinese witch hazel, *Kerria japonica* (Japanese rose), *Ligustrum obtusifolium* (border privet), or *Osmanthus heterophyllus* 'Variegatus' (holly olive) can dissipate the wind's force and slow it down.

City gardeners may also face compacted soil and pollution in soil and air. To improve the soil and make it more hospitable for your plants, double dig the beds and add humus, in the form of compost, well-rotted manure, or peat moss. In some areas, park departments or similar public agencies give away composted leaf humus; check with your local government.

As a last resort for badly polluted soil, plant in containers filled with potting mix. Container plants recommended for city conditions include dogwood, holly, *Andromeda* (bog rosemary), hydrangea, laurel, rhododendron, witch hazel, dicentra, corydalis, daylily, epimedium, hosta, begonia, and impatiens.

THE ART OF ILLUSION

Artful design expands the visual size of a tiny urban shade garden nestled amid buildings. An oakleaf hydrangea, hostas, and ground covers flower copiously in the scant summer sun; vines and espaliers soften the enclosing walls; and a small pond and waterfall highlight the island plantings.

Planting and Caring for Your Garden

Shade gardens not only give you invitingly cool, sheltered spaces, but also leave you plenty of time to relax in them. You'll spend far fewer hours maintaining a shady area than you would a sunny garden. Weeding, for example, is a minor chore, and the garden requires considerably less fertilizing and water.

To enjoy shade's bounty, however, you must pay a certain price up front. Growing plants successfully in the shade produced by either trees or structures means you must get the plants off to the best start possible. A key task will be to prepare just the right setting and soil for your chosen plants. One approach is shown in this Charlottesville, Virginia, garden, where the homeowner overcame drainage problems and soil compacted with tree roots by building a raised bed to support a variety of shade-loving plants. The following pages present detailed information on this and many other techniques for planting gardens that will thrive in all sorts of shade situations.

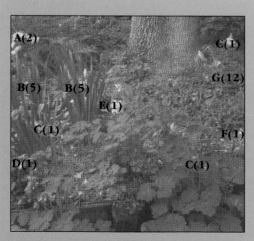

A. *Dicentra spectabilis
   'Alba' (2)*
B. *Narcissus 'Ice Follies' (10)*
C. *Aquilegia caerulea (3)*
D. *Lamium maculatum
   'Roseum' (1)*
E. *Aquilegia caerulea 'Alba' (1)*
F. *Hosta crispula (1)*
G. *Vinca minor (12)*

The key lists each plant type and the total quantity needed to replicate the garden shown opposite. The letters and numbers above refer to the type of plant and the number sited in an area.

Putting in a Shade Garden

Once you have designed your garden and selected plants, it is time to prepare the site for their arrival. As a preliminary step, if you already have mature trees on your property, complete any necessary heavy pruning and tree removal *(pages 82-85)* before installing more plants. The success of your garden will depend on careful preparation of the soil, which begins with learning how to test it—a relatively simple affair that will yield great dividends later.

Knowing Your Soil

Three aspects of soil are of prime importance to shade gardeners: structure, fertility, and pH, or acidity/alkalinity balance. A soil's structure—the way soil particles cling together and the size and frequency of air spaces between them—affects its drainage, ability to hold nutrients, and penetrability to growing roots. It is determined largely by the mix of different rock particles that make up the soil, the largest being sand, then silt, then clay. Good soil structure also requires the presence of considerable organic matter—living microorganisms and dead plant material—which help the soil form into crumbly, irregular, slightly moist shapes that allow for the optimum passage of air, water, nutrients, and roots.

Fertility refers to the amount of nutrients in the soil. A testing laboratory will perform a thorough analysis of your soil's fertility and pH and suggest specific amendments to improve it. Your Cooperative Extension Service can recommend a reputable lab near you. Once the soil has been professionally tested, you can perform an annual retest yourself using a relatively inexpensive kit available at nurseries and garden centers.

Your soil's pH is determined by the type of rock sediment it contains, as well as by organic matter. For instance, limestone in the soil produces high alkalinity; the rich, moist, decayed organic matter called humus produces high acidity. Nurseries and garden shops sell inexpensive kits that read pH. Once you know the pH level, you can either select plants suited to the soil as is or modify the acidity/alkalinity balance with the addition of amendments. Lime will raise the pH—make the soil more alkaline—while sulfur and organic matter will lower it.

Preparing the Soil for Shade Plants

Unless your shade garden has been thoroughly worked over a period of many years, you will probably need to improve the soil. But the effort and expense you put in will pay off handsomely. In good-quality soil, your plants will grow more vigorously and be more disease resistant.

In a naturally shady environment—a woodland—falling leaves and needles decompose into humus, which continuously replenishes the soil and feeds the trees. The picture differs, however, in most backyards. Moved by a spirit of tidiness, gardeners often remove the very plant debris that

A FLOWERY CARPET
The thick growth of star-like leaves and delicate white flowers of Galium odoratum (sweet woodruff) forms a colorful carpet at the foot of a rough-barked Norway spruce. This tough ground cover spreads quickly by aboveground stems and competes well with roots of trees and shrubs. The aromatic blossoms brighten shady areas for several weeks in early spring.

produces humus. If you do this, you will have to compensate by amending the soil before the initial planting and by adding hefty amounts of mulch each year. Humus can be found in many forms, but the commonest are garden compost, peat moss, and leaf mold.

Soil Amendments for a Shade Garden

Ideal shade soil will be rich in plant nutrients, light in structure—made up of roughly equal proportions of sand and a silt/clay mix, as well as generous amounts of humus—and mildly acid to near neutral, with a pH between 5 and 6.5.

If your soil is too sandy, improve its structure by adding 2 parts humus and decomposed manure to 1 part soil. If it is heavy with clay, add 1 part salt-free coarse sand to 1 part soil. Amendments must be thoroughly worked into the top 8 to 10 inches of soil. If the garden is reasonably small, you can do this by hand with a spading fork. If it is large, it is probably more practical to use a rototiller.

The best time to do the job is in the spring, after the ground has thawed. Never work the soil when it is wet; compacting will destroy its structure. After you have worked organic matter and other necessary amendments into the soil, you should try to let the plot settle for a few weeks. If you don't have the time, go ahead and put in your plants, tamping down the soil by hand around each as you set it in place. The remaining soil will settle on its own. As you work in the garden, take care not to step on prepared soil, since it is easily compacted. Walk, stand, and kneel on steppingstones or boards temporarily laid down for that purpose.

To speed drainage, dig the hole 4 inches deeper than twice the depth of the rootball and line the bottom with 4 inches of pebbles. Cover the pebble layer with 4 inches of soil mix made up of 1 part original soil, 4 parts compost or other humus, and 1 part pebbles. Set the crown of the plant slightly above the soil level and fill with soil mix. Tamp down firmly, water and tamp down again, then cover with mulch.

Planting amid Tree Roots

To grow herbaceous plants at the foot of a mature tree, the soil must be relatively free of roots—unless you are willing to cut away some roots, a method of last resort. To find out how thickly grown the roots are, push a shovel into the ground. If the blade is stopped by a mesh of roots, move to a new spot and try again until the shovel penetrates at least as deep as the length of the blade.

If your situation requires you to chop through a major root, take care not to overstress the tree. Don't cut away more than about 10 percent of the total root network, and have the crown pruned back a proportionate amount. After you finish digging, place landscape mesh around the perimeter of the hole to slow down encroachment by new root growth from the tree.

Drainage must always be checked in such soil. Dig a hole twice as wide and deep as the rootball you are planting and fill it with water. If the water doesn't drain away after 15 minutes, either improve the drainage *(above)* or put in plants that tolerate boggy conditions.

Helping Plants Move Up in the World

Vines and espaliered shrubs can dress up a bare wall or fence or create a handsome effect on a trellis. In a few square feet of rich, well-drained soil at the foot of the vertical surface, you can plant and train any one of many climbing species. Some, such as ivy, attach themselves to almost any surface with aerial roots. Others twine around supports or grow twining tendrils and will need wires or a trellis to climb.

If your surface is wood, you can nail steel vine eyes into it and string wire through them. For brick or stone, use screw eyes. Braided wire gives the longest-lasting support; galvanized wire may need tightening every other year. For nontwining lightweight vines, individual supports are available that can be cemented, nailed, or screwed onto a flat surface. Since stucco and vinyl walls may be damaged by nails or screws, it is best to erect a trellis in front of them. You can buy small trellises at garden centers or build larger ones yourself.

Climbing plants can be guided up a wall in varied patterns, such as repeating diamonds (above). First, install the wire supports—about 12 to 16 inches apart—then till and amend the soil and put in plants.

To mount an eye in brick (above) or stone, drill a hole at a mortar intersection and tap in an expandable metal plug. Screw into it a sturdy eye that will extend 4 to 6 inches from the wall. Thread wire through the eye and wrap it around once. Attach stems loosely to the wire with plastic ties.

For heavy, woody climbers, build a wooden trellis with pressure-treated posts and latticework (left). Site it at least 6 inches from the wall and complete the installation before planting the climber. Nail the lattice to the uprights, add a 2-by-4 support across the top, and top off the posts with metal caps. For maximum strength, set the trellis supports in concrete footings (above). Dig a hole 6 by 6 inches square and 2 feet deep. Place a 4-by-4 post in the hole, fill with concrete, and prop the post; use a level to make sure it's vertical. Slope the concrete surface away from the post for drainage.

Fixing Drainage Problems

Test the soil for drainage by digging a hole 10 inches deep and 12 inches square. Pour in a gallon of water and time how long it takes to drain away. If it takes 15 minutes or more, the soil has poor drainage that should be corrected before planting. If it drains very rapidly, say in 5 minutes or less, you will need to add humus to hold moisture.

If drainage is slow, remove the soil to a depth of 18 to 24 inches, refill with 4 to 6 inches of pebbles, then fill the rest with 4 parts humus mixed with 1 part soil and 1 part pebbles or coarse sand. Never use sand to lighten and loosen clay soil that is wet, however, as the cure may be worse than the disease; sand is prone to bond with wet clay to form cement. If drainage is especially poor, you may have to consider installing a system of drain tiles or pipes. A much simpler and less expensive solution is to build a raised bed.

Raised Beds

To construct a raised bed, you need only put up an enclosure of the chosen height made from lumber, stone, or brick, or you can simply build up a mound that slopes down to the surrounding grade. Fill the bed with equal parts soil, humus, and pebbles. The soil should be at least 4 inches deep for ground covers and 6 to 8 inches deep for most perennials. You can build a raised bed over tree roots without harming the tree, as long as no more than one-third of the root system is covered and the bed is kept at least 2 feet away from any tree trunk. Line the bottom of the bed with landscape mesh to prevent—or at least slow—encroachment by tree roots.

Planting Directly under Trees

It is possible to install flower beds under large shade trees without building a raised bed *(page 75, bottom),* but you'll have to take several factors into consideration: How much light and rain will the trees' canopy of leaves allow through? How thick and shallow are the tree roots? Even if enough light and rain reach the soil, shallow tree roots can be an almost prohibitive problem. Tree roots do not grow straight down into the earth, as is commonly believed. They grow in the top 18 inches of soil, spreading out far beyond the drip line. Roots can quickly invade flower beds and sap all the water and nutrients from them.

Maples, sycamores, and beeches are among the worst offenders and almost wholly preclude any understory planting. Some trees, however, such as oaks and conifers, have deeper-growing roots and can coexist well with other plantings. Many small trees, with a mature height of under 20 feet, also are amenable to underplantings, as their smaller root systems are less invasive.

If you find relatively root-free areas under trees where you can place a plant, you are in luck; some

A SHOWY GREETING FOR CALLERS
Climbing where it will, this 'Comtesse de Bouchaud' clematis has worked its way up the iron railing of a shady entranceway to a home in Kingwood, New Jersey. This hybrid blooms late in the season.

77

BRIGHTENING A TREE BASE
'Hyperion' daylilies, bearing scented yellow blossoms from late spring to midsummer, bloom beneath a river birch in Charlottesville, Virginia. Hosta cultivars flank the tree at the rear and upper right.

of the most beautiful landscape scenes are made up of lush plants in the shade of handsome trees. For such a garden to thrive, consider thinning the tree crown to allow more dappled sunlight through (*page 85, top*).

If your space is so limited that every square foot must be made to count, you may be able to garden beneath shallow-rooted trees, but the method is a drastic one and will take some muscle power. You can create planting and growing room by exposing a large root near the trunk and cutting it out with an ax or hatchet. Since new tree roots will penetrate this bed within a season or two—even if you line the hole with landscaping mesh—limit your plantings to annuals, and reclear the bed each year.

Putting Your Plants into the Ground

Choose a time to plant when temperatures are not too high, such as in the late afternoon. Before placing a plant in a hole, loosen its rootball, splitting it in half at the bottom and spreading the halves. Cut back any discolored roots. The single most important point to remember about shade plants is to set the crown of the plant no deeper than it was in the container. Always err on the side of raising the crown. Shade plants are accustomed to light, airy humus and cannot tolerate being smothered under soil. Pamper the new addition with extra water until it is established. If the soil has been prepared well, perennials and woody plants will not need additions of fertilizer the first year. Annuals can be fertilized halfway through the growing season.

TIPS FROM THE PROS

Letting Moss Have Its Way

If you want to keep some open space on your property but your attempts to cultivate a turf-grass lawn in the shade are being subverted by moss, give in to nature and let the moss take over. Moss thrives in the shade in moist clay soil with a pH of about 5.5. You can hurry up the conversion by spreading garden sulfur; 4 pounds per 100 square feet will lower the soil pH by about 1.5 points. Once the moss is established, it will spread steadily, covering the area with a green carpet that needs no mowing or fertilizing. To fill in bare spots in an established moss lawn, transplant small clumps of moss in early spring. First moisten the soil and loosen it with a hoe or three-pronged cultivator. Then lay the patches in the bare spots, patting them firmly into the soil so that no air spaces remain. Keep the area moist for a few weeks, covering it with wet burlap if the weather turns hot and dry.

Maintaining a Shade Garden

Although a shade garden, like all good gardens, will require some hard work initially, you can expect that once established it will be a relatively low-maintenance affair. Shady conditions discourage weeds, pests, and diseases, all of which proliferate in sunshine. It's true that it can be difficult to keep an abundant supply of nutrients and water in shady soil, where trees tend to soak up what's available. But many shade plants have evolved under such hardships and are fairly tolerant of dry spells. If the plants are sited and spaced in accordance with their light and soil requirements, they will need relatively little feeding, watering, and pruning.

Mulch

Despite being protected from the drying heat of direct sunlight, a shade garden will still need a liberal coating of mulch, first to replenish the soil with the right nutrients and then to help it retain its often meager supply of moisture. To approximate in city and suburban gardens the naturally rich woodland soil most shade plants evolved in, you will have to add generous amounts of organic mulch every spring—at least a 3-inch layer. This will not only provide nutrients and lower the pH somewhat but will also keep soil cool and moist, protect shallow roots, and discourage weeds.

You can find many kinds of mulch at garden shops and nurseries, but the best is available for free. Leaves collected from your lawn and your neighbors' lawns and run through a leaf shredder provide excellent mulch. Other mulches include compost, shredded fir bark, pine needles, and pine bark. The last is the favorite of many gardeners because it adds the most nutrients and acid to the soil and has an attractive appearance and fragrance.

Fertilizing and Watering

A shade garden will need regular fertilizing after its first year, especially in the spring. Amendments such as compost and rotted manure improve soil structure and promote the growth of beneficial microorganisms, but they will not supply enough nitrogen, phosphorus, and potassium, the major nutrients needed by all plants.

To boost the growth of your plants, use a slow-release organic granular fertilizer formulated to provide a complete and balanced menu of nutrients. Fertilizers made with inorganic chemical compounds, while faster acting than organic ones, can harm earthworms and soil microorganisms, which are beneficial in a shade garden. If you are fertilizing plants under trees, apply twice the recommended amount. The trees will take half of it.

Root feeding—a technique that brings fertilizer directly to tree roots—is a tonic for trees and shrubs that can be done every 3 to 5 years, although professionals tend to recommend more frequent feeding. If you have many trees and shrubs you may wish to hire an arborist to carry it out. If you do the job yourself, use an auger to drill holes 18 to 24 inches apart in a circle around the drip line. Drill several inches down into the soil, taking care not to injure large roots. Continue

A SHADE-PRODUCING ALTERNATIVE
Instead of the usual tree or shrub, two clumps of Miscanthus sinensis 'Zebrinus' (zebra grass) provide a comfortable, shady environment for the pink-and-green caladiums in this New Jersey garden. Zebra grass grows up to 6 feet tall; in winter it dies to the ground but if not cut back remains as a pleasing winter shape.

drilling holes in concentric circles 2 feet apart until you are two-thirds of the way in toward the trunk. Prepare dry or liquid fertilizer according to the directions on the package, and divide the total amount among the holes. Water thoroughly to prevent root burn.

Even though plants in the shade do not face harsh, moisture-evaporating sun, rainfall may be prevented from reaching them by tree canopies or high walls, and the rain that does get through is often soaked up by competing tree roots. As a result, you can't assume that even ample rainfall has met your plants' needs.

Most plants need 1 inch of water every 7 to 10 days. Always water deeply: Light watering is harmful as it encourages shallow root growth, which makes plants more vulnerable to drought. Recent plantings need to be kept moist so their root systems can develop; established ones do better if you let the soil dry out moderately between waterings.

Pests and Diseases

Even in a shade garden, pests and diseases can arise at any time, and early detection makes control easier. Conduct a weekly patrol through your garden, looking for anything awry—dead or un-

healthy leaves, unusual growth, poor color. Slugs, snails, and black vine weevils can be a particular menace because they prefer the cool, moist environment shade often provides. Powdery mildew disease and other fungal diseases thrive in poorly drained soil that stays damp too long or in crowded conditions that hinder air circulation, both common shade-garden conditions. Deer, rabbits, and voles can be a problem in suburban and woodland gardens.

For every pest and disease there is a control measure. The first measure to consider is prevention—making wise plant choices and using proper gardening techniques. New hybrids and cultivars bred for pest and disease resistance are increasingly available at local nurseries. Well-nourished soil with good structure, the right pH balance, and good drainage will nurture plants that are better able to resist attack by many insects and diseases. Watering the soil directly while keeping the foliage dry prevents the spread of fungal spores. Another anticipatory measure is to collect leaves and plant debris in the fall to prevent overwintering of spores and eggs. Chemical controls against pests and diseases should always be the last resort.

The best defense against four-footed critters is a physical barrier. A 6-foot-high fence may dissuade deer; enclosing plant roots in wire mesh will pre-

TIMETABLE FOR SHADE PERENNIAL, SHRUB, AND TREE CARE

ZONES 2 - 7

TYPE OF CARE	COOL SPRING	COOL SUMMER	COOL AUTUMN	COLD WINTER	WARM SPRING	
PLANTING	Plant perennials and flowering shrubs.		Plant and transplant trees and shrubs, except for bare-rooted stock. In early autumn, divide and replant perennials. Plant shade-tolerant spring bulbs.		Plant perennials and flowering shrubs.	
FERTILIZING	Feed young trees and shrubs. Fertilize plants growing in soil mix, container plants, and plants near roots of mature trees.	Using a slow-release fertilizer, feed container plants and plants in competition with nearby tree roots.	Feed young ornamentals and trees.		Fertilize ornamentals, container plants, and plants near roots of mature trees.	
CULTIVATION	Remove protective boughs, winter leaves, and other mulch from flower beds when the weather settles. Keep boughs nearby in case freezing weather returns. Apply summer mulch to all plants.	Water plants deeply during dry spells. Pay extra attention to newly installed plants and plants near large trees.		Mulch or screen delicate plants. If perennials have been heaved out, replant them. Container plants and plantings beneath eaves may need occasional watering, especially in bright, windy weather.	Remove protective boughs, leaves, and other mulch from flower beds when the weather becomes settled.	
PRUNING	Prune out dead or broken branches, suckers, and water sprouts on trees. Cut back to the ground fern fronds, epimediums, grassy-leaved shade plants, and evergreen perennials with old leaves. Prune to shape and thin spring-flowering shrubs and broad-leaved evergreens after they flower. Prune and train vines.	Pinch new shoots of perennials and spring-flowering shrubs for compact growth. Prune flowering trees. Prune summer-flowering shrubs to shape and thin; for compact growth, pinch off tips. Shear or shape needle-leaved trees and shrubs. In early summer, prune bleeding trees (yellowwood, maple, and birch) and do basal pruning of evergreens.		Prune nonbleeding deciduous trees. Prune evergreen branches for holiday decorations and reuse as winter mulch. In late winter, prune fruit trees, roses, and broad-leaved evergreens.	Prune out dead or broken branches, suckers, and water sprouts on trees. Cut back to the ground fern fronds, epimediums, grassy-leaved shade plants, and evergreen perennials with old leaves. Prune to shape and thin out spring-flowering shrubs and broad-leaved evergreens after they flower. Prune and train vines.	
PEST AND DISEASE CONTROL	Put out snail and slug traps. Spray for preventive control of pests or diseases found the previous year. Begin weekly checks for signs of pests and diseases.		Collect and discard any garden debris or leaves of plants that had pests or disease to remove overwintering spores and eggs.	Apply dormant oil.	Check all plants for pests and diseases. Put out snail and slug traps. Spray for preventive control of pests or diseases found the previous year.	

vent burrowing animals from reaching them. See the Troubleshooting Guide *(pages 92-95)* for detailed information about shade garden problems, and contact your Cooperative Extension Service to learn about particular problems in your area.

Handling Autumn Leaves

The natural mulch created in autumn by fallen leaves protects trees and woodland plants from extreme winter temperatures and sunburn. Only on lawns must leaves be removed, to keep them from smothering the delicate blades. The drawbacks to leaves as a winter mulch are that they tend to blow about and look untidy, they hinder winter cultivation, and they may harbor pests and diseases that will erupt in force the following spring.

Because of these problems, many gardeners prefer to gather up their leaves in autumn. The leaves can be composted until next autumn or left in a heap to decompose into leaf mold. Another option, if you don't have a reason to suspect the presence of pests or diseases, is to shred the leaves and respread them, making a tidy mulch.

If you keep leaves on perennials through the winter, be sure to rake or blow them away in early spring to clear the way for new shoots to emerge.

Providing Winter Protection

Many broad-leaved evergreens that grow in the shade of deciduous trees get burned by sun and wind in the winter when they lose their protective cover. Needled evergreens grown near the limits of their hardiness zones or facing severe winters are also susceptible to harm. To prevent damage, select plants that are appropriate to your zone and plant them on the lee side of a wall or a well-established needled evergreen. If this isn't possible, you can erect a windbreak or cover them with a protective mulch.

Cover perennials to prevent their being heaved out of the soil when cold temperatures and bright sunlight alternately freeze and warm the earth. Evergreen boughs make an excellent cover, keeping the ground evenly cold. Since the coldest season begins in January, you can wait until after Christmas, and then collect boughs from your neighbors' Christmas trees to cover the plants.

Snow, acting as an insulating blanket, makes a fine mulch. By all means shovel extra snow onto perennial beds. But if heavy snow accumulates on evergreens, shake or brush it off. Ice that has formed on leaves should be left to melt naturally.

Z O N E S 8 - 1 1		
WARM SUMMER	**WARM AUTUMN**	**WARM WINTER**
Plant trees and shrubs.	Plant trees and shrubs. Divide and replant shade perennials. Plant shade-tolerant spring bulbs.	Plant and transplant bare-root trees and shrubs.
Fertilize container plants and plants in competition with nearby tree roots.	Feed young shrubs and trees in late autumn.	
Mulch plants and water deeply during dry spells. Pay extra attention to the watering needs of newly added plants and plants near large trees.		Mulch to cover perennials and shrubs. If plants have been heaved out by frost, replant them. Container plants and plantings beneath eaves may need occasional watering, especially in bright, windy weather.
Pinch new shoots of spring-flowering shrubs and perennials for compact growth. Prune flowering trees. Prune summer-flowering shrubs to shape and thin; for compact growth, pinch off tips. Shear or shape needle-leaved trees and shrubs.	Prune roses, woody vines, and many flowering shrubs.	Prune deciduous trees, but not the sap-bleeding trees, such as yellow-wood, maple, and birch. Prune evergreen branches for holiday decorations and reuse as winter mulch.
Check and prune out fire blight. Check and spray for black vine weevils.	Collect and discard garden debris and leaves of plants that had pests or disease to remove overwintering spores and eggs.	Remove all garden debris, fallen leaves, and fallen blossoms. Apply dormant oil.

Pruning

Pruning is vital for any garden, and especially a shady one, where space and light are at a premium. Make a habit of checking your garden weekly for signs of weeds, undesirable growth, or plant parts damaged by pests or diseases. With judicious pruning, your garden will benefit from better air circulation, increased sunlight, and the removal of unhealthy, uncontrolled, or overcrowded growth.

A bit of practice will enable you to wield loppers and shears with artistry and skill to prune shrubs and low tree branches. For any major tree pruning your property might need, the information presented in this section will enable you to deal knowledgeably with professional arborists.

When to Prune

Diseased growth or other problems should be pruned out as soon as the problem is discovered, regardless of the time of year. Pruning for other purposes, however, should be done during specific seasons suitable to each plant.

Timing varies greatly from genus to genus. For instance, shrubs that flower on the previous season's wood should be pruned just after the blossoms fade, while shrubs that bloom on new growth should be pruned in early spring, before the new shoots emerge. Even within a single genus, such as clematis, there are three different ways to prune, depending on the species or cultivar.

The consequences of untimely pruning are all undesirable: stimulating weak new growth, removing the coming year's blossoms, or making the plant vulnerable to disease and stress. See the chart on pages 80-81 for broad guidelines for pruning different types of plants. If you are still in doubt about your plants, check with your local extension service or botanical garden.

Pruning to Rejuvenate

Many shrubs grow from a network of stems that increase in number and size every year. If left unattended for a number of years, the stems tend to become either dense and overcrowded or tall and lanky, which eventually weakens them and spoils

Pruning for Health

Check your trees and shrubs regularly for signs of disease and unhealthy growth; the sooner these problems are dealt with the better. Starting at ground level, look for a girdling root **1** that wraps around the trunk at the base; if not pruned away, it will eventually choke the tree. Suckers **2** and water sprouts **3** , which often erupt after heavy pruning, are unproductive growth that should be snipped away without delay. Dead limbs **4** should be removed, for they are entry points for rot, pests, and diseases. Stubs **5** and diseased branches **6** can be pruned back to healthy tissue at any time except when the plant is wet, since disease spreads most easily in moist tissue. If you suspect disease, ask your extension agent for tips on preventing the infection's spread. A double leader **7** is easy to lop off when small, but if it is left to grow, two heavy trunks will result that might someday split the tree right in two.

Deadheading Rhododendrons

The bountiful blossoms of frothy pink Rhododendron 'Centennial Celebration' *suggest what rewards can be gained by intervening in a plant's growth processes.*

Pinching off spent rhododendron flowers *can double or triple the number of blossoms next year as well as make the bush more compact. Remove dead blossoms and developing seed pods by bending the woody stem, just above where new buds are forming, and pulling gently until it snaps (below). With the seed pods gone, growth will be concentrated in the new buds. After a few weeks, when the buds have grown out about 4 inches, pinch off the last inch or so of that growth to encourage more shoots to sprout (bottom).*

the appearance of the plant. Such old shrubs can be revitalized with careful thinning.

For shrubs that flower on the previous year's growth, such as forsythia, remove about a third of the primary stems immediately after flowering, selecting first the stems with problems and then the largest, most unsightly ones, and cutting them right down to the ground. This kind of pruning will cure overcrowding and poor air circulation and increase the plant's vigor and blooming capacity.

Use sharp loppers or shears to make clean cuts as close to the ground as possible, or back to the trunk. Do not leave stubs, which will decay and invite disease. Remove all young basal growth or suckers, except for one or two vigorous new stems, which will grow up to replace the pruned ones. This process, repeated over a few years, will completely rejuvenate the shrub.

Shrubs that have become densely overgrown and those, such as *Cornus alba* 'Sibirica' (redstem

LIMBING UP FOR FLOWERY ABUNDANCE
Pruning away the lower growth on a pair of Umbellularia californica *(Oregon myrtle) trees (above, left) in a redwood forest in Sonora County, California, opened up enough area for a woodland garden bursting with colorful flowers, including a snowy-blossomed* Rhododendron yakusimanum, *yellow* Primula bulleyana *(Yunnan candelabra), and blue* Aquilegia vulgaris *(columbine).*

83

Pruning for More Light

A densely leafy tree that blocks out the sun—as depicted above—can be pruned to allow the passage of dappled light. Before pruning, the tree has a thick canopy, with branches growing almost to the ground. Two techniques—limbing up *(above, right)* and thinning *(opposite)* let progressively greater amounts of light reach plants beneath the tree.

Limbing Up

Removing the lower limbs of a tree not only allows sunlight through but also gives the tree a more pleasing shape. The task is easier when the tree is small, but it can be done even on mature trees. You can remove as many limbs from the trunk as necessary, provided you don't take off more than one-third of the total crown—including, of course, any thinning you wish to do higher up.

To remove a heavy limb cleanly, without tearing the bark, saw halfway up from below (1), *about a foot from its base. Just beyond this cut, saw down* (2) *till the limb breaks off. Remove the stub by sawing down just beyond the collarlike bulge around the base* (3).

dogwood), whose habit is to grow shoots from a spreading clump will benefit by being cut back hard to the base, or to a selected framework of young shoots, in early spring. Most shrubs that flower on new growth fall into this category.

Pruning for Appearance

By understanding a few principles of plant growth, you can learn how to stimulate and redirect growth to improve the appearance and blossoming potential of your plants. The new tips of plant stems, for example, release hormones that inhibit the growth of buds lower down on the stem. When you prune back these shoots, the hormone is no longer released, lower buds are no longer kept from growing, and the plant becomes bushier. This cutting back, also called shearing, can be done to perenni-

als, ground covers, vines, and shrubs. The wholesale lopping of the ends of branches or foliage keeps plants compact and prevents them from going to seed. Another technique is to remove faded blossoms before they go to seed. This is called deadheading *(page 83);* it keeps plants low and compact and promotes continued flowering of annuals and perennials in the current year and more flowering in shrubs and trees the following year.

Pruning to Increase Sunlight

As lovely as large shade trees may be, they can leave the ground underneath quite dark. Pruning can thin out the canopy, letting in the breeze and allowing dappled light to reach your garden floor. Pruning of large trees is a major undertaking that should be done only by a licensed and insured ar-

Thinning

Before you let anyone take a saw to the crown of a tree, plan out the cuts with an eye to symmetry. Study the tree in winter, when its structure is revealed. Look first for diseased or damaged limbs (illustration, page 82). Then identify any undesirable growth: branches that are overcrowded, rubbing against each other, growing toward the center of the tree, crossing, growing downward, or growing against an obstruction. If after removing these limbs you wish to thin the crown even more, space the cuts to maintain symmetry—as shown at right in the well-pruned version of the original tree opposite.

The finished product of thinning is often called lacing for its graceful effect (right). The remaining branches are well spaced, and all of them now grow outward and upward. Fewer branches mean that more sunlight and air can pass through, contributing to the health of the tree itself as well as to the plants underneath.

Limbs highlighted in black (below) are, for some of the reasons outlined at left, good candidates for thinning. Cuts should be made flush with the branch collar, taking care not to cut into it.

borist. Your part in the operation is to know what you want to achieve and, in general terms, how that should be done. Two kinds of pruning are used to increase sunlight under a tree: Crown thinning, in which limbs are removed from various places in the middle and upper reaches of the tree; and limbing up, or crown lifting, in which all limbs are removed from the lowest part of the trunk (above and opposite). Tree pruning must be done in moderation; never remove more than a third of the total canopy in one season, and give the tree at least 3 years to recover before pruning again.

Removing Trees

The best gardens are those that have been planned with the next 20 years of growth in mind. Sometimes gardeners who began with plantings that ap-

peared quite thin on the ground when new now contemplate their property with dismay as trees and shrubs crowd each other and stifle the growth of newer, smaller understory plants.

It is never too late to rectify the situation, however. Assess the merits of each of your trees, considering the future growth and the types of roots and shade they produce. Then draw up a long-range plan to gradually replace crowded or undesirable trees with smaller or deeper-rooted ones.

Before cutting, stand back and survey your land. Visualize how the landscape might look if various trees were removed. An overgrown grove might be transmuted into a kind of natural cathedral, for example, by removing interior trees and leaving tree-trunk pillars on the sides and an arched canopy of foliage for the ceiling. Or a way might be cleared through a crowded wood lot, the surviving trees on either side creating a tree-lined path.

Answers to Common Questions

Voles have just eaten my $20 hostas—sucked them right into the ground. They also destroyed my hardy cyclamen bulbs. I've tried baits, poisons, and traps to little avail. Can you help?

Voles love many shade plants and dig shallow tunnels to get to them—but they don't like digging through stony soil. Go to your building supply store or garden center and buy the sharpest-edged pea-sized gravel you can find. Spread a 2- to 3-inch layer over the entire area you wish to protect and then incorporate it thoroughly into the top 10 inches of soil with a spading fork. It is best to prepare whole areas before planting, but you can also spot-treat the soil around prize specimens.

How can I prevent red spider infestations on my astilbes? A miticide I used killed most of the foliage.

Moisture-retentive soil and an inch of water a week during drought are essential for astilbes, especially in warm climates. Dryness and sun are an open invitation to red spider infestations. If dull green leaves and characteristic webbing show that an infestation has occurred, spray the undersides of the leaves often with a forceful stream of water to knock off the pests.

For insect problems in my shady garden, including aphids, thrips, and whiteflies, can you recommend a spray that will not harm the environment—or me?

All sprays can be harmful if not properly used, but one relatively safe kind is marketed under different brand names as insecticidal soap. Made up of various formulations of potassium salts of fatty acids, they kill by penetrating the shells of soft-bodied insects, causing dehydration and quite rapid death. They cannot penetrate eggs already laid, so a few repeat sprayings at 7- to 10-day intervals are necessary to kill emerging larvae and achieve complete control.

I once read something about trees being vulnerable to damage from winter sun. It's hard to imagine how sun could harm a bare tree, but I have some fine young trees in my yard and I'd like to know if I should be concerned for them.

In winter, trees may be afflicted by a condition called sunscald. With shade-making foliage gone from deciduous shrubs and trees, rays from the afternoon sun can cut through frosty winter air to strike low on the western side of tree trunks with great intensity. The sun can heat and dry out the bark enough to separate it from underlying layers, damaging tissue and cracking the bark open to create pathways for insect invasion and disease. If you don't have evergreens or structures to provide afternoon shade for your trees, you may have to wrap or whitewash their lower trunks to protect them.

My outside sitting area is shaded by day, but I enjoy it the most at night during the hot summer months. How can I add horticultural interest for this very special time?

A few wonderful shade garden plants are made for these conditions. The pure white lilylike flowers of *Hosta plantaginea* open fully at night to release a honey-scented fragrance. Nicotianas are also fragrant at night. If you have a spot nearby that receives several hours of sun, be sure to put in the hauntingly fragrant *Ipomoea alba* (moonflower) vine, with its enormous white blossoms that open around sunset and glow in the moonlight. Look also for new *Hemerocallis* cultivars called nocturnal bloomers, which keep their blossoms open into evening, and extended bloomers, whose flowers stay open for up to 2 days.

I built a shaded flagstone terrace where the roots of a nearby maple restricted my gardening efforts. Now I spend too much time pulling weeds between the stones. Can I plant anything in these spaces to reduce maintenance and add interest?

Plant the narrowest crevices with *Sagina subulata* (Corsican pearlwort), a fine plant for paving areas with its creeping mossy evergreen foliage and tiny white spring flowers. In wider spaces you can establish *Mentha requienii* (Corsican mint), with ground-hugging leaves that emit a delicious fragrance of peppermint when trod upon occasionally, and *Mazus reptans,* a creeper with purple-blue to white flowers. For extra interest, but not to be walked on, consider *Lysimachia nummularia* 'Aurea' (creeping Jenny), with rounded yellow leaves and yellow blossoms in summer, or one of the several cultivars of *Ajuga,* with colored or variegated foliage.

What can I plant to give me lots of fragrance in my shade garden?

You should rely upon a succession of plants through the seasons and avoid the many species that are fragrant only at close range. From late winter to early spring, cultivars of *Hamamelis mollis* and *H.* x *intermedia* waft their enticing fragrance over the awakening landscape. As spring progresses, *Viburnum carlesii* (Koreanspice viburnum) will add its own tangy scent. Few plants are more fragrant from midspring to early summer than azaleas. One of the best is *Rhododendron arborescens* (sweet azalea). In summer, mass plantings of night-fragrant *Hosta plantaginea* and annuals such as *Lobularia maritima* (sweet alyssum) and the night-fragrant nicotianas are very effective. Finish up in autumn with another native, *Hamamelis virginiana*.

I am learning the art of arranging flowers. What shade garden plants will give me distinctive materials for seasonal creations?

All the shrubs and small trees mentioned in this book will yield either flowers, foliage, or fruit for your work. In addition, among the herbaceous plants, hostas are outstanding for the size, color, and texture of their foliage, as are *Bergenia, Ligularia, Polygonatum,* ferns, and *Heuchera* cultivars. For flowers, some of the best shade garden plants are *Aconitum, Alchemilla* (lady's-mantle), *Aquilegia, Cimicifuga, Dicentra, Digitalis, Lobelia, Mertensia,* and *Narcissus.* Flowers to avoid because of short vase life are *Anemone* x *hybrida* cultivars, most *Astilbe* cultivars, and hellebores kept in hot rooms.

I would like to have several types of foxgloves in my shade garden, but it's hard to tell much about their longevity from nursery catalogs. Which ones will I have to replace often?

Digitalis grandiflora is the longest lived of the perennial foxgloves and the showiest, producing sturdy stems with creamy yellow 2-inch-long blossoms in late spring. It does well for about 5 years before needing to be divided for rejuvenation. *Digitalis lutea* and *D. lanata* (Grecian foxglove) live for a few years but require more frequent division to remain vigorous. The popular *D.* x *mertonensis* should be divided every year to keep it going. *Digitalis purpurea* is a biennial, and although it may self-seed, for reliability's sake it must be renewed every year from seed-raised plants.

I need a low-maintenance, live-forever ground cover that will produce a good display of bloom in spring and be attractive the rest of the growing season. What can you recommend?

Although you seem to be asking a lot, *Brunnera macrophylla* should fit all your requirements. Through much of the spring it generously produces sprigs of porcelain blue blossoms on 18-inch stems. When flowering wanes, the very handsome heart-shaped, somewhat rough and hairy leaves increase steadily in size until they are 6 to 8 inches wide about midsummer. This foliage forms dense, weed-resistant foot-high mats of exceptionally bold texture. Plant them in partial shade, give them ample room to expand, and interplant other varieties chosen for textural contrast.

I don't have a very good eye for ferns—one sort looks pretty much like another to me. Can you point me to a few easily grown ferns that would stand out from all the others?

For a big, bold fern, plant *Matteuccia struthiopteris*. In moist dappled shade it can reach 5 feet in height, and with its vaselike shape and sentinel-like habit, a group of three about a yard apart would produce a lasting memory. If you are after color, there is nothing like *Athyrium nipponicum* 'Pictum', with beautiful silver variegations and touches of burgundy and mauve on light green fronds. It forms dense mats fairly rapidly and is one of the best ground-cover ferns. In Zones 7 to 10, you are missing a treat if you don't have a specimen or two of *Lygodium japonicum* (Japanese climbing fern). From a basal clump this plant annually produces a tangle of wiry stems that can climb a fence or trellis to a height of 6 feet or more. It lends a graceful, delicate, unmistakable touch to any garden.

What is the longest-blooming perennial I can plant in my shade garden?

In all but the hottest, driest parts of the country, the plant you seek is undoubtedly *Corydalis lutea*. It starts to bloom fairly early in spring and continues producing its small clusters of pendant tubular yellow flowers until the onset of hard frost.

My shade garden really goes into the doldrums in summer. Although I plant drifts of impatiens and begonias, I miss the individuality and charm of blooming perennials and shrubs at this time. What can I plant to enliven the scene?

In addition to the unlimited potential of daylilies, here are a dozen stalwart perennials to bridge your early-to-late-summer flower gap: *Aconitum napellus, Astilbe* x *arendsii* cultivars, *Chelone lyonii* (pink turtlehead), *Chrysogonum virginianum, Cimicifuga racemosa* (black cohosh) and *C. americana* (American bugbane), *Dicentra eximia* cultivars and hybrids, hosta, *Ligularia dentata* 'Desdemona', *Lilium* (lily), *Physostegia virginiana* (false dragonhead) cultivars, *Stokesia laevis* (Stokes' aster), and *Thalictrum rochebrunianum* (lavender mist meadow rue). Two very hardy native shrubs for outstanding blossoms in July are *Aesculus parviflora* (bottle-brush buckeye) and *Rhododendron prunifolium* (plum-leaved azalea), a real beauty with blossoms of glowing orange-red.

The towering white spires of bloom on my Cimicifuga racemosa dominate my shade garden at the height of summer. I couldn't do without it and am prompted to ask: Does this wonderful plant have other relatives I should try?

All *Cimicifuga* (bugbane) produce numerous small, fluffy white flowers made up mainly of stamens and opening from rounded pearl-like buds. Your *C. racemosa* starts the progression of bloom in midsummer. A bit later you could expect the slender, arching spikes of *C. americana* to light a woodland scene when little else is in flower. This species grows about 8 feet tall and tolerates dense shade but is happier in bright full shade. *Cimicifuga simplex* (Kamchatka bugbane) is the last species to bloom, in October in most areas, and continues for a good 3 weeks where frost does not intervene. It produces very fluffy stalks of fragrant flowers that arch in a distinctive manner.

I've had no luck luring hummingbirds to my shade garden. Most plants recommended for this purpose seem to be sun lovers, and others bloom only briefly. Do you have any suggestions?

One of the best plants to attract every hummingbird in the neighborhood is *Lonicera sempervirens* (trumpet or coral honeysuckle). It is also one of the most beautiful and longest-flowering vines you can bring into the garden. Train it up a trellis, where it will grow 10 to 15 feet high. The 2-inch-long blossoms are scarlet with orange throats and appear in great numbers from midspring to fall. The plant succeeds in bright full shade, although it will blossom better if exposed to a few hours of sun a day. It is hardy to Zone 4.

Can you suggest a low-maintenance group of plants for a striking but elegant spring color combination in my shade garden?

Start to paint your picture with *Dicentra spectabilis*. This garden aristocrat produces many arching racemes of heart-shaped pink flowers with tips that curve in the manner of a lyre. Mature plants can be a yard across, so the number you use will depend upon the size of your garden. Next, plant *Mertensia virginica*, which bears loose, pendulous clusters of ¾-inch-long porcelain blue bells above pale green foliage. Add some bright contrast to this delicate color combination with the warm yellow daisylike flowers of *Doronicum* 'Miss Mason' (leopard's-bane). All three of these plants die down in summer but can be easily grown through a ground cover of *Vinca minor*. Expansive hostas, ferns, and daylilies are also effective later in the season to mask the disappearing act.

PLANT CHARACTERISTICS

My Helleborus niger grow well, but they refuse to flower until mid-March. Is the winter here in Zone 5 too cold for them?

Myth, misconception, and sheer fantasy about the bloom period of the optimistically named Christmas rose abound in the gardening literature. Extreme cold is only a partial answer; commencement of flowering also depends on genetics and varies considerably from plant to plant. North of Zone 6, cold can prevent blossoms from opening early, even though buds may have emerged at the onset of winter. Only in Zones 7 to 9 might Christmas roses bloom during any part of Advent, and then only if the gardener is lucky enough to have obtained an early-flowering form.

I find that Helleborus orientalis blossoms wilt rapidly in my floral arrangements. Is there any way I can enjoy these lovely flowers indoors?

Make a sharp 2-inch cut on the side of each stem while it is immersed in the water of its container. This will prevent airlock in the water-conducting vessels of the stems and expose extra surface for water uptake, giving Lenten roses an excellent vase life in a cool room. Alternatively, you could remove the stems and float the blossoms among suitable greenery in shallow containers.

My epimediums are growing very slowly and not forming the excellent ground cover I expected. The soil and light conditions seem just right. What could the problem be?

Epimediums include both mat-forming and clump-forming types. The best for ground-cover use are the mat formers, which have elongated rhizomes that spread rapidly and produce tight, virtually weedproof growth. You probably have a clump former; these spread slowly or not at all. In order of preference, the best mat-forming epimediums for medium to large plantings are: *E.* x *versicolor* 'Sulphureum', *E. perralderanum,* and *E. pinnatum* var. *colchicum.* For small patches of ground cover with close initial spacing try *E.* x *cantabrigiense* (mats), *E. grandiflorum* and its cultivars (clumps), *E.* x *rubrum* (clumps), and *E.* x *youngianum* cultivars (clumps). Unsuitable species for ground cover include *E. diphyllum, E. pubigerum,* and *E.* x *warleyense.*

I like to grow ajugas because they seem to cope well with root competition from trees and shrubs in my shade garden. I notice that some spread rapidly and others do not. Which are which?

Two very distinct growth types exist among the bugleweeds. The ground-covering *A. reptans* and its cultivars are stoloniferous, sending aboveground stems in all directions, each producing a plantlet at its tip that quickly roots into place and repeats the process. *Ajuga pyramidalis* and *A. genevensis* are rhizomatous. They also spread, but slowly by way of underground stems to form noninvasive clumps rather than mats. Blue-flowering *A. pyramidalis* is the slowest to increase and is entirely safe in the tightest border situations.

A friend wants to give me some begonias that she says will be hardy in my Zone 6 shade garden. This sounds impossible to me. Can you tell me if such a plant exists?

The amazing *Begonia grandis,* from China, is fully hardy as far north as Philadelphia, usually survives in sheltered spots in the New York City area, and often succeeds in somewhat colder regions with the help of a winter mulch. *Begonia grandis* is a very beautiful plant with large, nearly heart-shaped leaves 4 to 5 inches long, pale green above and lightly tinged reddish purple below. The plants are densely branched and produce an abundance of light pink flowers in late summer.

CULTIVATION

On my large new property I visualize a woodland garden carpeted by numerous low-maintenance ground covers. But good hostas, ferns, epimediums, and the like are expensive, and I need many. How can I plant the garden I want and still keep up with my mortgage payments?

First, inspect plants in their containers at the nursery to see how many separate plants you can divide them into; a container that will yield 10 plants for the price of one is bound to help your cause. Second, till a piece of ground and get a nursery bed going even before you start to design and construct your garden. Most young plants you put in can be divided into three or more after the year or so it will take for your permanent garden areas to be ready for them. Establish your initial beds with drifts of five to 10 or more young plants. Enjoy these beds for a few seasons as you slowly acquire other plants and plan the next expansion of your garden. Those initial five or 10 plants you transferred from the nursery bed will have increased to yield divisions at a nearly geometric ratio. Within a few years you should have ample material to plant quite large areas, and you will probably even have enough left over to give to the neighbors.

The potted plants I grow on my shaded terrace never have that lush, overflowing look that I see in pictures in books and magazines. What am I doing wrong?

The secret is to be *very* generous initially with the number of plants used in each pot, regularly pinch back new buds on plants that require it to promote bushy growth, never let the soil dry out completely, and use a freely draining potting mix that contains a slow-release fertilizer. After 2 months, start applying a liquid fertilizer every 10 to 14 days. By early to midsummer your containers should be spilling over with lush growth.

Long-spurred varieties of aquilegia are favorites in my shady spring garden, but they don't seem to live very long for me. Can you give me any tips on how to manage my plantings?

The average life of most of the fancy columbine hybrids is about 3 years, though an unwanted legacy of mongrel self-sown seedlings often emerges in their wake. Many gardeners replenish their plantings every few years from nursery plants; seedlings are also easy to raise from commercial seed produced through careful hand pollination. Columbines are easily established in light, loamy soil from plantings made either in early spring or late summer. For superior vigor and appearance, prevent seed formation by cutting the plants back to basal foliage soon after blooming has ceased. An insect pest, the leaf miner, can be controlled to some extent by spraying with malathion in early or mid-May, by picking and discarding occasional affected leaves, or by cutting the plant back to the ground.

My astilbes seem to have lost their vigor, and their flower spikes are fewer and only half the size they were several years ago. What am I doing wrong?

Astilbes are greedy feeders. They need to be planted in fertile, acid soil rich in organic matter. Subsequently, annual side dressings of rotted manure, a 5-10-15 fertilizer, or a slow-release pelleted-type fertilizer in early spring will lengthen their effective life and assure maximum bloom. To keep the flowers coming abundantly, divide and reset the plants in thoroughly worked ground every 3 years. In hot climates, shade them from scorching sun.

I'm starting a woodland shade garden, but the site has lots of poison ivy. How should I get rid of it?

Use great caution in removing this plant, as even people who have always been immune to it can develop a sensitivity. Direct contact, contaminated clothing or pet fur, even smoke from burning plants all must be avoided. With a long-handled hoe, uproot small plants as soon as you notice them. Spray larger plants with the herbicide glyphosate; repeat if necessary. If the poison ivy has ascended a tree, cut its stems near the base with a long-handled pole saw and treat the basal portions with herbicide. Wearing washable cloth gloves or a double layer of disposable latex gloves, dig a hole about 2 feet deep and bury all cut-down and dead plant parts. If you are particularly sensitive or if the infestation is large, seek professional help to eradicate the plants.

Some of my rhododendrons have become overgrown. Can I cut them back? If so, when can I do this?

Rhododendrons usually need little or no pruning unless they get out of bounds, or if the growth becomes sprawly with long stretches of stem devoid of leaves. Then they will require drastic action. Cut back entire branches to within 2 feet of the ground, all at one time, just after the flowers have faded. You should see new sprouts from previously dormant buds on the old stems in about 4 to 8 weeks, but sometimes resprouting does not occur and the entire plant is lost. If this causes concern with a choice cultivar, you can elect a more conservative approach by removing one-third of the branches at a time over a 3-year period.

I greatly admire Japanese anemones but have never grown them. What care do they need?

Whether you mean *Anemone hupehensis* var. *japonica* or *A.* x *hybrida*, which share that common name, Japanese anemones must have rich soil to which liberal amounts of humus have been added. Perfect winter drainage is equally necessary. They tolerate considerable sun in cool climates, but bright full shade or partial shade is ideal in milder areas. In Zone 5, lay down a light winter mulch around the crowns just after the soil has frozen. A summer mulch is beneficial in areas with long, hot summers. Water plants frequently during dry periods.

A tall bamboo clump in my garden is taking up too much space and starting to send up canes among my flowers and shrubs. Can I control its growth?

Some bamboo species can push up new shoots 10 or more feet from the parent plant. But you can easily control such wayward growth early in the season by breaking off the new shoots with your foot or a spade as soon as they appear above ground, which will stop their forward march in its tracks. Repeat the process if new growth occurs later in the season. You can use the same method to eradicate an established grove of bamboo, but it will take considerable effort and patience. Cut down all growth in winter or early spring. As new shoots appear, kick them over or cut them as close to the ground as possible with your mower; destroy subsequent growth as the season progresses. It may take several growing seasons for food reserves in the roots to be exhausted and the plants to die.

Can I prune my camellia? It looks just fine, but is outgrowing its space and starting to block the view from my window.

Camellias almost never need pruning to grow and flower well—rather, they are cut back because they have outgrown a space that was too small for their potential growth in the first place. Some gardens are filled with hacked-up shrubs whose natural grace and elegance have been sacrificed because the gardener who put them in was unaware of the plants' ultimate size. Your camellia can be cut back very hard into old growth to reduce its size. But you will be without blooms for a few years, and the plant will surely grow back with renewed vigor to block your view again.

Troubleshooting Guide

Shade gardens are less prone than sunny ones to pests and diseases, but they are not immune. To keep problems in check, regularly inspect your plants for warning signs. Remember that lack of nutrients, improper pH levels, and other external conditions can cause diseaselike symptoms. If wilting or yellowing appears on a group of neighboring plants, the cause is probably environmental; pest and disease damage is usually more random.

In general, good fertility, drainage, and air circulation will help prevent infection, and you should consider using beneficial insects, such as ladybugs and lacewings, that prey on pests. Natural solutions to garden problems are best, but if you must use chemicals, be careful to treat only the affected plant. Try to make do with horticultural oil, insecticidal soap, and the botanical insecticide neem; these products are the least harmful to beneficial insects and will not destroy the soil balance that is the foundation of a healthy shade garden.

PESTS

PROBLEM: Leaves curl, are distorted in shape, and may have a black, sooty appearance. A clear, sticky substance often appears on stems and leaves. Buds and flowers are deformed, new growth is stunted, and leaves and flowers may drop.

CAUSE: Aphids are pear-shaped, semitransparent, wingless sucking insects about ⅛ inch long; they may be green, yellow, red, pink, black, or gray. Infestations are severest in spring and early summer, when the pests cluster on tender new shoots, the undersides of leaves, and around flower buds. Winged forms appear when colonies become overcrowded. Aphids secrete honeydew, a sticky substance that fosters the growth of a black fungus called sooty mold.

SOLUTION: Spray plants frequently with a steady stream of water from a garden hose to knock aphids off and discourage them from returning. Introduce ladybugs or lacewings, which eat aphids, into the garden. In severe cases, prune off heavily infested areas and spray with insecticidal soap, horticultural oil, pyrethrins, or rotenone.
SUSCEPTIBLE PLANTS: VIRTUALLY ALL.

PROBLEM: In spring, plants may be severely stunted or fail to develop new growth. Leaves yellow, wilt, and curl up; needles turn yellow then brown. Branches or entire plants, especially young ones, may die. Shrubs may go limp and turn brown, and can be pulled easily from the ground. In summer, large holes or notches appear along leaf margins, or leaves are eaten to the midrib.

CAUSE: Black vine weevils are ⅜-inch-long, black or brown, hard-bodied, winged yet flightless insects with a long, jaw-tipped snout. In early spring, the white, ¼-inch grubs, which do the most harm, feed on roots and girdle plants near the soil surface. In early summer, adult weevils feed on foliage at night and hide in leaf debris or cracks in the soil during the day.

SOLUTION: In the spring, remove and destroy infested young plants. At night in summer, pick adults off plants or shake them onto a drop cloth. Remove weeds and fallen leaves around plants and shrubs in the early fall. Cultivate soil to expose overwintering larvae. Drench soil with beneficial nematodes. Spray with pyrethrins or rotenone, or dust with sabadilla.
SUSCEPTIBLE PLANTS: PRIMARILY WOODY PLANTS SUCH AS ANDROMEDA, AZALEA, CAMELLIA, HEMLOCK, MOUNTAIN LAUREL, RHODODENDRON, VIBURNUM, AND YEW.

PROBLEM: Leaves become stippled or flecked, then discolor, curl, and wither. Webbing may appear, particularly on undersides of leaves and on the branches of shrubs and trees.

CAUSE: Mites are pinhead-sized, spiderlike sucking pests that can be reddish, pale green, or yellow. They are a major problem in hot, dry weather, and several generations may occur in a single season. Eggs, and the adults of some species, overwinter in sod and bark and on weeds and plants that retain foliage.

SOLUTION: Keep plants watered and mulched, especially during hot, dry periods. Regularly spray the undersides of leaves, where mites feed and lay eggs, with either a strong stream of water or a diluted insecticidal soap solution, which controls nymphs and adults but not eggs. Remove and destroy heavily infested leaves, branches, or entire plants. Introduce predators such as ladybugs and green lacewing larvae. Horticultural oil, neem, or pyrethrins can be applied. *SUSCEPTIBLE PLANTS: ALL.*

PROBLEM: Ragged holes appear in leaves, especially those near the ground. New leaves and entire young seedlings may be eaten. Telltale shiny silver streaks appear on leaves and garden paths.

CAUSE: Slugs and snails are serious pests in the shade garden, favoring such an environment over hot, sunny conditions. They prefer damp, cool locations and are most damaging in summer, especially in wet regions or during rainy years.

SOLUTION: Keep the garden clean to minimize hiding places. Handpick or trap slugs and snails by placing saucers of beer near plants. Slugs will also collect under grapefruit halves or melon rinds. Salt kills slugs and snails but may damage plants. Poison bait is available at garden centers and can be applied at dusk; reapply after rain or watering. Strips of coarse sand or cinders placed around beds will deter both slugs and snails. Spading in spring destroys dormant slugs and eggs. *SUSCEPTIBLE PLANTS: VIRTUALLY ALL, PARTICULARLY THOSE WITH YOUNG OR TENDER FOLIAGE. HOSTA IS ESPECIALLY SUSCEPTIBLE.*

D I S E A S E S

PROBLEM: Leaves thicken as bladder-shaped galls form on all or part of leaves or flowers. Soft when young, the galls eventually harden and darken. During the process, a white velvety layer appears on each gall's surface.

CAUSE: Azalea leaf gall, a fungal disease, spreads rapidly during periods of warm, wet weather in late spring. The white velvety layer produces spores. The fungus overwinters in infected tissue.

SOLUTION: Though unsightly, leaf gall is seldom a serious threat. Handpick and destroy galls, preferably before the white sporulating layer appears. Improve air circulation and avoid overhead watering in spring. Plant less susceptible species and cultivars. If infestation has been severe in previous years, spray plants with a copper fungicide just before the leaves unfurl and again 2 to 3 weeks later. *SUSCEPTIBLE PLANTS: AZALEA ESPECIALLY. SIMILAR SYMPTOMS CAUSED BY OTHER GALL-FORMING FUNGUS SPECIES OCCUR ON CAMELLIA, JAPANESE ANDROMEDA, MOUNTAIN LAUREL, AND RHODODENDRON.*

PROBLEM: Azalea and rhododendron buds or flower petals develop small, pinhead-sized rounded spots that are white on colored flowers, brown on white flowers. Camellia flower petals develop brown streaks and blotches. The brown markings enlarge and spread rapidly until the entire flower turns brown and collapses.

CAUSE: Azalea petal blight and camellia petal blight, both fungal diseases, occur during spring blooming time, when high humidity, rain, dew, or heavy fog persists. Symptoms can be distinguished from normal fading, because flowers turn brown almost overnight. The fungus over-winters as black fruiting bodies.

SOLUTION: There are no chemical controls. Remove and destroy infected flowers and buds, and rake up any debris on the ground under the shrub. Avoid overhead watering while plants are in flower. Clean up debris in fall; spores overwinter in dead flowers and debris. *SUSCEPTIBLE PLANTS: AZALEA, CAMELLIA, RHODODENDRON.*

PROBLEM: A brownish gray moldy growth appears on flowers and foliage. Stalks are weak and flowers droop. Buds may not open. Discolored blotches appear on leaves, stems, and flowers. Stem bases rot. Plant parts eventually turn brown and dry up. Flowering plants are most affected.

CAUSE: Botrytis blight, also known as gray mold, is a fungus disease that thrives in moist air and cool temperatures —typical shade-garden conditions. The blight survives the winter as hard black lumps in the soil or on dead plant parts.

SOLUTION: Limit watering to early in the day and avoid overhead watering. Place plants only in well-drained soil. Thin out plants so they get more light and air. Cut off and destroy all infected plant parts and collect and destroy infected leaves. Spray with Bordeaux mixture—a traditional antifungal treatment originally used in vineyards—or a fungicide containing chlorothalonil. *SUSCEPTIBLE PLANTS: FLOWERING PLANTS ARE MOST AT RISK.*

PROBLEM: Leaves turn yellow. Angular pale green or yellow blotches appear on upper leaf surfaces, with corresponding gray or tan fuzzy growths that resemble tufts of cotton forming on the undersides. Leaves wilt, turn brown, and die.

CAUSE: Downy mildew, a disease caused by a fungus, thrives in cool, wet weather and appears most often in late summer and early fall. Spores are spread by wind, rain, insects, and infected seed.

SOLUTION: Grow resistant varieties. Do not water plants overhead after morning. Space plants and thin stems to improve air circulation. Remove and destroy infected plant parts, or the entire plant if the infection is severe, and any debris. Spray with a copper fungicide, sulfur, Bordeaux mixture, mancozeb, or chlorothalonil. *SUSCEPTIBLE PLANTS: MANY.*

PROBLEM: Yellow spots that progress to brown may appear on leaves. Damage occurs between leaf veins. Eventually the leaf dies and becomes brittle. Young foliage curls and twists; growth is stunted. Symptoms appear first on older leaves, then move up the plant. Flowers and buds may be affected.

CAUSE: Foliar nematodes are microscopic worms that feed on the surface of young leaves and the interior of mature ones. They thrive in warm, humid summers. Wet conditions help them migrate on films of water to infect other plants and soil.

SOLUTION: Remove and destroy plants that are seriously infected; pick and destroy all leaves showing symptoms, as well as the leaves immediately surrounding them. Avoid watering foliage, since splashing water can spread the disease. Do not plant susceptible plants in infested soil.
SUSCEPTIBLE PLANTS: MOST TYPES, PARTICULARLY AZALEA, BEGONIA, CYCLAMEN, FERNS, HOSTA, IRIS, LILY, PRIMROSE, AND MANY WOODLAND PLANTS.

PROBLEM: A white powdery growth appears on leaves, buds, and, occasionally, shoots. Infected parts may distort and curl, then turn yellow and drop off. Plant growth is stunted.

CAUSE: Powdery mildews are fungus diseases that thrive when nights are cool and days are hot. The diseases are most noticeable in late summer and fall, particularly in very shady sites. In fall, fruiting bodies form on the mildew, starting out as tan-yellow specks before turning dark brown-black.

SOLUTION: Plant mildew-resistant varieties. Susceptible plants should be moved to an area that receives more sun; improve air circulation by spacing plants adequately or by thinning overcrowded growth. Spray plants daily with water, which kills spores. In the fall, cut infected perennials to the ground and discard. Spray plants with a solution of baking soda, or apply summer oil or an antitranspirant, which will decrease the loss of water through the leaves.
SUSCEPTIBLE PLANTS: MANY.

PROBLEM: Upper leaf surfaces have pale yellow or white spots, and undersides are covered with orange or yellow pustules. Leaves wilt or shrivel and hang down along the stem, but do not drop off. Pustules may become more numerous, destroying leaves and occasionally the entire plant. Plants may be stunted.

CAUSE: Rust, a fungus disease, is a problem in late summer and early fall and is most prevalent when nights are cool and humid. Rust spores are spread easily by wind and splashing water and overwinter on infected plant parts.

SOLUTION: Buy rust-resistant varieties whenever possible. Water early in the day and avoid wetting leaves. Remove and destroy infected plant parts in the fall and again in the spring. Spray with sulfur, lime sulfur, Bordeaux mixture, propiconazole, triadimefon, or triforine during the growing season.
SUSCEPTIBLE PLANTS: VIRTUALLY ALL.

PROBLEM: Plants suddenly lose their color, turn yellow, and wilt. Stems and branches may die back, or the whole plant may die. Roots are damaged or deformed and have knotty growths and swellings.

CAUSE: Soil nematodes—colorless microscopic worms that live in the soil and feed on plant roots—inhibit a plant's intake of nitrogen. Damage is at its worst in warm, moist soils. Nematodes overwinter in infected roots or soil and are spread by soil, transplants, and tools.

SOLUTION: Only a laboratory test will confirm the presence of soil nematodes. Be suspicious if roots are swollen or stunted. There are no chemical controls; dispose of infected plants and the soil that surrounds them, or solarize the soil. Plant resistant species and cultivars. Add nitrogen fertilizer.
SUSCEPTIBLE PLANTS: VIRTUALLY ALL.

RED	DIGITALIS X MERTONENSIS
	HEMEROCALLIS 'ED MURRAY'
	PRIMULA JAPONICA 'MILLER'S CR
	PULMONARIA MONTANA 'BOWLES
	RODGERSIA PINNATA 'SUPERBA'
PINK	ANEMONE BLANDA 'PINK STAR'
	ASTILBE CHINENSIS 'FINALE'
	BEGONIA GRANDIS SSP. EVANSIA
	CONVALLARIA MAJALIS VAR. ROS
	CYCLAMEN REPANDUM
	GERANIUM X OXONIANUM 'CLAR
	HYACINTHOIDES HISPANICA 'RO
	PHLOX STOLONIFERA 'PINK RID
	PULMONARIA MONTANA 'BARFIE
	RODGERSIA PINNATA
	TIARELLA CORDIFOLIA 'SLICK R
PURPLE/LAVENDER	ASTILBE CHINENSIS VAR. TAQUE
	BLETILLA STRIATA 'ALBOSTRIAT
	HEUCHERA AMERICANA 'PEWTE
	HOSTA 'HONEYBELLS'
	HOSTA VENUSTA
	PHLOX X 'CHATTAHOOCHEE'
	PHLOX DIVARICATA 'DIRIGO IC
	PULMONARIA OFFICINALIS 'RUB
	VIOLA ODORATA 'ROYAL ROBE'
BLUE	ACONITUM CARMICHAELII 'ARE
	ANEMONE BLANDA
	BROWALLIA SPECIOSA 'POWDE
	BRUNNERA MACROPHYLLA 'VAR
	CORYDALIS FLEXUOSA 'BLUE PA
	GERANIUM X 'JOHNSON'S BLUE'
	LOBELIA ERINUS 'CRYSTAL PAL

[1] TENDER ANNUAL

Table columns grouped as: **ZONES** (Zone 3–10), **SOIL** (Dry, Well-Drained, Moist), **LIGHT** (Full Shade, Dappled Shade, Partial Shade, Full Sun), **BLOOMING SEASON** (Spring, Summer, Fall, Winter), **PLANT HEIGHT** (Less Than 1 Ft., 1-3 Ft., More Than 3 Ft.), **NOTED FOR** (Form, Foliage, Fragrance, Flowers, Fruit).

		ZONES								SOIL			LIGHT				BLOOMING SEASON				PLANT HEIGHT			NOTED FOR				
		Z3	Z4	Z5	Z6	Z7	Z8	Z9	Z10	Dry	Well-Dr.	Moist	Full Shade	Dappled Shade	Partial Shade	Full Sun	Spring	Summer	Fall	Winter	<1 Ft.	1-3 Ft.	>3 Ft.	Form	Foliage	Fragrance	Flowers	Fruit
GREEN	MERTENSIA VIRGINICA	✓	✓	✓	✓	✓	✓				✓	✓	✓	✓	✓		✓					✓					✓	
	PULMONARIA SACCHARATA 'ROY DAVIDSON'		✓	✓	✓	✓					✓	✓			✓		✓					✓			✓		✓	
	ARISAEMA RINGENS			✓	✓	✓	✓	✓			✓	✓	✓				✓					✓					✓	✓
	HELLEBORUS ARGUTIFOLIUS				✓	✓					✓	✓			✓		✓					✓			✓		✓	
	NICOTIANA LANGSDORFII[1]					✓	✓				✓	✓			✓			✓				✓				✓	✓	
MULTICOLOR	ACONITUM X CAMMARUM 'BICOLOR'	✓	✓	✓	✓	✓					✓	✓		✓	✓			✓	✓			✓	✓			✓	✓	
	AQUILEGIA CANADENSIS	✓	✓	✓	✓	✓	✓				✓	✓	✓	✓	✓		✓					✓					✓	
	CYCLAMEN HEDERIFOLIUM			✓	✓	✓	✓	✓			✓	✓	✓	✓				✓	✓	✓	✓					✓		✓	
	DICENTRA SPECTABILIS		✓	✓	✓	✓					✓	✓	✓	✓	✓		✓					✓					✓	
	HELLEBORUS LIVIDUS				✓	✓					✓	✓	✓		✓		✓					✓			✓		✓	
	LOBELIA ERINUS 'RIVIERA BLUE SPLASH'[1]	✓	✓	✓	✓	✓	✓	✓	✓	✓	✓	✓		✓	✓	✓	✓	✓			✓						✓	
	TRICYRTIS HIRTA		✓	✓	✓	✓					✓	✓			✓				✓			✓					✓	
	VIOLA CUCULLATA 'FRECKLES'		✓	✓	✓	✓	✓				✓				✓		✓				✓						✓	
GROUND COVERS, GRASSES, AND FERNS	ADIANTUM HISPIDULUM				✓	✓	✓				✓	✓	✓								✓			✓	✓			
	AJUGA PYRAMIDALIS 'METALLICA CRISPA'	✓	✓	✓	✓					✓	✓	✓	✓	✓	✓	✓	✓				✓			✓	✓		✓	
	ASARUM EUROPAEUM		✓	✓	✓	✓					✓	✓		✓							✓			✓	✓			
	ATHYRIUM NIPPONICUM 'PICTUM'		✓	✓	✓	✓					✓	✓										✓		✓	✓			
	CAREX MORROWII 'VARIEGATA'			✓	✓	✓	✓				✓	✓	✓	✓								✓		✓	✓			
	CHRYSOGONUM VIRGINIANUM VAR. VIRGINIANUM		✓	✓	✓	✓	✓				✓	✓	✓	✓	✓		✓	✓			✓						✓	
	CYRTOMIUM FALCATUM			✓	✓	✓	✓	✓			✓	✓	✓									✓		✓	✓			
	DENNSTAEDTIA PUNCTILOBULA	✓	✓	✓	✓	✓				✓	✓		✓	✓	✓							✓		✓	✓			
	DRYOPTERIS ERYTHROSORA		✓	✓	✓	✓					✓	✓										✓		✓	✓			
	EPIMEDIUM X VERSICOLOR 'SULPHUREUM'		✓	✓	✓	✓	✓				✓	✓	✓	✓		✓					✓				✓		✓	
	HAKONECHLOA MACRA 'AUREOLA'		✓	✓	✓	✓					✓	✓	✓	✓								✓		✓	✓			
	LAMIUM MACULATUM 'BEACON SILVER'		✓	✓	✓	✓	✓				✓	✓		✓	✓		✓				✓				✓		✓	
	LIRIOPE MUSCARI 'VARIEGATA'			✓	✓	✓					✓	✓		✓	✓	✓					✓				✓		✓	✓
	MATTEUCCIA STRUTHIOPTERIS	✓	✓	✓							✓	✓	✓										✓	✓	✓			
	MAZUS REPTANS			✓	✓	✓	✓				✓	✓			✓	✓	✓	✓			✓				✓		✓	
	OPHIOPOGON JAPONICUS 'KYOTO DWARF'			✓	✓	✓					✓	✓	✓	✓	✓						✓			✓	✓			
	OSMUNDA CINNAMOMEA	✓	✓	✓	✓	✓	✓					✓	✓										✓	✓	✓			
	POLYSTICHUM SETIFERUM 'DIVISILOBUM'		✓	✓	✓	✓					✓	✓										✓		✓	✓	✓		
	WOODWARDIA FIMBRIATA					✓	✓	✓			✓	✓	✓											✓	✓	✓		

[1] TENDER ANNUAL

Guide to Woody Plants

Organized by plant type, this chart provides information needed to select species and varieties that will thrive in the particular conditions of your garden. For additional information on each plant, refer to the encyclopedia that begins on page 104.

SHRUBS

Plant	Zone 3	Zone 4	Zone 5	Zone 6	Zone 7	Zone 8	Zone 9	Zone 10	Dry	Moist	Shade	Partial Shade	Full Sun	Spring	Summer	Fall	Winter	Under 3 Ft.	3–6 Ft.	6–10 Ft.	10–30 Ft.	More Than 30 Ft.	Form	Foliage	Flowers	Fruit	Bark
ABELIA X GRANDIFLORA 'PROSTRATA'			✓	✓	✓	✓	✓			✓		✓	✓		✓			✓					✓	✓	✓		
ARDISIA CRENATA				✓	✓	✓	✓		✓	✓									✓					✓		✓	
AUCUBA JAPONICA 'PICTURATA'				✓	✓	✓	✓		✓	✓	✓	✓	✓							✓				✓		✓	
BERBERIS JULIANAE			✓	✓	✓					✓	✓	✓	✓	✓						✓				✓	✓	✓	
BUXUS MICROPHYLLA 'TIDE HILL'	✓	✓	✓	✓	✓	✓						✓						✓						✓			
CAMELLIA JAPONICA 'BERENICE BODDY'				✓	✓	✓			✓	✓	✓	✓	✓			✓				✓				✓	✓		
CAMELLIA 'WINTER'S INTERLUDE'			✓	✓	✓				✓	✓	✓	✓	✓			✓	✓		✓					✓	✓		
CERCIS CHINENSIS 'AVONDALE'			✓	✓	✓	✓			✓	✓	✓	✓	✓	✓					✓						✓	✓	
CORNUS X RUTGERSENSIS 'STARDUST'			✓	✓	✓				✓	✓	✓	✓	✓	✓						✓	✓				✓	✓	
CORYLOPSIS GLABRESCENS		✓	✓	✓	✓					✓	✓	✓	✓	✓						✓				✓			
DANAE RACEMOSA				✓	✓				✓	✓	✓					✓			✓				✓	✓		✓	
DAPHNE MEZEREUM	✓	✓	✓	✓	✓					✓	✓	✓		✓			✓	✓							✓	✓	
DAPHNE ODORA				✓	✓	✓				✓	✓	✓					✓	✓							✓	✓	
ENKIANTHUS CAMPANULATUS 'ALBIFLORUS'		✓	✓	✓						✓			✓							✓				✓	✓		
ENKIANTHUS PERULATUS		✓	✓	✓	✓				✓	✓	✓	✓	✓						✓					✓	✓		
EUONYMUS FORTUNEI 'EMERALD GAIETY'	✓	✓	✓	✓	✓			✓	✓	✓	✓	✓							✓				✓	✓			
FATSIA JAPONICA					✓	✓			✓	✓	✓					✓				✓			✓	✓	✓	✓	
FOTHERGILLA GARDENII 'MOUNT AIRY'		✓	✓	✓	✓					✓		✓	✓	✓					✓				✓	✓	✓		
FOTHERGILLA MAJOR	✓	✓	✓	✓	✓					✓		✓	✓	✓						✓				✓	✓		
GAULTHERIA SHALLON		✓	✓	✓	✓				✓	✓	✓		✓						✓	✓				✓	✓		
HAMAMELIS MOLLIS 'GOLDCREST'			✓	✓	✓				✓	✓	✓	✓				✓				✓		✓	✓	✓		
HAMAMELIS VERNALIS		✓	✓	✓	✓			✓	✓	✓	✓	✓	✓			✓			✓					✓	✓		
HYDRANGEA ARBORESCENS 'GRANDIFLORA'	✓	✓	✓	✓	✓	✓				✓	✓	✓			✓				✓						✓		✓
HYDRANGEA QUERCIFOLIA 'SNOWFLAKE'		✓	✓	✓	✓	✓				✓	✓	✓	✓		✓					✓				✓	✓		✓
HYPERICUM 'HIDCOTE'			✓	✓	✓			✓		✓	✓	✓	✓	✓				✓							✓	✓	✓
ILLICIUM FLORIDANUM			✓	✓	✓				✓	✓	✓	✓	✓	✓						✓				✓	✓	✓	
JASMINUM NUDIFLORUM			✓	✓	✓			✓	✓			✓	✓				✓		✓				✓		✓		✓
KALMIA LATIFOLIA 'BULLSEYE'		✓	✓	✓	✓	✓	✓			✓	✓	✓	✓	✓	✓					✓				✓	✓		

		ZONES								SOIL		LIGHT			BLOOMING SEASON				PLANT HEIGHT					NOTED FOR				
	Plant	Zone 3	Zone 4	Zone 5	Zone 6	Zone 7	Zone 8	Zone 9	Zone 10	Dry	Moist	Shade	Partial Shade	Full Sun	Spring	Summer	Fall	Winter	Under 3 ft	3-6 ft	6-10 ft	10-30 ft	More than 30 ft	Form	Foliage	Flowers	Fruit	Bark
SHRUBS	KALMIA LATIFOLIA 'TIDDLYWINKS'		✓	✓	✓	✓	✓	✓			✓	✓	✓	✓	✓	✓				✓				✓	✓	✓		
SHRUBS	KERRIA JAPONICA 'PLENIFLORA'		✓	✓	✓	✓	✓	✓		✓	✓		✓	✓	✓						✓			✓		✓		✓
SHRUBS	KERRIA JAPONICA 'VARIEGATA'		✓	✓	✓	✓	✓	✓		✓	✓		✓	✓	✓				✓							✓		✓
SHRUBS	LAURUS NOBILIS					✓	✓	✓	✓	✓	✓		✓	✓		✓							✓			✓		✓	
SHRUBS	LEUCOTHOE FONTANESIANA 'RAINBOW'		✓	✓	✓	✓	✓				✓	✓	✓	✓	✓					✓				✓	✓	✓		
SHRUBS	LIGUSTRUM JAPONICUM				✓	✓	✓	✓			✓	✓	✓	✓	✓						✓				✓	✓		
SHRUBS	MAGNOLIA VIRGINIANA			✓	✓	✓	✓	✓			✓		✓	✓	✓	✓							✓			✓	✓		
SHRUBS	MAHONIA AQUIFOLIUM			✓	✓	✓	✓				✓	✓	✓		✓					✓					✓	✓	✓		
SHRUBS	MYRICA PENSYLVANICA	✓	✓	✓	✓	✓				✓	✓	✓	✓	✓	✓					✓				✓	✓		✓	✓
SHRUBS	NANDINA DOMESTICA 'MOYER'S RED'			✓	✓	✓	✓			✓	✓	✓	✓	✓	✓					✓				✓	✓	✓	✓	
SHRUBS	OSMANTHUS HETEROPHYLLUS 'VARIEGATUS'				✓	✓	✓			✓	✓	✓	✓	✓			✓			✓					✓	✓		
SHRUBS	PIERIS FLORIBUNDA		✓	✓	✓						✓	✓	✓	✓	✓					✓				✓	✓	✓		
SHRUBS	PIERIS JAPONICA 'FLAMINGO'			✓	✓	✓					✓	✓	✓	✓	✓					✓				✓	✓	✓		
SHRUBS	PITTOSPORUM TOBIRA					✓	✓	✓	✓	✓	✓	✓	✓	✓	✓						✓			✓	✓	✓		
SHRUBS	PRUNUS LAUROCERASUS 'ZABELIANA'			✓	✓	✓	✓				✓	✓	✓	✓	✓					✓				✓	✓	✓		
SHRUBS	RHODODENDRON 'BLUE PETER'			✓	✓	✓					✓	✓	✓	✓	✓						✓				✓	✓		
SHRUBS	RHODODENDRON CALENDULACEUM			✓	✓	✓					✓	✓	✓	✓	✓						✓					✓		
SHRUBS	RHODODENDRON SCHLIPPENBACHII		✓	✓	✓	✓					✓	✓	✓	✓	✓					✓					✓	✓		
SHRUBS	RHODODENDRON 'VULCAN'S FLAME'			✓	✓	✓					✓	✓	✓	✓	✓					✓					✓	✓		
SHRUBS	SARCOCOCCA CONFUSA				✓	✓					✓	✓	✓					✓		✓				✓	✓		✓	
SHRUBS	SKIMMIA JAPONICA				✓	✓					✓	✓	✓		✓					✓					✓	✓	✓	
SHRUBS	STEWARTIA OVATA VAR. GRANDIFLORA			✓	✓	✓	✓	✓			✓		✓			✓						✓			✓	✓		
SHRUBS	TAXUS CUSPIDATA 'DENSA'		✓	✓	✓	✓					✓	✓								✓				✓	✓		✓	
SHRUBS	VIBURNUM SIEBOLDII		✓	✓	✓						✓	✓	✓	✓	✓							✓			✓	✓		
TREES	ACER CIRCINATUM				✓	✓	✓	✓			✓	✓	✓		✓							✓		✓	✓	✓	✓	✓
TREES	ACER PENSYLVANICUM	✓	✓	✓	✓	✓					✓	✓	✓	✓	✓							✓			✓	✓		✓
TREES	CERCIS CANADENSIS 'FOREST PANSY'				✓	✓	✓	✓			✓	✓	✓	✓	✓							✓			✓	✓		
TREES	CORNUS FLORIDA 'CHEROKEE CHIEF'			✓	✓	✓	✓				✓	✓	✓	✓	✓							✓			✓	✓	✓	
TREES	CORNUS NUTTALLII					✓	✓	✓			✓	✓	✓	✓	✓							✓			✓	✓	✓	
TREES	HALESIA MONTICOLA 'ROSEA'		✓	✓	✓	✓	✓				✓	✓	✓	✓	✓								✓	✓	✓	✓	✓	✓
TREES	HALESIA TETRAPTERA		✓	✓	✓	✓	✓				✓	✓	✓	✓	✓								✓	✓	✓	✓	✓	✓
TREES	ILEX OPACA 'OLD HEAVY BERRY'			✓	✓	✓	✓	✓			✓	✓	✓	✓	✓								✓		✓		✓	

Category	Name	Zone 3	Zone 4	Zone 5	Zone 6	Zone 7	Zone 8	Zone 9	Zone 10	Dry	Moist	Shade	Partial Shade	Full Sun	Spring	Summer	Fall	Winter	Under 3 ft.	3-6 ft.	6-10 ft.	10-30 ft.	More than 30 ft.	Form	Foliage	Flowers	Fruit	Bark
TREES	ILEX VERTICILLATA	✓	✓	✓	✓	✓	✓	✓			✓	✓	✓	✓	✓						✓			✓			✓	
	ILLICIUM PARVIFLORUM				✓	✓	✓				✓	✓	✓	✓	✓							✓			✓		✓		
	LIRIODENDRON TULIPIFERA		✓	✓	✓	✓	✓				✓		✓	✓									✓	✓	✓	✓	✓		
	MAGNOLIA 'ELIZABETH'			✓	✓	✓	✓				✓		✓	✓	✓								✓				✓	✓	
	MAGNOLIA X LOEBNERI 'BALLERINA'		✓	✓	✓	✓	✓				✓		✓	✓	✓								✓				✓	✓	
	OSMANTHUS FRAGRANS						✓	✓			✓	✓	✓	✓	✓			✓					✓				✓		
	PINUS PONDEROSA	✓	✓	✓	✓						✓		✓	✓										✓	✓	✓			✓
	PRUNUS CAROLINIANA			✓	✓	✓	✓	✓			✓	✓	✓	✓	✓								✓		✓	✓	✓		
	QUERCUS RUBRA		✓	✓	✓	✓	✓				✓		✓	✓										✓	✓	✓			
	STEWARTIA PSEUDOCAMELLIA			✓	✓	✓					✓		✓	✓			✓						✓				✓		✓
	STYRAX OBASSIA			✓	✓	✓	✓				✓		✓	✓		✓	✓						✓		✓	✓	✓		
	TAXUS BACCATA				✓	✓					✓		✓	✓	✓								✓		✓	✓	✓	✓	
	TSUGA CANADENSIS	✓	✓	✓	✓	✓					✓	✓	✓	✓										✓	✓	✓			
GROUND COVERS	ARDISIA JAPONICA				✓	✓	✓				✓	✓	✓				✓			✓					✓	✓	✓	✓	
	ARDISIA JAPONICA 'ITO FUKURIN'				✓	✓	✓				✓	✓	✓					✓		✓					✓	✓	✓	✓	
	EUONYMUS FORTUNEI 'KEWENSIS'		✓	✓	✓	✓	✓					✓	✓	✓						✓					✓	✓			
	GAULTHERIA PROCUMBENS	✓	✓	✓	✓	✓					✓	✓	✓				✓			✓						✓	✓	✓	
	HYPERICUM CALYCINUM			✓	✓	✓	✓			✓		✓	✓	✓			✓			✓							✓		
	MAHONIA REPENS			✓	✓	✓	✓	✓			✓	✓	✓			✓				✓						✓	✓	✓	
	PACHYSANDRA TERMINALIS 'GREEN CARPET'		✓	✓	✓	✓	✓				✓	✓	✓			✓				✓					✓	✓	✓		
	SASA PALMATA			✓	✓	✓	✓				✓	✓	✓	✓					✓						✓				
	SASA VEITCHII				✓	✓					✓	✓	✓	✓					✓						✓				
	VINCA MAJOR 'VARIEGATA'		✓	✓	✓	✓					✓	✓	✓	✓												✓	✓		
VINES	AKEBIA QUINATA		✓	✓	✓	✓	✓			✓	✓	✓	✓	✓	✓							✓				✓	✓	✓	
	ARISTOLOCHIA MACROPHYLLA			✓	✓	✓	✓				✓	✓	✓			✓							✓			✓			
	CLEMATIS 'THE PRESIDENT'				✓	✓	✓				✓	✓	✓	✓		✓							✓				✓		
	X FATSHEDERA LIZEI					✓	✓	✓			✓	✓					✓						✓			✓		✓	
	GELSEMIUM SEMPERVIRENS 'PRIDE OF AUGUSTA'				✓	✓	✓	✓			✓	✓	✓	✓	✓								✓				✓		
	HEDERA COLCHICA 'DENTATA-VARIEGATA'			✓	✓	✓	✓	✓			✓	✓	✓	✓										✓		✓			
	HEDERA HELIX 'NEEDLEPOINT'				✓	✓	✓	✓	✓		✓	✓	✓	✓										✓		✓			
	HYDRANGEA ANOMALA VAR. PETIOLARIS		✓	✓	✓	✓					✓	✓	✓	✓		✓								✓			✓		✓
	JASMINUM OFFICINALE 'GRANDIFLORUM'					✓	✓				✓	✓		✓	✓		✓	✓					✓	✓			✓		

A Zone Map of the U.S. and Canada

A plant's winter hardiness is critical in deciding whether it is suitable for your garden. The map below divides the United States and Canada into 11 climatic zones based on average minimum temperatures, as compiled by the United States Department of Agriculture. Find your zone and check the zone information in the plant selection guide *(pages 96-101)* or the encyclopedia *(pages 104-151)* to help you choose the plants most likely to flourish in your climate.

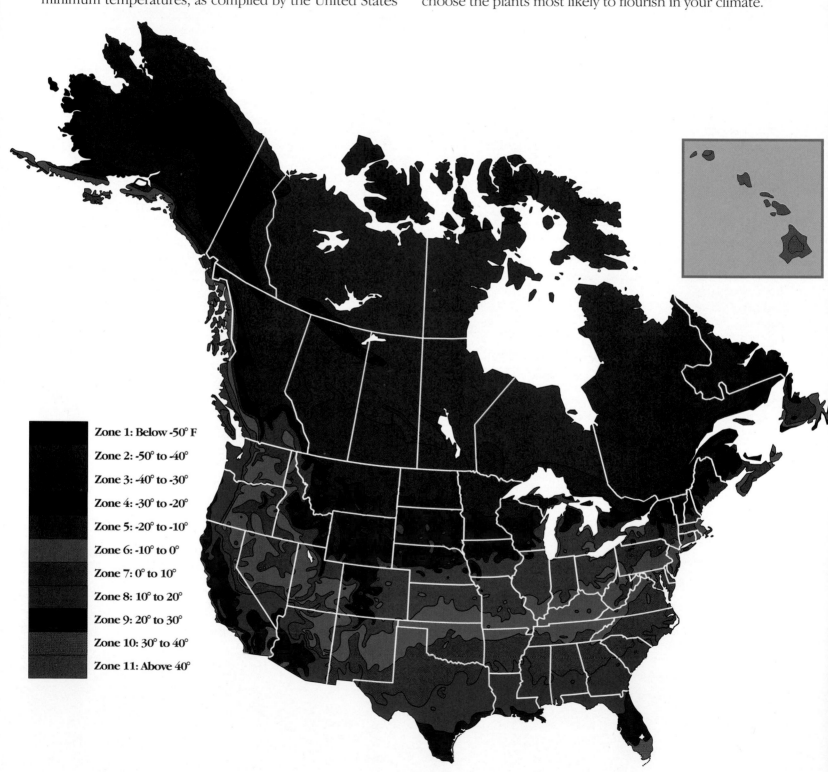

Zone 1: Below -50° F

Zone 2: -50° to -40°

Zone 3: -40° to -30°

Zone 4: -30° to -20°

Zone 5: -20° to -10°

Zone 6: -10° to 0°

Zone 7: 0° to 10°

Zone 8: 10° to 20°

Zone 9: 20° to 30°

Zone 10: 30° to 40°

Zone 11: Above 40°

Cross-Reference Guide to Plant Names

Alumroot—*Geranium maculatum*

Alumroot—*Heuchera*

Andromeda—*Pieris*

Angel-wings—*Caladium*

Anise (anise tree)—*Illicium*

Arrowwood—*Viburnum*

Azalea—*Rhododendron*

Balsam—*Impatiens*

Bamboo—*Sasa*

Barberry—*Berberis*

Barberry—*Mahonia aquifolium*

Barrenwort—*Epimedium*

Bayberry—*Myrica*

Bishop's hat—*Epimedium*

Black alder—*Ilex*

Black dragon—*Ophiopogon*

Bleeding heart—*Dicentra*

Bluebell—*Hyacinthoides*

Bluebells—*Mertensia*

Box (boxwood)—*Buxus*

Bugleweed—*Ajuga*

Busy Lizzy—*Impatiens*

Checkerberry—*Gaultheria*

Chinese orchid—*Bletilla*

Chocolate vine—*Akebia*

Christmas berry—*Ardisia*

Christmas rose—*Helleborus niger*

Columbine—*Aquilegia*

Coral bells—*Heuchera*

Coralberry—*Ardisia crenata*

Cornelian cherry—*Cornus mas*

Cowslip—*Mertensia*

Cowslip—*Primula*

Cowslip—*Pulmonaria*

Cranesbill—*Geranium*

Daffodil—*Narcissus*

Daylily—*Hemerocallis*

Dead nettle—*Lamium*

Devilwood—*Osmanthus*

Dogwood—*Cornus*

Dragonroot—*Arisaema*

Dutchman's-breeches—*Dicentra*

Dutchman's-pipe—*Aristolochia*

Elephant's-ear—*Caladium*

False cypress—*Chamaecyparis*

False miterwort—*Tiarella*

False Solomon's-seal—*Smilacina*

False spikenard—*Smilacina*

Fern (chain)—*Woodwardia*

Fern (Christmas)—*Polystichum*

Fern (cinnamon)—*Osmunda*

Fern (hay-scented)—*Dennstaedtia*

Fern (hedge)—*Polystichum*

Fern (holly)—*Polystichum*

Fern (interrupted)—*Osmunda*

Fern (Japanese holly)—*Cyrtomium*

Fern (lady)—*Athyrium*

Fern (maidenhair)—*Adiantum*

Fern (ostrich)—*Matteuccia*

Fern (royal)—*Osmunda*

Fern (shield)—*Dryopteris*

Fern (shield)—*Polystichum*

Fern (wood)—*Dryopteris*

Fetterbush—*Leucothoe*

Fetterbush—*Pieris*

Fiddleheads—*Osmunda*

Foamflower—*Tiarella*

Foxglove—*Digitalis*

Fumewort—*Corydalis*

Funkia—*Hosta*

Golden-ray—*Ligularia*

Goldenstar—*Chrysogonum*

Green and gold—*Chrysogonum*

Hardy orchid—*Bletilla*

Heavenly bamboo—*Nandina*

Helmet flower—*Aconitum*

Hemlock—*Tsuga*

Holly—*Ilex*

Holly (false)—*Osmanthus*

Indian turnip—*Arisaema*

Inkberry—*Ilex glabra*

Ivy—*Hedera*

Ivy—*Parthenocissus*

Jack-in-the-pulpit—*Arisaema*

Japanese rose—*Kerria*

Jasmine—*Gelsemium*

Jasmine—*Jasminum*

Jerusalem sage—*Phlomis*

Jerusalem sage—*Pulmonaria*

Jessamine—*Gelsemium*

Jessamine—*Jasminum*

Judas tree—*Cercis*

Laurel (Alexandrian)—*Danae*

Laurel (American, mountain)—*Kalmia*

Laurel (Australian)—*Pittosporum tobira*

Laurel (cherry)—*Prunus*

Laurel (drooping)—*Leucothoe*

Laurel (English)—*Prunus laurocerasus*

Laurel (Japanese, spotted)—*Aucuba*

Laurel (swamp)—*Magnolia virginiana*

Laurel (true, bay)—*Laurus*

Leather flower—*Clematis*

Lenten rose—*Helleborus orientalis*

Lily-of-the-field—*Anemone*

Lily-of-the-valley—*Convallaria*

Lily-of-the-valley bush—*Pieris japonica*

Lilyturf—*Liriope*

Lilyturf—*Ophiopogon*

Lungwort—*Mertensia*

Lungwort—*Pulmonaria*

Mandrake—*Podophyllum*

Maple—*Acer*

Marlberry—*Ardisia japonica*

May apple—*Podophyllum*

Mondo grass—*Ophiopogon*

Monkshood—*Aconitum*

Mountain camellia—*Stewartia*

Oak—*Quercus*

Olive—*Olea*

Olive—*Osmanthus*

Paper plant—*Fatsia japonica*

Periwinkle—*Vinca*

Persian violet—*Cyclamen*

Plantain lily—*Hosta*

Privet—*Ligustrum*

Ragwort—*Ligularia dentata*

Redbud—*Cercis*

Roanoke-bells—*Mertensia*

Rockfoil—*Saxifraga*

Rock geranium—*Heuchera*

Sedge—*Carex*

Siberian bugloss—*Brunnera*

Silver bell—*Halesia*

Snakeroot—*Asarum canadense*

Snowbell—*Styrax*

Snowdrop—*Galanthus*

Snowdrop tree—*Halesia*

Snowdrop tree—*Styrax*

Snowflake—*Leucojum*

Solomon's-seal—*Polygonatum*

Spurge—*Euphorbia*

Spurge—*Pachysandra*

St.-John's-wort—*Hypericum*

Storax—*Styrax*

Sweet bay—*Laurus nobilis*

Sweet box—*Sarcococca*

Toad lily—*Tricyrtis*

Tobacco—*Nicotiana*

Tulip tree—*Liriodendron*

Umbrella leaf—*Diphylleia*

Umbrella tree—*Magnolia*

Virginia creeper—*Parthenocissus*

Virgin's-bower—*Clematis*

Wild ginger—*Asarum*

Wild sweet William—*Phlox*

Windflower—*Anemone*

Winter aconite—*Eranthis*

Winterberry—*Ilex*

Winter creeper—*Euonymus fortunei*

Wintergreen—*Gaultheria*

Winter hazel—*Corylopsis*

Witch alder—*Fothergilla gardenii*

Witch hazel—*Hamamelis*

Wolfsbane—*Aconitum napellus*

Woodbine—*Parthenocissus*

Yellow bleeding heart—*Corydalis lutea*

Yellow waxbells—*Kirengeshoma*

Yew—*Taxus*

Encyclopedia of Plants

Presented here in compact form is pertinent information on most of the plants mentioned in this volume. Each genus is listed alphabetically by its Latin botanical name, followed by pronunciation of the Latin and, in bold type, its common name or names. If you know a plant only by a common name, see the cross-reference chart on page 103 or the index.

A botanical name consists of the genus and a species, both usually printed in italics. Species may also have common names, which appear in parentheses, and many species contain one or more cultivars, whose names appear between single quotation marks. An "x" preceding the name indicates a hybrid.

"Hardiness" refers to the zones described on the USDA Plant Hardiness Zone Map for the U.S. and Canada (page 102). Annuals designated "tender" cannot tolerate frost; bulbs designated "tender" must be dug up in fall for winter storage or grown in pots, except in warm zones.

Abelia
(a-BEE-li-a)
ABELIA

Abelia x grandiflora 'Francis Mason'

Hardiness:	*Zones 6-10*
Plant type:	*shrub*
Height:	*3 to 6 feet*
Interest:	*flowers, foliage*
Soil:	*moist, well-drained, acid*
Light:	*partial shade to full sun*

Abelia forms a broad, dense mound with arching branches that bear dainty funnel-shaped summer flowers at a time when most other shrubs have stopped blooming. Small lustrous leaves provide interesting texture for the landscape.

Selected species and varieties: *A.* x 'Edward Goucher'—pink-purple flowers and bronzy foliage in fall. *A.* x *grandiflora* (glossy abelia)—6 feet tall and wide, bearing a profusion of white flowers flushed with pink from early summer till frost and glossy leaves turning purplish bronze in fall; 'Francis Mason' has leaves with rich yellow borders and green centers maturing to all yellow; 'Prostrata' grows 1½ to 2 feet tall, with spreading habit, with white flowers and leaves that are red when new, turning purple-green in fall and winter.

Growing conditions and maintenance: Abelias are easy to grow but do best when leaf mold or peat moss has been added to the soil. Plant them where they will receive some sun and protection from winter winds. Full shade results in less bloom and a more open habit. Prune cold-injured branches in late winter or early spring. Flowers form on new growth.

Acer
(AY-ser)
MAPLE

Acer circinatum

Hardiness:	*Zones 3-9*
Plant type:	*large shrub or small tree*
Height:	*15 to 25 feet*
Interest:	*foliage, bark*
Soil:	*moist, well-drained, slightly acid, fertile*
Light:	*bright full shade to full sun*

Although maples come in all sizes, some species make good understory trees that work well in naturalized areas.

Selected species and varieties: *A. circinatum* (vine maple)—15 to 25 feet tall and almost as wide, the twisting branches often growing horizontally before turning upward, and bearing leaves up to 7 inches wide that turn red to orange in fall on red twigs that remain showy in winter, along with red-winged seed capsules and clusters of tiny red-purple early-spring-blooming flowers; Zones 6-9. *A. palmatum* (Japanese maple)—up to 25 feet tall with an equal or greater width, its fine-textured foliage appearing in reds and purples in some of its many cultivars; can be trained as a tree or bush; Zones 5-8. *A. pensylvanicum* (striped maple)—15 to 20 feet tall, with white-striped green bark when young, 5- to 7-inch leaves that are pinkish when young and yellow in fall, yellow flowers in spring; Zones 3-7.

Growing conditions and maintenance: These maples like cool, humus-rich soils. Vine maple tolerates moderately dry to very moist soils. Mulch the base of striped maple to minimize mower damage.

Aconitum
(ak-o-NY-tum)
MONKSHOOD

Aconitum x bicolor 'Spark'

Hardiness: *Zones 3-8*

Plant type: *perennial*

Height: *2 to 4 feet*

Interest: *flowers*

Soil: *moist, well-drained, fertile*

Light: *full to partial shade*

The vivid hues of monkshoods and their glossy dark green deeply cut leaves make striking additions to any perennial border or naturalized area. Blooming in summer when there are few other blue flowers in the garden, the tall spikes of flowers also make excellent cuttings. *Caution:* All parts of the plant are poisonous.

Selected species and varieties: *A. anthora*—clusters of yellow flowers on 2-foot stems. *A.* x *bicolor* 'Spark'—violet-blue flowers on 4-foot stems in mid- to late summer. *A.* x *cammarum* 'Bicolor'—2 to 4 feet tall with blue-and-white flowers. *A. carmichaelii* 'Arendsii' (azure monkshood)—large blue flowers on 3- to 4-foot stems. *A. napellus* (common monkshood, Turk's-cap)—4 feet tall with indigo blue flowers; 'Carneum' has pink flowers.

Growing conditions and maintenance: Though monkshoods prefer shade as a rule, they especially need it during hot summer afternoons. They tolerate full sun only in constantly moist soil in cool climates. Add peat moss, compost, or leaf mold to soil before planting, and space plants 1½ feet apart. Taller varieties need staking. Divide clumps in spring or fall.

Adiantum
(ad-ee-AN-tum)
MAIDENHAIR FERN

Adiantum pedatum

Hardiness: *Zones 2-10*

Plant type: *perennial*

Height: *8 inches to 3 feet*

Interest: *foliage*

Soil: *moist, well-drained, fertile*

Light: *dense to bright full shade*

Maidenhair ferns add airiness and texture to rock gardens and naturalized areas. Black, or sometimes chestnut, stripes accent the delicately etched green fronds. Slowly creeping on rhizomes, these mostly deciduous ferns form colonies.

Selected species and varieties: *A. capillus-veneris* (common maidenhair, dudder grass)—1- to 2-foot-tall arching fronds; Zones 7-10. *A. hispidulum* (rosy maidenhair, Australian maidenhair)—erect, finely textured fronds, rosy as they unfurl, growing to 1 foot tall with hairy stripes; Zones 8-10. *A. pedatum* (northern maidenhair, five-fingered maidenhair)—slightly arching, branched and fan-shaped fronds, 10 to 18 inches tall, on chestnut brown stripes, spreading slowly; Zones 2-8. *A. venustum* (evergreen maidenhair)—graceful, lacy, arching fronds 8 to 12 inches long; Zones 5-8.

Growing conditions and maintenance: Ferns do best in sites that mimic the moisture and shade of their native woodland settings. Amend soil with leaf mold or peat moss before planting, and top-dress with bone meal every year. Propagate by dividing rhizomes in spring.

Ajuga
(a-JOO-ga)
BUGLEWEED

Ajuga reptans 'Burgundy Glow'

Hardiness: *Zones 3-9*

Plant type: *perennial*

Height: *3 to 12 inches*

Interest: *foliage, flowers*

Soil: *well-drained*

Light: *bright full shade to full sun*

A reliable ground cover for areas where grass will not grow, bugleweed forms a thick mat of crinkled, often colorful foliage ideal for banks, bulb beds, rock gardens, and under trees. Flowers appear in spikes in spring or early summer.

Selected species and varieties: *A. genevensis* (Geneva bugle)—blue, pink, or white spring flowers on erect 6- to 12-inch stems atop green leaves; Zones 4-9. *A. pyramidalis* (pyramid bugle)—blue flowers 4 to 6 inches tall, less invasive than other species; Zones 3-9; 'Metallica Crispa' [also listed as 'Crispa'] has iridescent purplish bronze wrinkled leaves and blue flowers. *A. reptans* (carpet bugle)—a fast spreader 4 inches tall with 10-inch flower stems in spring; Zones 3-8; 'Bronze Beauty' has bronze-purple leaves and blue flowers; 'Burgundy Glow', green, white, and pink variegated leaves with blue or purple flowers in spring.

Growing conditions and maintenance: Bugleweed grows well in almost any soil. For complete cover in one growing season, plant *A. reptans* in well-drained acid loam about 6 inches apart. This species may become invasive.

Akebia
(a-KEE-bee-a)
CHOCOLATE VINE

Akebia quinata

Hardiness:	*Zones 4-8*
Plant type:	*ground cover or climbing vine*
Height:	*20 to 40 feet*
Interest:	*foliage, fruit*
Soil:	*well-drained*
Light:	*full shade to full sun*

Akebia is equally good at covering ground or walls, quickly twining around anything close at hand. With its semi-evergreen foliage, it offers multiseason interest to the landscape. Fruit pods, usually a bright, rich purple, dangle abundantly from the plant in fall; in the spring, small fragrant flowers peep out from the new foliage. A good choice for a trellis or pergola, akebia can also provide quick cover of an eyesore in the landscape.

Selected species and varieties: *A. quinata* (five-leaf akebia)—attractive, dark blue-green compound leaves with five leaflets, each to 3 inches long, nearly masking dark purple fragrant flower racemes that are hard to see from a distance, followed by purple fruit pods up to 4 inches long that ripen in late summer and leaves that usually hold their color until the first hard freeze.

Growing conditions and maintenance: A tough, vigorous plant, akebia tolerates nearly any growing conditions and can easily choke out other plants. Pruning is required to keep it under control.

Anemone
(a-NEM-o-nee)
WINDFLOWER

Anemone hupehensis 'September Charm'

Hardiness:	*Zones 4-8*
Plant type:	*bulb*
Height:	*4 inches to 5 feet*
Interest:	*flowers, foliage*
Soil:	*well-drained, fertile*
Light:	*partial to bright full shade*

Anemone's showy flowers adorn shady perennial beds, borders, naturalized areas, and rock gardens, and are stunning when planted in masses. Members of the buttercup family, anemones come in many varieties and provide durable bloom through three seasons. Flowers are 1 to 3 inches wide and have single or double rows of sepals, rather than petals. Shades of blue, pink, red, white, and rose are available. The mounds of fernlike foliage on branched stems provide textural interest in the landscape. Many varieties are natural spreaders and work well as a ground cover in bulb beds or on banks difficult to cultivate.

Selected species and varieties: *A. blanda* (Grecian windflower)—4 to 6 inches high, bearing blue 2-inch-wide flowers in midspring over distinctly divided leaves; reliably hardy to Zone 6; 'Charmer' has dark pink flowers; 'Pink Star', large light pink flowers; 'Radar', mauve blooms with white centers; 'White Splendour', very large, pure white flowers. *A. canadensis* (meadow anemone)—to 2 feet tall, with rosettes of maplelike leaves beneath 1½-inch-wide white flowers

from late spring to early summer that make it a good ground cover. *A. hupehensis* (dwarf Japanese anemone)—1½ to 3 feet tall, bearing flowers that are red outside, pink inside, in 15-flowered cymes from late summer to fall; Zones 6-8; 'September Charm' [sometimes attributed to *A.* x *hybrida*] is 30 inches tall with silvery pink flowers; var. *japonica* (Japanese anemone) bears pink semi-double flowers; Zones 6-8. *A.* x *hybrida* (Japanese anemone)—1 to 4 feet tall,

Anemone blanda

with 2- to 3-inch-wide flowers blooming from late summer to midfall; Zones 4-8; 'Honorine Jobert' grows to 4 feet tall with simple 2- to 3-inch white flowers; 'Krimhilde' has salmon flowers on stems 24 to 30 inches tall; 'Königin Charlotte' ('Queen Charlotte') is 3 feet tall with semidouble silvery pink flowers; 'Prinz Heinrich' ('Prince Henry') has deep rose semidouble flowers on 3-foot stems; 'Whirlwind' is 4 to 5 feet tall with semidouble white flowers.

Growing conditions and maintenance: Most anemones do best in humus-rich loam; add pebbles if soil is too heavy and amend with compost, leaf mold, or peat moss. Keep soil moist during growing period, drier during dormancy. *A.* x *hybrida* is intolerant of both summer drought and wet winter soil. *A. canadensis* tolerates any soil. Plant anemones where they will be protected from harsh winter winds, and apply a winter mulch in marginal zones. Because they don't naturally grow singly, anemones should be planted in groups, and can be divided in spring. Once established, they need little care. *A. canadensis* and *A.* x *hybrida* may become invasive, so give them lots of room.

Aquilegia
(ak-wil-EE-jee-a)
COLUMBINE

Aquilegia canadensis

Hardiness: *Zones 3-9*

Plant type: *perennial*

Height: *8 inches to 3 feet*

Interest: *flowers*

Soil: *moist, well-drained*

Light: *dappled to bright full shade*

This beautiful and delicate wildflower is ideal for perennial beds and naturalized areas. The flowers come in many colors and bicolors, appearing in spring on erect stems; they are nodding or upright and consist of a short tube surrounded by five petals and backward-projecting spurs of varying lengths. The blue-green compound leaves fade early. Many species have a life span of only 3 to 4 years.

Selected species and varieties: *A. canadensis* (Canadian columbine, wild columbine)—1 to 3 feet tall, with nodding flowers consisting of yellow sepals, short red spurs, and yellow stamens that project below the sepals; Zones 3-8. *A. flabellata* 'Nana Alba' (fan columbine)—8 to 12 inches tall, with pure white nodding flowers 2 inches wide with spurs to 1 inch long and leaflets having broad lobes. *A. x hybrida* 'Crimson Star'—30 to 36 inches tall, bearing bright red and white upright flowers with long spurs.

Growing conditions and maintenance: Columbines require good drainage; for heavy soils, work pebbles in before planting. Because they are deep rooted, columbines are difficult to transplant.

Ardisia
(ar-DEES-ee-a)
ARDISIA

Ardisia crenata

Hardiness: *Zones 7-10*

Plant type: *small shrub or ground cover*

Height: *8 inches to 6 feet*

Interest: *foliage, flowers, fruit*

Soil: *moist, well-drained, acid, fertile*

Light: *bright full shade*

A lovely low evergreen for shady areas, ardisia has glossy dark green serrated leaves that are tapered at both ends and clustered at the ends of stems. Small star-shaped flowers are borne in racemes in summer, followed by berries that persist into winter.

Selected species and varieties: *A. crenata* (Christmas berry, coralberry, spiceberry)—shrublike growth to 6 feet tall with lustrous foliage and bright red berries; Zones 7-10. *A. japonica* (marlberry)—mat-forming ground cover, 8 to 12 inches tall with lustrous dark green toothed leaves, 1½ to 3½ inches long, that are pink when new, white flowers in summer and red berries in the fall; variably hardy to Zone 5 but best in Zones 7-9; 'Hakuokan' is one of the largest cultivars and has broad, white leaf margins; 'Ito Fukurin', light, silvery green leaves thinly edged in white; 'Nishiki', rosy pink leaf margins that turn yellow with age.

Growing conditions and maintenance: Amend soil with leaf mold, peat moss, or compost. Provide protection from harsh winter winds. Variegated forms are less cold hardy than the green ones.

Arisaema
(a-ri-SEE-ma)
JACK-IN-THE-PULPIT

Arisaema sikokianum

Hardiness: *Zones 4-10*

Plant type: *bulb*

Height: *15 inches to 2 feet*

Interest: *flowers, fruit, foliage*

Soil: *moist, well-drained, slightly acid, fertile*

Light: *dappled to full shade*

Arisaema has a curious-looking flower with a broad shield (spathe) that rises behind the sexual parts (spadix). Blooms appear in spring below glossy leaves. Clusters of red berries ripen in fall. Use in naturalized areas and perennial borders.

Selected species and varieties: *A. candidissimum*—20 inches tall, fragrant, bearing a green-striped white or pink spathe and single leaves; hardy to Zone 6. *A. ringens*—20 inches tall, with a helmet-like spathe that is green with white stripes outside, dark purple with white stripes inside; hardy to Zone 5. *A. sikokianum*—16 to 24 inches tall with a spadix that rises above the spathe, which is dark purple or green with white or green veins outside, white inside; hardy to Zone 5. *A. triphyllum* (Indian turnip, dragonroot)—15 to 24 inches tall with a bronze-purple spathe.

Growing conditions and maintenance: Arisaemas like humus-rich soil in bright shade with no afternoon sun. Intolerant of drought, they can withstand wet soil if it is well drained. Mulch the less hardy types for winter, or dig the corms and store in damp spaghnum moss or peat.

Aristolochia	*Arum*	*Asarum*
(a-ris-to-LO-kee-a)	*(AY-rum)*	*(a-SAR-um)*
DUTCHMAN'S-PIPE	**ARUM**	**WILD GINGER**

Aristolochia macrophylla	*Arum italicum 'Pictum'*	*Asarum europaeum*

Hardiness: *Zones 4-8*

Plant type: *woody vine*

Height: *30 feet*

Interest: *foliage*

Soil: *moist, well-drained*

Light: *partial to bright full shade*

Dutchman's-pipe is a vigorous twining vine with glossy dark green heart-shaped deciduous leaves up to 10 inches long. Hidden in the overlapping foliage are dark flowers that look like small pipes with fluted edges. Valued for its fast growth, aristolochia has long been used for shading a porch, covering a trellis for privacy, or concealing an unsightly wall.

Selected species and varieties: *A. macrophylla* [also classified as *A. durior*] (pipe vine)—4- to 10-inch heart- or kidney-shaped leaves masking purplish brown, yellow-throated flowers in early summer.

Growing conditions and maintenance: Aristolochia does well in bright to medium or partial shade. It tolerates any average garden soil but performs with more vigor if compost is applied to its base in spring. Water during droughts. New plants need training during the first year.

Hardiness: *Zones 5-9*

Plant type: *bulb*

Height: *12 to 18 inches*

Interest: *fruit, foliage, flowers*

Soil: *moist, well-drained, fertile*

Light: *full to partial shade*

Arum makes a good specimen plant for perennial borders and woodland areas. Because of its clumping habit, it also makes a fine container plant. The broad, arrow-shaped leaves emerge in fall and, in milder zones, remain all winter. Calla-like flowers in shades of cream, green, or purple top 18-inch erect, leafless stalks in spring or early summer and precede upright clusters of colorful berries. *Caution:* All parts of the plant are poisonous.

Selected species and varieties: *A. italicum* (Italian arum)—creamy to yellow flowers in late spring followed by upright clusters of orange-red berries in summer on a 12- to 18-inch-high clump of foot-long, glossy green leaves with pale veins; 'Marmoratum' has very large leaves marbled in yellow-green; 'Pictum' (painted arum) has whitish green flowers with purple spots and red-orange fruit that appears after the dark green leaves, which are marbled with gray and cream, have faded away.

Growing conditions and maintenance: Arum is easily grown; given a slightly acid loam and protection from afternoon sun, it may spread quickly. Top-dress lightly with compost or organic fertilizer in fall.

Hardiness: *Zones 4-8*

Plant type: *ground cover*

Height: *5 to 10 inches*

Interest: *foliage, fragrance*

Soil: *moist, fertile*

Light: *full shade*

The low-growing perennial wild gingers—particularly the evergreen forms—make good ground covers for medium to deep shade. The small, dark spring flowers are mostly insignificant, hidden beneath the foliage. Rhizomes and crushed leaves carry a ginger fragrance.

Selected species and varieties: *A. canadense* (snakeroot, Canadian wild ginger)—mat-forming, 7 or more inches tall, with heart-shaped 3- to 7-inch-wide deciduous leaves that are reddish hued in spring, then turn bronze-green. *A. europaeum* (European wild ginger)—5 to 10 inches tall, with evergreen leaves 2 to 3 inches wide; Zones 4-7. *A. hartwegii* (Sierra wild ginger)—marbled evergreen leaves 1½ to 5 inches long; hardy to Zone 5. *A. shuttleworthii* [also listed as *Hexastylis shuttleworthii*] (mottled wild ginger)—8 inches tall with evergreen leaves that are usually mottled with silver.

Growing conditions and maintenance: Wild ginger needs slightly acid, humus-rich soil and protection from direct sun. *A. canadense* can also grow in slightly calcareous or limy soils. Propagate by division or from root cuttings.

Astilbe
(a-STIL-bee)
PERENNIAL SPIREA

Astilbe chinensis var. taquetii 'Purple Lance'

Hardiness: *Zones 3-9*

Plant type: *perennial*

Height: *8 inches to 4 feet*

Interest: *flowers, foliage*

Soil: *moist, well-drained, fertile*

Light: *bright full shade to full sun*

Feathery plumes in many colors make astilbe one of the treasures of a shade garden. Depending on variety, blooms appear through summer and into early fall atop 1- to 4-foot stalks. The 6- to 18-inch-high foliage, consisting of finely divided fernlike leaves, adds a medium-fine texture to the landscape. Some varieties are nearly as ornamental in seed as they are in flower. Astilbe can be used as a background accent to shorter perennials, or to grace water features. The dwarf forms work well tucked into rock gardens and border fronts.

Selected species and varieties: *A.* x *arendsii* (false spirea)—a hybrid group, to 4 feet tall, with pink, salmon, red, white, and lavender varieties; Zones 4-9; 'Fanal' has carmine red flowers on 2-foot stems with bronzy leaves in early to midsummer; 'Feuer' ('Fire') bears coral red flowers on 30-inch stems in late summer; 'Red Sentinel', 3-foot-tall brilliant red flowers and reddish green leaves in midsummer; 'White Gloria' ('Weisse Gloria'), white plumes to 2 feet in late summer. *A. chinensis* (Chinese astilbe)—to 2 feet tall, with white, rose-tinged, or pur-

plish blooms; 'Finale' grows 18 inches tall with light pink blooms; 'Pumila' (dwarf Chinese astilbe) produces mauve-pink flowers in narrow plumes on 8- to 12-inch stems in late summer and spreads by stolons for a good ground cover; Zones 3-8; var. *taquetii* 'Purple Lance' ('Purpulanze') (fall astilbe) grows 4 feet tall with purple-red flowers; 'Superba', 3 to 4 feet tall with lavender-pink or reddish purple spikes that bloom from late summer to fall over bronze-

Astilbe chinensis 'Pumila'

green, somewhat coarse foliage. *A. simplicifolia* (star astilbe)—a compact species with simple leaves having several cultivars from 12 to 20 inches tall in white and several shades of pink; Zones 4-8. *A. thunbergii* 'Ostrich Plume' ('Straussenfeder')—salmon pink plumes to 3 feet in midsummer.

Growing conditions and maintenance: In hot climates, astilbe requires shade, where the soil does not dry out; in cooler climates, partial or full sun is acceptable if the soil is moisture retentive. Select an area that has good drainage, and enrich the soil with compost, peat moss, or leaf mold. Astilbe is a heavy feeder, so take care not to plant under shallow-rooted trees. Allow soil to dry out in the winter. Apply a high-phosphorus fertilizer such as 5-10-5 each spring. Plants will multiply quickly and lose vigor as they become crowded. Divide clumps every 2 or 3 years to rejuvenate.

Athyrium
(a-THER-ee-um)
ATHYRIUM

Athyrium nipponicum 'Pictum'

Hardiness: *Zones 4-7*

Plant type: *perennial*

Height: *1 to 3 feet*

Interest: *foliage*

Soil: *moist, well-drained*

Light: *full shade*

Athyriums are deciduous woodland ferns that thrive in even the deepest shade. Arising in clumps, the light green fronds are finely divided and grow upright or gracefully arched. These delicately textured plants work well as accents, space fillers, background plants, or beside water. By late summer, the foliage tends to look worn before it dies back in the fall.

Selected species and varieties: *A. filix-femina* (lady fern)—2 to 3 feet tall, with reddish, brownish, or tan stalks and erect, twice-pinnate fronds 6 to 9 inches wide and often wider. *A. nipponicum* [also classified as *A. goeringianum*] 'Pictum' (painted lady fern)—12 to 18 inches tall with divided fronds, gray-green foliage flushed with maroon only on the upper half of maroon stems; hardy to Zone 4.

Growing conditions and maintenance: Although lady ferns perform best in the slightly acid, rich loam of their native woodland settings, they accept a wide range of soil types and are among the easiest of all ferns to grow. Locate them out of windy areas, as the fronds are easily broken. The painted lady fern needs less light than almost any other fern.

Aucuba
(aw-KEW-ba)
AUCUBA

Aucuba japonica 'Picturata'

Hardiness: *Zones 7-10*

Plant type: *evergreen shrub*

Height: *5 to 10 feet*

Interest: *foliage, fruit*

Soil: *moist, well-drained, fertile*

Light: *full to partial shade*

Aucuba is a broad-leaved evergreen that can thrive in, and brighten, the densest shade. The leathery leaves, from 3 to 8 inches long, are lustrous, and many varieties are heavily variegated with bold splashes of yellow. The sexes are divided in aucuba: Female plants bear ½-inch-long scarlet berries that are often hidden by the foliage. Aucuba is useful as an accent or foundation planting.

Selected species and varieties: *A. japonica* (spotted laurel, Japanese laurel)—leaves are dark and lustrous in all seasons on semiupright branches; 'Crassifolia' is a male plant with large dark green leaves; 'Crotonifolia' has large leaves finely sprinkled with yellow; 'Picturata' leaves have a splash of yellow in the center and yellow specks elsewhere.

Growing conditions and maintenance: Shade—even in winter—helps Japanese aucuba hold its color; in the South, some leaves may turn black in direct sun. While it is tolerant of almost any soil, it will do best with high levels of organic matter.

Begonia
(be-GO-nee-a)
BEGONIA

Begonia grandis ssp. evansiana

Hardiness: *Zones 6-10*

Plant type: *perennial*

Height: *6 inches to 3 feet*

Interest: *flowers, foliage*

Soil: *moist, well-drained, fertile*

Light: *partial to bright full shade*

Prized for their flowers that bloom continuously from late spring to fall, begonias provide vivid color in planters and borders. The mounded foliage comes in rich green, bronze, and reddish tones.

Selected species and varieties: *B. grandis* [sometimes classified *B. grandis* ssp. *evansiana*] (hardy begonia, Evans's begonia)—2- to 3-foot branching stems with clusters of pale pink blooms in summer and large toothy leaves that are green with red veins above and red below; Zones 6-9; 'Alba' has white flowers. *B. semperflorens-cultorum* (wax begonia)—6 to 12 inches tall, with bronze to green leaves and white, pink, or red 1-inch-wide single or double flowers alone or in clusters, blooming nonstop all summer; 8- to 10-inch-tall hybrid series has medium-sized camellia-like flowers on basal branching stems that reduce the top-heaviness of the species; Zones 6-10.

Growing conditions and maintenance: Begonias prefer light, open shade. Generously mix compost or peat moss into the soil. Hardy begonias need winter mulch north of Zone 8. North of Zone 6, bring wax begonias inside before frost.

Berberis
(BER-ber-is)
BARBERRY

Berberis julianae

Hardiness: *Zones 5-8*

Plant type: *evergreen shrub*

Height: *3 to 8 feet*

Interest: *flowers, fruit, foliage*

Soil: *moist, well-drained, slightly acid*

Light: *bright full shade to full sun*

The barberries are dense, thorny shrubs with bright yellow flowers in spring and colorful berries that may persist into fall. They make excellent barrier plants.

Selected species and varieties: *B. julianae* (wintergreen barberry)—6 to 8 feet tall with glossy deep green leaves 1½ to 2½ inches long that sometimes turn bronze or deep red in winter and showy yellow flower clusters in spring followed by blue-black oval berries on yellow stems; Zones 6-8. *B. triacanthophora* [also classified as *B. wisleyensis* or *B.* x *wisleyensis*] (three-spine barberry)—open form 3 to 5 feet tall with yellow stems setting off narrow 1- to 2-inch-long bright green leaves, accenting pale yellow or white flowers flushed with red outside that appear pink from a distance and bluish black fruit. *B. verruculosa* (warty barberry)—3 to 6 feet tall, producing 1-inch-long lustrous dark green leaves with white beneath that turn purplish to mahogany in fall and winter and violet-black berries.

Growing conditions and maintenance: Locate barberries where they will be out of desiccating winds, and water during dry periods. They accept pruning.

Bletilla
(ble-TIL-a)
BLETILLA

Bletilla striata

Hardiness: *Zones 5-9*

Plant type: *bulb*

Height: *8 to 20 inches*

Interest: *flowers*

Soil: *moist, well-drained, fertile*

Light: *full shade*

One of the few orchids that can be grown outdoors, bletilla produces sprays of light rosy purple flowers in late spring or early summer just above broad, pointed, papery leaves that have prominent parallel veins. Bletilla is useful as a specimen, in group plantings, or as a container plant.

Selected species and varieties: *B. striata* (Chinese orchid, Chinese ground orchid, hyacinth orchid, hardy orchid)—8 to 20 inches tall, with nodding deep pink or rosy purple flowers, up to 1½ inches across, borne in terminal racemes of six to 10 above dark green pleated leaves; 'Alba' has creamy white flowers; 'Albostriata', leaves bearing longitudinal white stripes that stay attractive throughout the season and purple to rosy purple flowers.

Growing conditions and maintenance: Bright shade and rich moist loam are best for bletilla. Locate a site that is protected from wind. Work peat moss or compost into the soil, and plant no more than 2 inches deep. Water during dry periods; drought can result in diminished or no bloom the following spring. Propagate by dividing the pseudobulbs.

Browallia
(bro-WALL-ee-a)
BUSH VIOLET

Browallia speciosa

Hardiness: *tender*

Plant type: *annual*

Height: *1 to 5 feet*

Interest: *flowers, foliage*

Soil: *moist, well-drained, fertile*

Light: *bright full to partial shade*

Browallia produces star-shaped flowers in blue, lavender, or white all summer long above glossy bright green foliage. The compact bush and trailing forms are ideal for shade bedding, edgings, planters, window boxes, and rock walls.

Selected species and varieties: *B. speciosa* (amethyst flower, sapphire flower)—stems to 5 feet tall bearing tube-shaped flowers about 2 inches across above 2½-inch leaves; 'Blue Bells' produces lavender-blue flowers on a 1-foot-tall plant that requires no pinching; 'Jingle Bells' includes a mixture of indigo blue, light blue, and snow white flowers from other cultivars; 'Powder Blue' has light blue blooms; 'Silver Bells', large sugar white flowers.

Growing conditions and maintenance: Flower color is best when browallia is shaded from afternoon sun. Mulch the plants to help maintain moisture, and do not overwater. Feed them lightly once a month; too much fertilizer will result in lush foliage but few flowers.

Brunnera
(BRUN-er-a)
BRUNNERA

Brunnera macrophylla

Hardiness: *Zones 4-8*

Plant type: *perennial*

Height: *12 to 18 inches*

Interest: *flowers, foliage*

Soil: *moist, well-drained*

Light: *partial to full shade*

Brunnera bears delicate sprays of tiny blue starlike flowers above bright green heart-shaped leaves that grow larger and darker with age and are sometimes mottled. The flowers, resembling forget-me-nots, and the loosely mounded foliage work well in perennial borders, rock gardens, and naturalized areas.

Selected species and varieties: *B. macrophylla* (Siberian bugloss)—a dense mound bearing loosely branched flower clusters in early to midspring on 12-inch stems over leaves up to 8 inches across with fuzzy stems; 'Langtrees' has leaf centers that are spotted with silver-gray; 'Variegata', leaves bearing bold splashes of cream-white; some are almost completely white.

Growing conditions and maintenance: Brunnera has few pests. Adaptable to a wide range of soils, it does best in moist loam but can tolerate drier sites. Space plants 1 foot apart. Brunnera prefers dense full shade in the South, partial shade in the North; hot afternoon sun tends to wilt the foliage and scorch the variegated forms. As clumps deteriorate, rejuvenate by dividing.

Buxus
(BUKS-us)
BOX, BOXWOOD

Buxus microphylla 'Wintergreen'

Hardiness: *Zones 4-9*

Plant type: *evergreen shrub*

Height: *2 to 20 feet*

Interest: *foliage*

Soil: *moist, well-drained*

Light: *bright full shade to full sun*

These long-lived shrubs are widely used for hedges and foundation plantings.

Selected species and varieties: *B. microphylla* (littleleaf boxwood)—very slow growing mound, 3 to 4 feet tall with an equal spread, producing medium green ⅓- to 1-inch-long leaves in summer that become yellowish to green-brown in winter; Zones 6-9; 'Tide Hill' grows slowly to 2 feet tall and 5 feet wide, with foliage that stays green all winter; Zones 4-9; 'Wintergreen' has small, light green leaves; Zones 4-9. *B. sempervirens* (common boxwood)—leaves ½ to 1 inch long on a slow-growing shrub, 15 to 20 feet in height with an equal or greater spread; Zones 5-8; 'Suffruticosa' is very slow growing, dense and compact, reaching 4 to 5 feet, with fragrant leaves; 'Vardar Valley' has a flat-topped habit, growing 2 to 3 feet tall with 4- to 5-foot spread and dark blue-green foliage; Zones 4-8.

Growing conditions and maintenance: Plant in wind-protected areas and mulch to keep roots cool and moist. Shade helps protect boxwoods from leaf burn in winter. Boxwoods do best in climates that do not have extreme heat or cold.

Caladium
(ka-LAY-dee-um)
ELEPHANT'S-EAR

Caladium bicolor 'White Queen'

Hardiness: *tender or Zones 10-11*

Plant type: *bulb*

Height: *1 to 2 feet*

Interest: *foliage*

Soil: *moist, well-drained*

Light: *partial to full shade*

Caladium's large leaves, shaped like arrowheads and 6 to 18 inches long, are colorfully patterned in various combinations of red, pink, white, and green. A good container plant, caladium is also excellent for mass plantings in shady borders.

Selected species and varieties: *C. bicolor* [formerly *C.* x *hortulanum*]—shieldlike leaves may be flat, wavy, or ruffled; 'Fannie Munson' has pink leaves with narrow green margins; 'Frieda Hempel', solid red leaves with green margins; 'Pink Beauty', soft pink leaves with rose-colored veins on a deep green background; 'White Queen' is 18 inches tall with red-veined, green-edged, whitish leaves 8 to 12 inches long.

Growing conditions and maintenance: Caladiums need ample water in the growing season and do poorly in low humidity. Feed with an all-purpose fertilizer during the growing season. Tender plants with tropical origins, they can be treated as perennials and naturalized only in the southern tip of Florida and in southwestern California. Elsewhere, however, they can be dug in the fall and stored during winter; divide before replanting.

Camellia
(kah-MEEL-ee-a)
CAMELLIA

Camellia sasanqua 'Yuletide'

Hardiness: *Zones 6-9*

Plant type: *large shrub or small tree*

Height: *6 to 25 feet*

Interest: *flowers, foliage*

Soil: *moist, well-drained, acid, fertile*

Light: *bright full shade to full sun*

Camellia has glossy deep green leaves and stunning red, white, or pink flowers.

Selected species and varieties: *C. japonica* (common camellia, Japanese camellia)—a 15- to 25-foot-tall pyramid having 3- to 5-inch-wide flowers in midfall for some varieties, winter or early spring for others; Zones 7-9; 'Adolph Adusson' has red semidouble flowers 4 inches wide in late fall or early winter; 'Berenice Boddy', light pink semidouble flowers with dark pink undersides in winter. *C. sasanqua* 'Yuletide'—6 to 10 feet tall, bearing 2- to 3-inch single red flowers with yellow stamens from fall to early winter. *C. oleifera* and *C. sasanqua* Ackerman selections—midfall flowers on a more cold-hardy plant 6 to 10 feet high; Zones 6-8; 'Snow Flurry' has white double blooms; 'Winter's Interlude', lavender-pink anemone-like flowers.

Growing conditions and maintenance: Camellias need shelter from hot midday sun, but too much shade or sun limits flowering. Plant in spring to allow cold hardiness to become established. Shallow rooted, camellias benefit from an application of mulch. Prune after flowering.

Carex
(KAY-reks)
SEDGE

Carex morrowii 'Variegata'

Hardiness: *Zones 5-9*

Plant type: *perennial*

Height: *1 to 3 feet*

Interest: *foliage*

Soil: *moist, well-drained, fertile*

Light: *bright full shade to full sun*

The mounds of gracefully arching grasslike leaves make sedge useful in the foreground of edgings and in rock gardens, where, as a single specimen or in groups, it lends texture and fluidity to the shady landscape.

Selected species and varieties: *C. buchananii* (leatherleaf sedge, fox-red sedge)—dense clumps of very narrow reddish bronze leaves to 20 inches high; Zones 8-9. *C. morrowii* 'Variegata' (variegated Japanese sedge)—12 to 18 inches tall, gracefully swirling moplike mounds, with leathery evergreen cream-and-green leaves ¼ to ½ inch wide; Zones 6-9. *C. pendula* (drooping sedge, giant sedge, sedge grass)—mounds 2 to 3 feet high with bright green, furrowed, usually evergreen leaves ¾ inch wide and 18 inches long; Zones 5-9.

Growing conditions and maintenance: Unlike true ornamental grasses, sedge is a native of woodland environments and performs well in shade. Avoid exposing *C. pendula* to dry, sunny conditions, particularly in winter. Propagate by dividing in spring.

Cercis
(SER-sis)
REDBUD, JUDAS TREE

Cercis canadensis 'Forest Pansy'

Hardiness: *Zones 4-9*

Plant type: *large shrub or small tree*

Height: *8 to 30 feet*

Interest: *flowers, fruit*

Soil: *moist, well-drained*

Light: *bright full shade to full sun*

An early and prolific spring bloomer, redbud is a good accent tree for shady areas. Large heart-shaped leaves appear after the flowers, and long green seed pods turn brown and persist into winter.

Selected species and varieties: *C. canadensis* (eastern redbud)—a small tree with a spreading crown 20 to 30 feet tall, bearing 5-inch-wide leaves that turn a subdued yellow in fall; 'Alba' has white flowers; 'Forest Pansy', red-purple leaves and pink-lavender flowers; hardy to Zone 7. *C. chinensis* (Chinese redbud)—a multitrunked shrub or tree 8 to 12 feet tall with upright growth and rose-purple flowers; Zones 6-9; 'Avondale' grows to 9 feet, with deep rose-purple flowers that bloom profusely. *C. reniformis*—usually 15 to 20 feet tall with glossy dark green leaves 2 to 4 inches wide and pale pink flowers; Zones 7-9; 'Oklahoma' has glossy leaves and wine red flowers.

Growing conditions and maintenance: Eastern redbud needs some sun in late winter and early spring for the the best flower production. In Zones 5-7, plant in spring; farther south, plant at any time from fall to spring.

Chrysogonum
(kris-AHG-o-num)
GOLDENSTAR

Chrysogonum virginianum

Hardiness: *Zones 5-9*

Plant type: *ground cover*

Height: *4 to 9 inches*

Interest: *flowers, foliage*

Soil: *moist, well-drained, fertile*

Light: *dappled to bright full shade*

Goldenstar produces bright yellow star-shaped flowers from spring to mid-summer amid lush green foliage. Each bloom consists of five ray florets around a yellow disk. Spreading by means of leafy runners along the ground, goldenstar forms a low, dense carpet, making it useful as a ground cover, for edging, or in a rock garden.

Selected species and varieties: *C. virginianum* var. *virginianum* (green and gold)—grows 6 to 9 inches tall in a mat-like habit with rich green, broadly serrated leaves that are triangular to oval, and 1- to 1½-inch-wide flowers that bloom well into summer in cooler zones, where there is sometimes a second flush before fall; var. *australe* is a rapidly spreading form 4 to 8 inches high.

Growing conditions and maintenance: Goldenstar grows well in average soil but benefits from the addition of organic matter such as leaf mold or peat moss. Once established, it tolerates occasional dryness. Site plants 1 foot apart for ground coverage. Mulch in colder zones to assist in overwintering. Propagate by division in spring.

Clematis
(KLEM-a-tis)
VIRGIN'S-BOWER

Clematis montana 'Elizabeth'

Hardiness: *Zones 3-8*

Plant type: *woody vine*

Height: *5 to 20 feet*

Interest: *flowers, foliage*

Soil: *moist, well-drained, fertile*

Light: *bright full shade to full sun*

The twining foliage of clematis forms the lush background for large, elegant flowers in blue, purple, pink, and white. Clematis has no true petals; the showy parts of the flower are the sepals. Many hybrids have been developed with extra large flowers up to 8 inches across. Leaves are 3 to 6 inches long and are medium to dark green. A vigorous climber with a scrambling habit, clematis is useful for trellises, rock walls, arbors, posts, and fences.

Selected species and varieties: *C. macropetala* 'Markham's Pink' [also called 'Markham'] (downy clematis)—8 to 10 feet tall with pink flowers 2½ to 4 inches across; hardy to Zone 5. *C. montana* (anemone clematis)—fast-growing species with late-spring white flowers to 2½ inches wide; 'Elizabeth' grows 12 to 20 feet high and yields 2½- to 3-inch-wide lightly vanilla-scented pink flowers; hardy to Zone 5; 'Tetrarose' has purplish pink flowers 3 inches across and bronze-green foliage; var. *rubens* grows 10 to 20 feet high and produces fragrant, deep rosy pink early-summer flowers, 2 to 2½ inches wide; Zone 5. Large-flowering hybrids include: 'Comtesse de Bouchard', 8 to 12 feet tall, bearing 5- to 6-inch pink flowers with yellow stamens and a touch of lavender, growing on new wood from June to August; hardy to Zone 6; 'General Sikorski', with reddish-centered, 4- to 6-inch-wide lavender flowers with cream-colored stamens; 'H. F. Young', 6- to 8-inch wide flowers in wedgewood blue with cream-colored stamens from early summer to fall; 'Marie Boisselot', 6- to 8-inch-wide flowers, growing on the previous

Clematis 'H. F. Young'

year's wood, that are pale pink when first unfurling, maturing to pure white with cream stamens and broad overlapping sepals that cause blooms to appear semi-double; 'Mrs. Cholmondeley', light blue flowers up to 8 inches across with four to six sepals, blooming on new wood from late spring to late summer; 'Perle d'Azur', sky blue flowers on new growth from late spring until frost, reaching 10 to 12 feet in height; 'The President', to 12 feet, with 6-inch-wide bluish purple flowers growing from early summer to fall on the previous year's wood; hardy to Zone 6.

Growing conditions and maintenance: Clematis grows best in neutral to slightly alkaline soil in dappled or partial shade. A north-facing location is ideal. To make sure the site is well drained, fill the planting hole with equal parts of soil, compost, and coarse sand. Roots must stay cool; mulch or underplant with shallow-rooted ground cover. Young plants need support and training. In spring and fall, feed with an all-purpose fertilizer; after the first year, fertilize every 10 days during bloom. If soil is naturally acid, add lime every year or two. Propagate from seed or from stem cuttings taken in summer.

Convallaria
(kon-va-LAIR-ee-a)
LILY-OF-THE-VALLEY

Convallaria majalis

Hardiness: *Zones 2-7*

Plant type: *perennial*

Height: *8 to 10 inches*

Interest: *flowers, fragrance, foliage*

Soil: *moist, well-drained, acid, fertile*

Light: *full to partial shade*

The incomparable fragrance and waxy, bell-shaped flowers of lily-of-the-valley make this a springtime favorite for woodland settings, borders, and shady rock gardens. A natural spreader, lily-of-the-valley makes an effective ground cover. The cut flowers are favored additions to arrangements and bridal bouquets.

Selected species and varieties: *C. majalis*—a vigorously growing species with five to 13 white flowers pendant from an 8-inch-tall wiry stalk that arises in late spring from a pair of tonguelike leaves 8 inches long and 1 to 3 inches wide that tend to look unkempt by late summer and die down early; 'Aureovariegata' has leaves with yellow stripes; 'Flore Pleno', double white flowers; var. *rosea*, dusty pink flowers.

Growing conditions and maintenance: Lily-of-the-valley blooms best if it is not sited in dense shade. Plant pips—single rhizomes with growth buds—4 to 6 inches apart from early to midfall. Top-dress with compost or complete fertilizer after the first frost. Once established, though, plantings do fine with a minimum of attention.

Cornus
(KOR-nus)
DOGWOOD, CORNEL

Cornus florida

Hardiness: *Zones 4-9*

Plant type: *large shrub or small tree*

Height: *10 to 45 feet*

Interest: *flowers, fruit, foliage, form*

Soil: *moist, well-drained*

Light: *bright full shade to full sun*

The dogwood, native to woodland edges, provides four-season interest—flowers in spring, bird-attracting berries from summer onward, autumn color, and a shapely, spreading silhouette in winter. Some species have attractive bark. Hybrids have been developed to thrive in almost any climate except for very hot and dry areas.

Selected species and varieties: *C. controversa* (giant dogwood)—30 to 45 feet tall and horizontally branched in tiers, with creamy white midspring flower cymes 3 to 7 inches across, red berries turning blue-black in late summer, and dark green leaves that sometimes turn purple in fall; Zones 5-7. *C. florida* (flowering dogwood)—the commonest of the dogwoods, 20 to 40 feet high with equal spread, blooming in spring with white petal-like bracts before the leaves unfurl and red fruit through late fall; hardy to Zone 5 if the nursery stock originated there; 'Cherokee Chief' has rosy red bracts and reddish new growth; 'Cloud Nine' is a slow grower with spreading habit and white overlapping bracts; 'Welchii' has leaves variegated green, pink, and white. *C. mas* (cornelian cher-

ry)—gray to brown flaking bark on a large multitrunked shrub or small tree that branches close to the ground and grows 20 to 25 feet tall and 15 to 20 feet wide, producing dark green semiglossy foliage with unreliable fall color, yellow flowers that open early and red fruit that appears in midsummer; Zones 4-8. *C. nuttallii*

Cornus controversa

(Pacific dogwood, mountain dogwood) —the West Coast version of *C. florida*, with flowers made up of four to eight white bracts, blooming in spring and sometimes again in late summer, orange to red berries, and yellow to red fall foliage; hardy to Zone 7. *C. racemosa* (panicled dogwood, gray dogwood)—10- to 15-foot-tall shrub with equal width, suckering from roots and covered with bark that is chestnut brown when young and grays with age, with flowers on 2-inch whitish cymes in late spring and white berries in late summer; Zones 4-8. *C.* x *rutgersensis*—resistant to dogwood borer and anthracnose, flowering in late spring after leaves appear; Zones 6-9; 'Aurora' has overlapping white bracts and blooms profusely; 'Stardust' forms a shrub to 15 feet with long arching branches and white flowers.

Growing conditions and maintenance: Flowering dogwood is susceptible to many pests and diseases. For optimum vigor, plant in acid soil high in organic matter, and mulch around base of the trunk to keep roots cool and eliminate mower damage. Pruning, if necessary, should only be done during dormancy; make cuts perpendicular to the ground. Giant dogwood likes moist, acid soils. *C. mas* and *C. racemosa* tolerate a variety of soils but prefer rich, well-drained sites.

Corydalis
(ko-RID-a-lis)
FUMEWORT

Corydalis flexuosa 'Blue Panda'

Hardiness: *Zones 5-8*

Plant type: *perennial*

Height: *8 to 15 inches*

Interest: *flowers, foliage*

Soil: *moist, well-drained*

Light: *dappled to bright full shade*

Corydalis is useful for edgings, rock gardens, and perennial beds. Spikes of small trumpet-shaped flowers bloom from midspring through summer. The fernlike foliage remains attractive throughout the growing season.

Selected species and varieties: *C. flexuosa* 'Blue Panda'—8- to 12-inch-tall mounds bearing bright blue flower spikes from late spring until frost. *C. lutea* (yellow corydalis, yellow bleeding heart)—a bushy, multistemmed plant 12 to 15 inches tall with ¾-inch-long yellow flowers flaring out from spikes above the foliage.

Growing conditions and maintenance: Corydalis grows best in light or dappled shade but will tolerate deep shade. For increased vigor, work organic matter such as compost, leaf mold, or peat moss into the soil before planting. Good drainage is essential. Apply an all-purpose fertilizer in spring. After 2 or 3 years, divide plants in early spring. Propagate by seeds or stem cuttings. Yellow corydalis self-seeds freely.

Corylopsis
(kor-ee-LOP-sis)
WINTER HAZEL

Corylopsis pauciflora

Hardiness: *Zones 5-8*

Plant type: *deciduous shrub*

Height: *4 to 15 feet*

Interest: *flowers, fragrance, foliage*

Soil: *moist, well-drained, acid*

Light: *bright full shade to full sun*

One of the first shrubs to flower in spring and one of the best for thick summer foliage, winter hazel is useful against bare walls or in informal shrub borders. Drooping panicles of fragrant yellow bell-shaped flowers appear before the leaves in April.

Selected species and varieties: *C. glabrescens* (fragrant winter hazel)—8 to 15 feet tall with similar spread, followed by oval, pointed, toothy leaves 2 to 4 inches long; Zones 5-8. *C. pauciflora* (buttercup winter hazel)—4 to 6 feet tall, with flowers in clusters of only 2 or 3, and leaves 1½ to 3 inches long; Zones 6-8. *C. sinensis* (Chinese winter hazel)—5 to 8 feet tall but may grow to 15 feet, bearing blue-green downy leaves 2 to 5 inches long and flowers in 2-inch drooping clusters.

Growing conditions and maintenance: Winter hazels grow best in light shade, but they need some sun in early spring to promote flowering. Protect from winter winds, sudden temperature dips, and spring frosts that can easily kill flower buds. Work leaf mold, peat moss, or compost liberally into the soil before planting. There is usually no need to fertilize.

Cyclamen
(SIK-la-men)
PERSIAN VIOLET

Cyclamen repandum

Hardiness: *Zones 7-9*

Plant type: *bulb*

Height: *3 to 6 inches*

Interest: *flowers, foliage*

Soil: *moist, well-drained, neutral to alkaline, fertile*

Light: *dappled to bright full shade*

The cyclamen that has long graced florists' shops also comes in hardy varieties that are suitable for shady gardens. The flowers are produced on naked stalks above round, heart-shaped leaves that are often mottled with silvery white. Cyclamen works well in rock gardens, borders, and planters.

Selected species and varieties: *C. coum*— 4 inches tall, with red, pink, or white flowers from winter to early spring and dark green to marbled foliage; 'Album' has pure white flowers. *C. hederifolium* [also classified as *C. neapolitanum*] (Neapolitan cyclamen, baby cyclamen)— 3 to 6 inches tall, with 5-inch leaves variable in form and color and pink or white flowers to 1 inch long in late summer and fall; 'Album' has white flowers with an occasional flush of pink. *C. repandum*— deep pink flowers in late spring or early summer and spotted leaves.

Growing conditions and maintenance: Tubers should be planted ½ inch deep and 6 to 8 inches apart in soil amended with organic matter.

Cyrtomium
(sir-TOH-mee-um)
CYRTOMIUM

Cyrtomium falcatum

Hardiness: *Zones 5-10*

Plant type: *perennial*

Height: *1 to 2 feet*

Interest: *foliage*

Soil: *moist, well-drained, fertile*

Light: *bright full shade*

Cyrtomium has toothy, hollylike, semi-evergreen fronds arranged in a circle and arching outward. Scattered amid rhododendrons or other evergreens, the medium-fine, leathery, glossy foliage adds textural interest to the shady landscape. In the North, it is often grown as a houseplant.

Selected species and varieties: *C. falcatum* (Japanese holly fern)—1 to 2 feet tall, with leathery, dark green coarsely serrated fronds having four to 10 pairs of pinnae about 3 inches long. *C. fortunei*—erect fronds to 2 feet high and up to 10 inches wide with 12 to 26 pairs of pinnae that taper sharply and are a paler green and less lustrous than those of Japanese holly fern and not as serrated.

Growing conditions and maintenance: Good drainage is particularly important in winter, when the cyrtomium can be subject to rot. Work leaf mold, peat moss, or compost into the soil when planting. In marginal zones, provide a site that is sheltered from winter winds and hard frost, and mulch heavily.

Danae
(DAY-nah-ee)
ALEXANDRIAN LAUREL

Danae racemosa

Daphne
(DAF-nee)
DAPHNE

Daphne x burkwoodii 'Carol Mackie'

Dennstaedtia
(den-STET-ee-a)
CUP FERN

Dennstaedtia punctilobula

Hardiness: *Zones 8-9*

Plant type: *evergreen shrub*

Height: *2 to 4 feet*

Interest: *foliage, fruit, form*

Soil: *moist, well-drained*

Light: *dappled to bright full shade*

The lustrous rich green leaves of Alexandrian laurel and its gracefully arching habit lend elegance and texture throughout the seasons. Related to butcher's-broom, this laurel arises bamboolike into sheaves of stems and leaves. Orange-red berries appear in the fall. The branches make long-lasting cuttings for indoor arrangements.

Selected species and varieties: *D. racemosa*—2 to 4 feet high and equally as wide, with long, pointed, rich green "leaves" that are actually flattened stems 1½ to 4 inches long and ¼ to 1½ inches wide, inconspicuous greenish yellow flowers, and showy berries that are ¼ to ⅜ inch in diameter.

Growing conditions and maintenance: Alexandrian laurel prefers light, open shade; direct hot sun can discolor leaves or, in winter, produce leaf burn. Supplement the soil with organic matter such as leaf mold or peat moss. Propagate by dividing.

Hardiness: *Zones 4-9*

Plant type: *shrub*

Height: *3 to 5 feet*

Interest: *flowers, fragrance, fruit, foliage*

Soil: *moist, well-drained, near neutral*

Light: *partial to bright full shade*

Daphnes are temperamental plants, but their intensely fragrant late-winter or early-spring flowers make them worthwhile. They can be either deciduous or evergreen. Birds love the red berries that appear in summer. *Caution:* All parts of the plant are poisonous to humans.

Selected species and varieties: *D. x burkwoodii* (Burkwood daphne)—3 to 4 feet high with an equal spread, producing clusters of fragrant, creamy white to pinkish spring flowers and semi-evergreen foliage; Zones 4-8; 'Carol Mackie' has leaves with creamy margins. *D. mezereum* (February daphne, mezereum)—3 to 5 feet high and wide, with lavender to rosy purple flowers that emerge in late winter to early spring before the semi-evergreen to deciduous leaves; Zones 4-8. *D. odora* (winter daphne)—3 feet high, densely branched, and evergreen, growing extremely fragrant rosy purple flowers in late winter to early spring; Zones 7-9.

Growing conditions and maintenance: Consider eventual spread; daphnes do not withstand transplanting. Despite the best care, however, daphnes may suddenly die for unknown reasons.

Hardiness: *Zones 3-8*

Plant type: *deciduous ground cover*

Height: *1½ to 3 feet*

Interest: *foliage*

Soil: *dry to moist, well-drained, slightly acid*

Light: *bright full shade to full sun*

Hay-scented fern forms wide-ranging, dense mats of finely textured light green fronds that smell like fresh-mown hay when crushed. A moderately fast growing ground cover, it is particularly useful for shady slopes and rocky areas that need filling in but are difficult to manage.

Selected species and varieties: *D. punctilobula* (hay-scented fern, boulder fern)—curved, pyramidal, very lacy fronds up to 36 inches long and 3 to 6 inches wide, covered with gland-tipped whitish hairs from which the scent emerges, the foliage turning yellow to brown in fall.

Growing conditions and maintenance: Although hay-scented fern grows best in slightly acid, loamy soils, it tolerates a wide range of soil conditions and, once it is established, can withstand summer drought. Give the plants plenty of room, setting them 2 feet apart. It requires little care but enjoys a springtime application of bone meal to the soil surface at the rate of 1 ounce per square yard. It spreads by slender, underground rhizomes; divide by separating the rhizomatous mats in spring.

Dicentra
(dy-SEN-tra)
BLEEDING HEART

Dicentra spectabilis 'Pantaloons'

Hardiness: *Zones 2-9*

Plant type: *perennial*

Height: *4 inches to 3 feet*

Interest: *flowers, foliage*

Soil: *moist, well-drained, fertile*

Light: *partial to bright full shade*

Bleeding heart's puffy flowers, ferny foliage, and arching habit work well in a perennial bed or rock garden. Various species offer bloom from spring till fall.

Selected species and varieties: *D. cucullaria* (Dutchman's-breeches)—4- to 10-inch plants bear yellow-tipped white flowers in spring. *D. eximia* (fringed bleeding heart)—pink to purple heart-shaped flowers in spring and summer on 18-inch stems amid blue-green foliage; 'Adrian Bloom' has red flowers and blue-green leaves; 'Luxuriant' blooms off and on until frost with red flowers on 8- to 18-inch stems. *D. formosa* (western bleeding heart)—9 to 12 inches tall, rose-purple blooms; 'Alba' has white flowers late spring to summer; 'Sweetheart' has white flowers on 1-foot stems. *D. spectabilis* (Japanese bleeding heart)—2 to 3 feet tall, with pink-and-white flowers in spring; 'Pantaloons' has white flowers.

Growing conditions and maintenance: Bleeding hearts do not tolerate dry or wet soils and falter in hot, muggy climates. *D. spectabilis* does not do well in Forida and along the Gulf Coast. Work organic matter liberally into the soil.

Digitalis
(di-ji-TAL-us)
FOXGLOVE

Digitalis x mertonensis

Hardiness: *hardy or Zones 3-8*

Plant type: *perennial, biennial, or annual*

Height: *2 to 5 feet*

Interest: *flowers*

Soil: *moist, well-drained, fertile*

Light: *partial to bright full shade*

Erect spikes of usually drooping, bell-shaped flowers bloom above foxglove's fuzzy, coarse foliage, which grows in basal rosettes. Foxgloves are often used as a background or border plant. They also make good cut flowers. The leaves produce an ingredient that is used for a heart stimulant. *Caution:* All parts of the plant should be treated as poisonous.

Selected species and varieties: *D. ferruginea* (rusty foxglove)—5 feet high with dark green basal foliage and very slender, yellowish flower spikes with rust-colored markings in midsummer; hardy to Zone 7. *D. grandiflora* (yellow foxglove)—2 to 3 feet tall and hairy, bearing 2-inch-long yellow flowers with brown spots on 8- to 12-inch spikes in late spring to early summer; perennial. *D. lutea* (straw foxglove)—a perennial with white to pale lemon yellow flowers on 2- to 3-foot stems blooming sporadically from early summer to fall. *D. x mertonensis* (strawberry foxglove)—grows 3 to 4 feet tall, with very large coppery rose flowers in late spring to early summer above glossy leaves, performing as a long-lived perennial only when frequently divided; Zones

3-8. *D. purpurea* (common foxglove)—a biennial growing 2½ to 5 feet tall with summer flowers up to 3 inches long in 1- to 2-foot one-sided spikes; 'Alba' has ivory white flowers; Excelsior Hybrids grow 3 to 5 feet tall and offer shades of red, pink, white, and yellow flowers that are borne around the spike and held out at right angles to the stem, enabling markings to be easily seen; Shirley Hybrids are 3 to 5 feet tall and have flowers in a choice of colors on one side of the spike; Foxy Hybrids are biennials frequently grown as annuals, 2 to 3 feet tall,

Digitalis purpurea Excelsior Hybrids

with rosettes of long, narrow leaves at the base of the stem as well as a few others scattered farther up and flowers available in many colors borne in 1-foot spikes, each plant producing nine to 10 flower stalks.

Growing conditions and maintenance: Although foxgloves are tolerant of a wide variety of soil types, they cannot weather drought or boggy conditions. Amend the soil with leaf mold, peat moss, or compost, and space plants 12 to 18 inches apart. Feed lightly once a month during the growing season with an all-purpose fertilizer. If exposed to afternoon sun, mulch to conserve moisture. Cull dead flower stems to encourage rebloom. Foxgloves, including the biennial forms, self-seed when conditions are good. The perennials are usually short-lived.

Diphylleia
(dy-FIL-ee-a)
DIPHYLLEIA

Diphylleia cymosa

Dryopteris
(dry-OP-te-ris)
WOOD FERN

Dryopteris erythrosora

Enkianthus
(en-kee-AN-thus)
ENKIANTHUS

Enkianthus campanulatus

Hardiness: *Zones 6-8*

Plant type: *perennial*

Height: *to 3 feet*

Interest: *flowers, fruit, foliage*

Soil: *moist, well-drained, fertile*

Light: *deep to bright full shade*

Diphylleia is a decorative plant useful for naturalizing in drifts under trees and large shrubs. Mammoth rounded, cleft leaves form the background for the cymes of white flowers with yellow stamens that appear in late spring or early summer. A month later, small powdery blue berries arrive.

Selected species and varieties: *D. cymosa* (umbrella leaf)—2- to 3-foot-tall stalks, with foliage emerging copper colored before turning light green, consisting of only two leaves, each with a cleft dividing the leaf in half, each half with five to seven lobes, as well as flowers that appear over the foliage in flat-topped clusters and later berries.

Growing conditions and maintenance: Diphylleia is easily grown in settings that duplicate its native woodlands. Work leaf mold, peat moss, or compost into the soil before planting. Propagate by division in spring or by sowing seed at harvest.

Hardiness: *Zones 3-8*

Plant type: *perennial*

Height: *1½ to 3½ feet*

Interest: *foliage*

Soil: *moist to wet, well-drained, fertile*

Light: *deep to bright full shade*

Native to moist woodlands or swamps but adaptive to the home garden, wood ferns give textural accents to rock gardens, shelter early bulbs, and provide soft backgrounds in perennial beds.

Selected species and varieties: *D. cristata* (narrow swamp fern, crested wood fern, crested fern)—erect plant with sterile arching ferns 18 to 30 inches tall, bearing 3- to 6-inch-wide dark green brittle fronds whose pinnae bend at midstem if fertile and whose sori are large and rusty brown; evergreen in Zones 6-7, hardy to Zone 3. *D. dilatata* (broad wood fern, broad buckler fern)—deep green fronds 2 to 3½ feet long, erect to arching and deciduous. *D. erythrosora* (Japanese shield fern, copper shield fern, autumn fern)—arching evergreen fronds 30 inches long, 8 to 12 inches wide, coppery when new and turning deep glossy green as they mature; hardy to Zone 5.

Growing conditions and maintenance: *D. cristata* grows well in moist soil, and it flourishes close to streams and ponds. Once established in soil that has been well amended with organic matter, wood ferns need little care.

Hardiness: *Zones 4-7*

Plant type: *large shrub*

Height: *6 to 30 feet*

Interest: *flowers, foliage*

Soil: *moist, well-drained, acid, fertile*

Light: *bright full shade to full sun*

Enkianthus provides drooping clusters of bell-shaped flowers in spring and vivid autumn foliage. Growing slowly to various sizes, enkianthus is useful as a specimen or for shrub borders.

Selected species and varieties: *E. campanulatus* (redvein enkianthus)—usually 8 to 12 feet tall but perhaps to 30 feet in the South, with open, horizontal branching to 20 feet wide and cream-colored, yellow, or pale orange ½-inch red-veined flowers borne in 3-inch clusters, opening before the leaves appear and lasting until the oval 3-inch leaves are fully formed; 'Albiflorus' is more compact than the species, with creamy white flowers and red-orange fall color. *E. perulatus* (white enkianthus)—grows to more than 6 feet, with flowers similar to those of redvein.

Growing conditions and maintenance: Add liberal amounts of leaf mold or peat moss to the soil before planting, giving enkianthus the same soil that rhododendrons need. The best fall color develops if the plant receives some afternoon sun. Propagate from stem cuttings or by layering—securing part of a branch to the ground until it takes root.

Epimedium
(ep-i-MEE-dee-um)
BARRENWORT

Epimedium x youngianum 'Roseum'

Hardiness: *Zones 4-8*

Plant type: *perennial*

Height: *8 to 12 inches*

Interest: *flowers, foliage*

Soil: *moist, well-drained, fertile*

Light: *partial to bright full shade*

Epimedium produces sprays of spurred flowers and heart-shaped leaves. Leaves are red as they unfurl, light green in summer, bronzy red in fall. Its slow creeping habit makes it a good ground cover.

Selected species and varieties: *E. grandiflorum* (longspur epimedium)—1 foot tall with pink blooms; 'Rose Queen' has large deep pink flowers in late spring; 'White Queen', white flowers. *E. pinnatum* ssp. *colchicum* (Persian epimedium)—yellow flowers above evergreen leaves turning bronze in winter. *E.* x *rubrum* (red barrenwort)—broad clumps to 12 inches tall, bearing flowers with red sepals and yellow petals. *E.* x *versicolor* 'Sulphureum' (bicolored barrenwort)—spreading mounds to 12 inches tall with pale yellow flowers. *E.* x *youngianum* (Young's barrenwort)—low-growing species with usually white blooms; 'Niveum' has nearly double pure white flowers; 'Roseum' has mauve-pink flowers.

Growing conditions and maintenance: Add peat moss or leaf mold to the soil and plant 8 to 10 inches apart in spring or fall. Mulch well. Remove dead growth before new foliage appears in spring.

Eranthis
(e-RAN-thus)
WINTER ACONITE

Eranthis hyemalis

Hardiness: *Zones 3-7*

Plant type: *bulb*

Height: *2 to 4 inches*

Interest: *flowers, foliage*

Soil: *moist, well-drained*

Light: *dappled shade to full sun*

A member of the buttercup family, winter aconites produce a ground-hugging carpet of yellow flowers in late winter or early spring. Each bloom is surrounded by a rosette of dark straplike foliage that lasts until midsummer. A rapid spreader, winter aconite quickly fills in spaces in rock gardens, bulb beds, and shrub borders and looks best in mass plantings and naturalized areas.

Selected species and varieties: *E. hyemalis*—bright yellow, cup-shaped flowers, 1½ inches wide, with six petals.

Growing conditions and maintenance: Site winter aconites in a wind-protected spot where they will receive partial shade during winter and full shade in summer. Soak the tubers for several hours before planting 2 to 3 inches deep in soil amended with organic matter in late summer or early fall. Water during extended dry periods. Winter aconites are easily propagated by division; move whole clumps, rather than individual tubers, after they have finished flowering. Fertilization is not necessary.

Euonymus
(yew-ON-i-mus)
SPINDLE TREE

Euonymus fortunei 'Emerald Gaiety'

Hardiness: *Zones 4-9*

Plant type: *woody vine or shrub*

Height: *4 inches to 20 feet*

Interest: *foliage*

Soil: *well-drained*

Light: *full shade to full sun*

Depending on the cultivar, euonymus can cover the ground, climb a wall or trellis, or serve as a low hedge. The dark green oval leaves stay green all winter.

Selected species and varieties: *E. fortunei* (winter creeper)—a ground cover or shrub to 20 feet tall, with oval leaves and pinkish blooms; 'Coloratus' grows 4 to 6 inches tall as a ground cover, with 1- to 2-inch dark green leaves turning purple in winter; 'Emerald Gaiety' forms a shrub to 4 or 5 feet tall or will climb a support and has white-edged leaves turning pink in winter; 'Kewensis' is a miniature version forming a low mat 4 to 5 inches high, with very narrow ¼- to ⅜-inch-long leaves; 'Minimus' is a low-growing form; var. *radicans* either trails or climbs, bears leaves 1½ to 2 inches long, and produces reddish fruit in fall. *E. japonicus* 'Albomarginatus' (Japanese spindle tree)—a somewhat stiff shrub usually 5 to 10 feet high and half as wide, with dark green leaves thinly edged in white; Zones 7-9.

Growing conditions and maintenance: Euonymus is tolerant of all but heavy, wet soils and, in the case of *E. fortunei* varieties, can tolerate the deepest shade.

Euphorbia
(yew-FOR-bee-a)
SPURGE

Euphorbia amygdaloides var. robbiae

Hardiness: *Zones 7-10*

Plant type: *perennial*

Height: *12 to 20 inches*

Interest: *foliage, flowers*

Soil: *well-drained to dry, sandy*

Light: *bright full shade to full sun*

A member of a large and variable family of mostly low, bushy, succulent plants with distinctive habit, spurge can be used in masses or as accent plants. As with poinsettia, to which it is related, the showy parts of spurge are the colorful bracts, or petal-like leaves, that surround the small flowers. *Caution:* The milky sap is caustic and may be poisonous.

Selected species and varieties: *E. amygdaloides* var. *robbiae* (wood spurge)—spreads quickly by stolons to form wide patches, bearing yellowish green bracts in late spring on the previous year's growth and glossy, leathery, dark green leaves that are clustered in rosettes at the tips of nonflowering stems.

Growing conditions and maintenance: Plant spurge in an area where its evergreen foliage can be sheltered from winter winds. It is tolerant of drought and poor soil. Rich, moist soil encourages rampant growth in an already vigorous plant. Spurge self-propagates by root sprouts and self-seeding.

Fatsia
(FAT-see-a)
FATSIA

Fatsia japonica

Hardiness: *Zones 8-10*

Plant type: *evergreen shrub*

Height: *6 to 10 feet*

Interest: *foliage, flowers, fruit*

Soil: *moist, slightly acid, fertile*

Light: *medium to bright full shade*

Fatsia forms a broad, rounded shrub whose huge, finger-shaped dark green leaves lend a tropical effect to the shade garden. Panicles of white flowers appear in fall, followed by black berries. Interesting for its textural effects, fatsia makes a good backdrop for smaller shrubs. In the North, fatsia is used as a houseplant.

Selected species and varieties: *F. japonica* (Formosa rice tree, Japanese fatsia, glossy-leaved paper plant)—6 to 10 feet high with equal spread, bearing seven- to nine-lobed leaves 6 to 14 inches across and white flowers; inconsistently hardy to Zone 8. x *Fatshedera lizei*—the result of a cross between fatsia and English ivy, a semiclimbing shrub or vine with five-lobed leaves 4 to 10 inches across and pale green flowers; hardy to Zone 8.

Growing conditions and maintenance: Fatsia's leaves may become brown if exposed to full sun or winter winds. At the northern limits of hardiness, site in a courtyard or against a wall for increased protection. Although it tolerates a wide range of soils, fatsia grows best in soil high in organic matter. Allow it plenty of room, and prune to discourage legginess.

Fothergilla
(faw-ther-GIL-a)
FOTHERGILLA

Fothergilla major

Hardiness: *Zones 4-9*

Plant type: *deciduous shrub*

Height: *3 to 10 feet*

Interest: *foliage, flowers*

Soil: *moist, well-drained, sandy, acid*

Light: *partial shade to full sun*

Fothergilla works well massed, in borders, and in foundation plantings. Fragrant white bottle-brush flowers appear in spring. The blue-green leaves turn a brilliant yellow, orange, and scarlet in fall.

Selected species and varieties: *F. gardenii* (witch alder, dwarf fothergilla)—a dense mound 3 feet tall and 4 feet wide with zigzag spreading branches bearing 1-inch-long white spikes before the appearance of 1- to 2-inch-long wedge-shaped leaves that are dark green above and bluish white below; Zones 4-9; 'Blue Mist' has a feathery, mounded habit with glaucous, bluish leaves and subdued fall colors; 'Jane Platt', narrow leaves and longer flower clusters than in the species; 'Mount Airy', an upright habit, with profuse flowers and excellent fall color. *F. major* [also classified as *F. monticola*] (large fothergilla)—upright growth 6 to 10 feet high with 2- to 4-inch white flower spikes tinged with pink, appearing with the oval to roundish dark green leaves that show brilliant fall colors; Zones 4-8.

Growing conditions and maintenance: Fothergilla does not tolerate limy soils. Virtually pest free, it requires little care.

Galanthus
(ga-LAN-thus)
SNOWDROP

Galanthus nivalis

Hardiness: *Zones 3-8*

Plant type: *bulb*

Height: *6 to 12 inches*

Interest: *flowers*

Soil: *moist, well-drained, fertile*

Light: *partial to bright full shade*

Snowdrops brighten otherwise dreary late-winter or early-spring landscapes with their white flowers over arching, dark green straplike leaves. Tougher than they look, snowdrops are unperturbed by snowfall. They are lovely when planted in drifts and are also useful in rock gardens and edgings.

Selected species and varieties: *G. elwesii* (giant snowdrop)—bluish green leaves to 4 inches high and 1½ inches wide, and 2-inch flowers with white outer petals, the inner ones brushed with green, blooming in winter or early spring on 1-foot stems; hardy to Zone 4. *G. nivalis* (common snowdrop)—leaves are ¼ inch wide below 1-inch-wide flowers on 6-inch stems in early spring, blooming slightly earlier than the giant snowdrop; Zones 3-8; 'Flore Pleno' has very large double flowers.

Growing conditions and maintenance: While snowdrops will grow in almost any garden soil, they do best in loam. Work leaf mold or peat moss into the soil before planting. Propagate by dividing the clumps after they finish flowering.

Gaultheria
(gawl-THER-ee-a)
GAULTHERIA

Gaultheria shallon

Hardiness: *Zones 3-7*

Plant type: *ground cover or shrub*

Height: *3 inches to 4 feet*

Interest: *foliage, fruit, fragrance*

Soil: *moist, well-drained, acid*

Light: *dappled to bright full shade*

Gaultheria forms a lustrous evergreen carpet for shady areas. Small bell-shaped flowers appear in spring amid clustered leaves that release their scent when crushed. Mint-flavored bright red berries develop later and remain into spring.

Selected species and varieties: *G. procumbens* (wintergreen, checkerberry, teaberry, mountain tea)—spreading carpet 3 to 6 inches tall, with waxy flowers that are mostly hidden by the 1- to 2-inch leaves, prominent berries ¼ to ½ inch wide, and foliage that is red when new, green in summer, and bronze in the fall; Zones 3-7. *G. shallon* (salal, shallon)—variable habit, including ground cover to 2 feet tall or shrub to 4 feet tall in normal landscape conditions, but grows to 8 feet in the Pacific Northwest woods, bearing 5-inch clustered, conspicuous leaves that stay glossy green all year, urn-shaped flowers in late spring, and purple-black berries; hardy to Zone 5.

Growing conditions and maintenance: Gaultheria thrives in humus-rich soil; supplement the soil with leaf mold or peat moss before planting. Mulch to maintain moisture.

Gelsemium
(jel-SEE-mee-um)
CAROLINA JASMINE

Gelsemium sempervirens

Hardiness: *Zones 6-9*

Plant type: *vine or ground cover*

Height: *to 20 feet*

Interest: *flowers, fragrance*

Soil: *well-drained*

Light: *bright full shade to full sun*

The fragrant flowers of Carolina jasmine bloom in spring amid shiny green leaves that tend to be evergreen in the warmer zones. Although it can be allowed to scramble upon itself, forming a loose mounding shrub or ground cover, it is best used as a climbing vine for trellises, porches, and fences. *Caution:* All parts of the plant are poisonous.

Selected species and varieties: *G. sempervirens* (false jasmine, evening trumpet flower)—yellow flowers with a funnel-shaped corolla and five rounded lobes, clustered in the axils of leaves that are 2 to 4 inches long; 'Pride of Augusta' has double flowers that bloom more profusely and for a longer period than the species.

Growing conditions and maintenance: Carolina jasmine, which grows naturally in roadside meadows and open woodlands in the South, needs little special care. Although it prefers moist soils rich in organic matter, it adapts to other conditions. The foliage is denser and the flowers more abundant when the plant receives some direct sun. If the vine gets top-heavy, prune back severely.

Geranium
(jer-AY-nee-um)
CRANESBILL

Geranium x 'Johnson's Blue'

Hardiness:	*Zones 3-9*
Plant type:	*perennial*
Height:	*10 to 36 inches*
Interest:	*flowers*
Soil:	*dry to moist, well-drained*
Light:	*partial to bright full shade*

Geraniums provide summer color for lightly shaded borders and rock gardens. Its deeply lobed leaves are as attractive as its long-lasting five-petaled flowers.

Selected species and varieties: *G. endressii* 'Wargrave Pink' (Pyrenean cranesbill)—forms medium green mounds to 15 inches tall producing 1-inch-wide salmon pink funnel-shaped flowers with broad, deeply notched petals; hardy to Zone 4. *G. x* 'Johnson's Blue'—15- to 18-inch-high mats, with 1½- to 2-inch blue flowers traced with darker blue veins, blooming profusely from spring to summer; hardy to Zone 5. *G. macrorrhizum* 'Album' (bigroot geranium)—a ground cover 10 to 12 inches tall, producing clusters of bluish white flowers with red calyxes from late spring to summer and sweetly musky, maple-shaped leaves that turn bright red and yellow in fall; hardy to Zone 3; 'Bevan's Variety' has deep magenta petals and deep red sepals; 'Ingwersen's Variety' is 10 to 15 inches tall with soft rose pink flowers; 'Spessart' has light- to dark-pink-petaled flowers in summer. *G. maculatum* (wild geranium, wild cranesbill, spotted cranesbill, alum-root)—openly branched, grayish, weedy foliage 1 to 2 feet high with pale lilac flowers 1 inch wide in late spring or early summer and maplelike leaves; Zones 3-7; 'Album' has white flowers. *G. x oxonianum* 'Claridge Druce'—a hybrid of *G. endressii* and *G. versicolor* 1½ to 3 feet tall with equal spread, gray-green foliage, and late-spring-to-fall-blooming pink-petaled flowers that have dark pink

Geranium versicolor

veins and white bases; Zones 4-9. *G. phaeum* (black widow)—forms large clumps via thick rhizomes, with bright green five- to seven-lobed leaves, often spotted reddish purple, and flowers that are dark purple-black or brownish, though sometimes white or pink, and are borne on 18- to 24-inch stems in summer; hardy to Zone 5. *G. versicolor*—to 2 feet tall, with spreading stems bearing roundish five-lobed leaves and white flowers with magenta veins, the petals deeply notched at the apex where they are also broadest; hardy to Zone 6.

Growing conditions and maintenance: Geraniums can grow in full sun to partial shade in cool areas but need afternoon shade in areas where the summers are hot. 'Johnson's Blue' and 'Claridge Druce' tolerate full sun. Provide all geraniums with protection from wind. *G. maculatum* prefers moist, rich soil, but *G. macrorrhizum*, *G. endressii*, and *G. versicolor* can tolerate dry shade and relatively infertile soil. Once established, geraniums develop long-lived colonies that require little care. Plants usually need to be divided every 4 to 5 years.

Hakonechloa
(hah-kon-eh-KLO-a)
HAKONECHLOA

Hakonechloa macra 'Aureola'

Hardiness:	*Zones 5-9*
Plant type:	*ornamental grass*
Height:	*12 to 18 inches*
Interest:	*foliage*
Soil:	*moist, well-drained, fertile*
Light:	*partial to bright full shade*

A slow-spreading deciduous ground cover, hakonechloa can also be used as an accent alone, in masses along walkways, or in borders and rock gardens. Breezes rustling through the foliage produce soft textural effects. Hakonechloa also makes a good container plant.

Selected species and varieties: *H. macra* 'Aureola' (golden variegated hakonechloa)—a 12- to 18-inch-high rhizomatous clump with arching habit, consisting of bamboolike stems that display 8-inch-long, tapering, cream-colored, bronzy-green-edged leaves that usually spill over in the same direction and become buff colored in fall, as well as inconspicuous open panicles of yellowish green flowers that appear in late summer or early fall.

Growing conditions and maintenance: Hakonechloa needs shelter from hot afternoon sun. Amend the soil liberally with organic matter such as compost, leaf mold, or peat moss before planting, and space plants 12 to 15 inches apart.

Halesia
(ba-LEE-zhi-a)
SILVER BELL

Halesia monticola

Hardiness: *Zones 4-8*

Plant type: *deciduous tree*

Height: *25 to 80 feet*

Interest: *flowers, bark, fruit*

Soil: *moist, well-drained, acid, fertile*

Light: *bright full shade to full sun*

Silver bell's dangling clusters of white bell-shaped flowers in spring appear before or with the dark yellow-green leaves, which hold their color until they turn yellow early in the fall. Green to brown four-winged fruits remain after the leaves have fallen. The furrowed and plated bark is gray, brown, and black. Silver bell serves well as an understory tree but can also be used to create shade for other plants.

Selected species and varieties: *H. monticola* (mountain silver bell)—60 to 80 feet tall with a usually conical habit displaying 1-inch-long flowers in two- to five-flowered clusters as the 3- to 6½-inch-long leaves begin to develop; 'Rosea' has pale rose-colored flowers. *H. tetraptera* [also classified as *H. carolina*] (Carolina silver bell, opossumwood)—a smaller, low-branched version of mountain silver bell 25 to 40 feet tall with a rounded crown 20 to 35 feet wide consisting of ascending branches with 2- to 4-inch leaves, flowers ½ to ¾ inch long, and fruits 1½ inches long.

Growing conditions and maintenance: Silver bells do best in soil supplemented with organic matter. They are pest resistant and require little maintenance.

Hamamelis
(ba-ma-MEL-lis)
WITCH HAZEL

Hamamelis japonica 'Zuccariniana'

Hardiness: *Zones 3-8*

Plant type: *large shrub or small tree*

Height: *6 to 20 feet*

Interest: *flowers, foliage, fragrance*

Soil: *well-drained to moist*

Light: *bright full shade to full sun*

Witch hazels brighten the fall and winter landscape with heavily fragrant yellow to red flowers on angular branches, sometimes appearing long after their colorful fall foliage has fallen. The two-valved, dry fruit capsules explode, propelling the black seeds many feet away.

Selected species and varieties: *H.* x *intermedia* 'Arnold Promise'—to 20 feet tall and wide with 1½-inch primrose yellow flowers in winter to early spring and gray-green foliage that becomes yellow, orange, or red in fall; 'Diane' grows 14 to 20 feet tall, bearing slightly fragrant orange-red flowers with purple-red calyxes and yellow-orange to red autumn foliage; 'Jelena' [sometimes called 'Copper Beauty'] has copper-colored flowers and orange-red fall foliage; 'Primavera', very fragrant prolific clear yellow flowers borne later than the species; 'Ruby Glow', coppery red to reddish brown flowers and orange-red fall foliage; all *H.* x *intermedia* are hardy to Zone 5. *H. japonica* 'Sulphurea' (Japanense witch hazel)—10 to 15 feet high and wide with open, flat-topped habit, producing yellow flowers with red calyx cups in late

winter and lustrous green leaves that turn yellow, red, and purplish in fall; hardy to Zone 5; 'Zuccariniana' has rich yellow flowers with a hint of green inside the calyx; hardy to Zone 5. *H. mollis* 'Goldcrest' (Chinese witch hazel)—an oval, broadly open large shrub or small tree 10 to 15 feet tall and wide with medium green leaves in summer that turn a vivid yellow to yellow-orange in fall and fragrant yellow flowers with red-brown calyx cups blooming for a long period in winter; reliably hardy to Zone 6; 'Pallida'

Hamamelis mollis

has a spreading habit and lustrous leaves, with yellow flowers suffused with a blush of chartreuse in late winter; hardy to Zone 5. *H. vernalis* (American witch hazel)—multistemmed, broad rounded outline 6 to 10 feet tall with a greater spread and very fragrant yellow to red flowers from late winter to early spring and medium to dark green foliage in summer turning golden yellow in fall; hardy to Zone 4; 'Carnea' has richly colored flowers with a red calyx and petals that are red at the base blending to orange at the tip. *H. virginiana* (common witch hazel)—large shrub to small tree 20 feet tall and equally wide with angular spreading branches and fragrant yellow flowers that emerge in mid- to late fall, sometimes just as its 4- to 6-inch leaves have turned yellow; hardy to Zone 3.

Growing conditions and maintenance: Common and American witch hazel can tolerate heavy, poorly drained clay. Give Chinese and Japanese witch hazels well-drained acid soil to which organic matter has been added. Prune *H.* x *intermedia* to encourage dense branching.

Hedera
(HED-er-a)
IVY

Hedera helix

Hardiness: *Zones 5-10*

Plant type: *evergreen woody vine*

Height: *6 inches to 100 feet*

Interest: *foliage*

Soil: *moist, well-drained*

Light: *full shade to full sun*

Ivies are perfect for carpeting shady banks and borders and, with their aerial roots, for climbing fences and posts. After climbing ceases at maturity, they produce yellowish green flowers 1½ to 2½ inches wide and poisonous black berries.

Selected species and varieties: *H. canariensis* (Algerian ivy, Canary ivy, Madeira ivy)—three- to seven-lobed dark green leathery leaves on dark red petioles; Zones 9-10; 'Variegata' has showy yellow or pale green streaks. *H. colchica* 'Dentata' (colchis ivy, fragrant ivy, Persian ivy)—a fast climber with slightly toothed leaves from 5 to 10 inches wide; hardy to Zone 6; 'Dentata-variegata' has creamy yellow margins. *H. helix* 'Cavendishii' (English ivy)—three- to five-lobed leaves 2 to 4 inches wide with creamy white margins; 'Gold Heart' has triangular leaves with a gold center; 'Needlepoint' is a very dense slow grower with dark green leaves ¼ to 1 inch wide.

Growing conditions and maintenance: Though ivy tolerates a wide variety of soil types, it benefits from a good start: Enrich the soil with organic matter and keep the plants moist until they are established.

Helleborus
(hell-e-BOR-us)
HELLEBORE

Helleborus niger

Hardiness: *Zones 4-9*

Plant type: *perennial*

Height: *1 to 2 feet*

Interest: *flowers, foliage*

Soil: *moist, well-drained, fertile*

Light: *bright full shade*

The cuplike flowers of hellebores offer such subtle variation in rich coloration that every plant carries a distinctive look. Most species are long-lived, consistent bloomers for borders and perennial beds. Depending on the species, they are stemmed or stemless plants with deeply lobed leaves that may remain evergreen if given winter protection. *Caution:* All parts of the plant are poisonous.

Selected species and varieties: *H. argutifolius* [also listed as *H. corsicus* and *H. lividus* ssp. *corsicus*] (Corsican hellebore)—shrubby growth 1 to 2 feet tall without rhizomes, with glossy, heavily toothed leaves having ivory veins and, sometimes, red margins and producing clusters of yellowish green cups in spring; Zones 6-8. *H. atrorubens*—produces dark red, brownish, or plum-colored flowers on 1½ foot stems in winter or early spring followed by deciduous leaves; hardy to Zone 6. *H. foetidus* (stinking hellebore)—2 feet tall and bearing small green bells edged with maroon over lobed, glossy black-green leaves that form rosettes around the flowers; some hybrids are well scented; hardy to Zone 6.

H. lividus—12 to 18 inches tall, similar to Corsican hellebore, but the 2-inch-wide greenish yellow cups are brushed with pink and gray and borne in clusters of 15 to 20 in spring over deeply toothed, purple-toned leaves; hardy to Zone 8. *H. niger* (Christmas rose)—highly variable in size and bloom time and color, but generally 12 to 15 inches tall, each

Helleborus orientalis

stalk bearing a seminodding, white or pinkish green flower almost 3 inches across in late fall to early spring; Zones 5-8; ssp. *macranthus* has unusually large flowers in winter and pale blue-green foliage; hardy to Zone 5. *H. orientalis* (Lenten rose)—bears cream, pale to deep pink, plum, brownish purple, chocolate brown, or nearly black flowers 2 inches wide in early to midspring on 18-inch plants; Zones 4-9.

Growing conditions and maintenance: Hellebores are adaptable to most garden soils, but they do best when leaf mold or peat moss has been added to the soil. Although near neutral or alkaline soils are considered ideal, many hellebores seem to do just as well under acid conditions. Space smaller species 1 foot apart, larger ones up to 2 feet apart. Hellebores form clumps and self-seed under suitable conditions. Most species develop rhizomes; the exception is Corsican hellebore, which cannot be cut back because of its unusual habit. Christmas rose appears to thrive and flower best when it receives ample water from spring to midsummer followed by a dry period in late summer. Stinking hellebores are especially tolerant of dry shade. Hellebore roots are brittle; take special care when dividing, which is best done in early summer.

Hemerocallis
(hem-er-o-KAL-is)
DAYLILY

Hemerocallis 'Cherry Cheeks'

Hardiness: *Zones 3-9*

Plant type: *perennial*

Height: *14 inches to 4 feet*

Interest: *flowers*

Soil: *well-drained*

Light: *bright full shade to full sun*

The trumpet-shaped flowers of daylilies are borne on tall stalks over thick clumps of arching, grasslike foliage. An assortment of hybrids can provide bloom from spring until frost. Pale colors, which tend to bleach in the sun, are especially good choices for the shade garden. Excellent for naturalizing, daylilies can be used as specimens and are magnificent in mass plantings. They are also useful beside streams and ponds and on steep banks. Planted in groups, they form a dense ground cover that chokes out most weeds. Some varieties have evergreen foliage where winters are mild.

Selected species and varieties: *H. citrina* (citron daylily)—fragrant light yellow blooms up to 6 inches long that hold through the night. *H. fulva* (orange daylily, tawny daylily, fulvous daylily)—a 4-foot clump bearing six to 12 flower trumpets per scape on vigorous plants in midsummer; 'Europa' is an extremely vigorous clone; 'Kwanzo' yields double flowers that bloom later than the species over occasionally white-striped foliage. *H. lilio-asphodelus* [also classified as *H. flava*] (lemon daylily, yellow daylily,

lemon lily)—4-inch-long lemon yellow blooms on somewhat weak and arching 2- to 3-foot scapes in late spring or early summer. *H.* hybrids—'Catherine Woodbury', to 30 inches tall, producing pale-pink-and-cream flowers with a flush of lavender in mid- to late summer; 'Cherry Cheeks', vivid raspberry pink flowers on 28-inch stems; 'Cornwall', large orange flowers; 'Ed Murray', 28-inch stems bearing deep black-red flowers 4½ inches across; 'Eenie Weenie', a long-flowering dwarf to 14 inches in yellow; 'Hyperion', fragrant medium-sized yellow flowers on 4-foot scapes; 'Oriental Ruby', large wine red flowers; 'Peach Fairy', 26 inches tall

Hemerocallis 'Ruffled Apricot'

with 2½-inch pink-melon blooms; 'Ruffled Apricot', 32 inches tall with large ruffled apricot-colored flowers; 'Stella de Oro', slightly ruffled, golden yellow bell-like flowers 2½ inches long on 18-inch scapes from early to late summer.

Growing conditions and maintenance: Daylilies need afternoon shade where summers are hot. Work organic matter such as peat moss or compost into the soil before planting to improve drainage, and add a handful of bone meal. Set the crown—where roots and stem meet—an inch below the soil surface. Mulch to conserve moisture and for winter protection. Apply an all-purpose feed such as 5-10-5 sparingly in spring; too much fertilizer will reduce flowering. Disease resistant and rugged, daylilies provide stunning results with minimal care. Increase by dividing the clumps in late summer or early spring.

Heuchera
(HEW-ker-a)
ALUMROOT

Heuchera micrantha 'Palace Purple'

Hardiness: *Zones 4-9*

Plant type: *perennial*

Height: *15 to 30 inches*

Interest: *flowers, foliage*

Soil: *moist, well-drained, fertile*

Light: *partial shade to full sun*

Its flowers and handsome lobed leaves make alumroot well suited for edgings, rock gardens, and perennial beds.

Selected species and varieties: *H. americana* (rock geranium)—to 3 feet tall, with mottled leaves turning solid green and with greenish white flowers; 'Pewter Veil' has 6-inch-wide silvery purple leaves with gray veins forming a 20-inch-high mound with purplish flowers; 'Ruby Veil' has leaves similar to 'Pewter Veil' but with red veins. *H.* 'Chocolate Ruffles'—20 inches high and wide, with white flowers on purple spikes and ruffled leaves 9 inches wide that are brown above, burgundy below. *H. micrantha* (small-flowered alumroot)—to 2 feet tall with panicles of whitish blooms; 'Palace Purple', 15 to 18 inches tall with creamy white flowers on 18-inch stems in midsummer above a mound of crinkled bronze-purple leaves with red-purple undersides; 'Ruffles' forms a 30-inch-wide mound of ruffled green leaves with white flowers.

Growing conditions and maintenance: Add peat moss, leaf mold, or compost to soil and avoid crowding plants. Divide in spring after flowering or in the fall.

Hosta
(HOS-ta)
PLANTAIN LILY

![Hosta 'Krossa Regal']

Hosta 'Krossa Regal'

Hardiness:	*Zones 3-9*
Plant type:	*perennial*
Height:	*5 inches to 3 feet*
Interest:	*foliage, flowers, fragrance*
Soil:	*moist, well-drained*
Light:	*partial to bright full shade*

Hostas are valued chiefly for their foliage—mounds of oval or heart-shaped green, blue, and gold leaves in a variety of sizes. They are useful as edging or border plants, as ground covers, and in mass plantings. The variegated and light green forms make beautiful accent plants and brighten shady corners.

Selected species and varieties: *H. decorata* (blunt plantain lily)—1 to 2 feet tall, with white-edged leaves 3 to 8 inches long and dark blue flowers. *H. fortunei* (Fortune's hosta, giant plantain lily)—to 2 feet tall, with 5-inch-long oval leaves and pale lilac to violet flowers; 'Albo-marginata' forms a 15- to 24-inch-high clump with white margins on 5-inch leaves. *H. lancifolia* (narrow-leaved plantain lily)—a 2-foot-high cascading mound of 4- to 6-inch-long leaf blades and 1- to 1½-inch blue-purple flowers in late summer; hardy to Zone 3. *H. plantaginea* (fragrant plantain lily)—fragrant pure white flowers 2½ inches wide open in late summer on 2½-foot stems above bright green heart-shaped foliage; Zones 3-8. *H. sieboldiana* (Siebold plantain lily)—2½ to 3 feet tall with 10- to 15-inch-long glaucous,

gray to blue-green puckered leaves and lavender flowers that bloom amid the leaves in midsummer; hardy to Zone 3; 'Big Mama' has blue puckered leaves and pale lavender flowers; 'Blue Umbrellas' grows 3 feet tall and 5 feet wide, with blue to blue-green leaves; 'Frances Williams', 32 inches tall and 40 inches wide with round, puckered, blue-green leaves having wide, irregular gold margins; var. *elegans* [also classified as *H. s.* 'Elegans'], 36 inches tall with lavender-white flowers that barely clear the large, dark blue puckered leaves. *H. tardiflora* (autumn plantain lily)—glossy dark green medium-sized leaves and large purple flowers on 1-foot scapes in fall. *H. tokudama*—

![Hosta 'Golden Tiara']

Hosta 'Golden Tiara'

18 inches tall and 40 inches wide, with cupped, puckered bluish leaves and white flowers in midsummer; 'Flavo-circinalis' grows to 18 inches tall and 50 inches wide with round, heavily puckered blue-green leaves that have irregular cream-and-yellow margins and white flowers in early summer. *H. undulata* var. *univittata* [also classified as *H. u.* 'Univittata'] (wavy-leaf shade lily, snow feather funkia)—2 to 3 feet tall and 3 feet wide, with broad white centers in medium green leaves and lavender flowers. *H. venusta* (dwarf plantain lily, pretty plantain lily)—5 inches tall and 8 inches wide with medium green leaves and light purple flowers. *H. hybrids*—'August Moon', to 12 inches tall, with small yellow puckered leaves and midsummer white flowers; 'Fringe Benefit', 36 inches tall and 42 inches wide, with broad cream-colored margins on green heart-shaped leaves and pale lavender flowers in early summer; 'Ginko Craig', an excellent ground

cover, 10 inches tall with narrow, white-edged, dark green lance-shaped leaves and lavender flowers in midsummer; hardy to Zone 4; 'Golden Tiara', a low, compact mound 6 inches high and 16 to

![Hosta sieboldiana 'Frances Williams']

Hosta sieboldiana 'Frances Williams'

20 inches wide bearing yellow-edged medium green heart-shaped leaves and purple flowers on 15-inch scapes in midsummer; 'Gold Standard', 15 inches tall with dark green margins on greenish gold leaves and lavender flowers on 3-foot scapes in mid- to late summer; 'Halcyon', 12 inches tall and 16 inches wide, with grayish blue heart-shaped leaves having wavy margins and distinct parallel veins and lilac-blue flowers blooming in late summer; 'Honeybells', fragrant lavender flowers and light green leaves to 2 feet tall; 'Krossa Regal', to 3 feet tall, with silvery blue leaves and 2- to 3-inch-long lavender flowers in late summer on 5-foot scapes; hardy to Zone 4; 'Royal Standard', full-sun-tolerant plant with fragrant white flowers on 30-inch stems in late summer to early fall; 'Shade Fanfare', lavender blooms on 2-foot scapes in midsummer above leaves with broad cream-colored margins.

Growing conditions and maintenance: Amend soil with leaf mold or compost. Consider the hostas' eventual spread before planting and set them far enough apart to allow for air circulation and avoid overcrowding. Water during dry spells. Remove flowers to promote leaf growth. The blue forms need bright shade in order to hold color. *H. plantaginea* is tender until established; in the northern part of its range, mulch or cover during the first winter. Once established, hostas are long-lasting and need little attention.

Hyacinthoides
(hy-a-sin-THOY-deez)
BLUEBELL

Hyacinthoides hispanica

Hardiness:	*Zones 5-10*
Plant type:	*bulb*
Height:	*to 20 inches*
Interest:	*flowers*
Soil:	*moist, well-drained, fertile*
Light:	*bright full shade to full sun*

Dainty bell-shaped flowers with splayed petals nod from stems above clumps of straplike foliage in spring. Excellent for naturalizing beneath trees, in mass plantings, and in borders with other bulbs, bluebells also make good container plants and are useful as cut flowers.

Selected species and varieties: *H. hispanica* [also classified as *Scilla campanulata* or *Endymion hispanicus*] (Spanish bluebell)—each 20-inch stem produces up to 15 flowers ranging from white to pink to violet above leaf straps that are 1 inch wide; hardy to Zone 5; 'Rose Queen' produces rose-colored flowers; 'White Triumphator', white flowers.

Growing conditions and maintenance: Bluebells can be naturalized as far as Zone 5. In colder areas, mulch in winter, or dig the bulbs and replant in spring. Bluebells are vigorous growers and successfully compete with tree roots. Amend soil with organic matter and plant 3 to 4 inches deep in the fall. Water regularly during dry periods, except in summer. Bluebells spread quickly by self-seeding and can often become weedy. Propagate by division.

Hydrangea
(hy-DRANE-jee-a)
HYDRANGEA

Hydrangea macrophylla 'Blue Wave'

Hardiness:	*Zones 3-9*
Plant type:	*deciduous shrub or vine*
Height:	*3 to 60 feet*
Interest:	*flowers, foliage, bark*
Soil:	*moist, well-drained, fertile*
Light:	*bright full shade to full sun*

The large and showy summer flowers on hydrangea's rotund shape work well in shrub borders and as specimens. The flower clusters consist of small, starlike fertile flowers in the center surrounded by larger sterile (or ray) flowers 1 to 1½ inches wide. Many forms offer attractive fall foliage. Exfoliating reddish brown bark provides winter interest.

Selected species and varieties: *H. anomala* var. *petiolaris* (climbing hydrangea)—climbs without support to 60 feet or more with fragrant white flowers 6 to 12 inches wide and attractive exfoliating bark; Zones 4-7. *H. arborescens* 'Annabelle' (wild hydrangea, sevenbark, smooth hydrangea)—3 to 5 feet tall and nearly as wide, with white flowers 10 to 12 inches across in summer and bright green finely toothed leaves 3 to 6 inches long with downy undersides; 'Grandiflora' (hills-of-snow) grows to 3 feet with blooms consisting almost entirely of large sterile white flowers that change to pink and tan. *H. macrophylla* (French hydrangea, bigleaf hydrangea)—3 to 6 feet tall with equal or greater spread and leaves to 8 inches long; Lacecap cultivars

produce globular flower heads 5 to 10 inches across, blooming pink in slightly acid to alkaline soils and blue in strongly acid soils; Zones 6-9. Selected Lacecaps: 'Bluebird' produces blue flowers and is commonly found on the Pacific Coast; 'Blue Billow', blue flowers in midsummer; 'Blue Wave', pink to rich blue blooms and bold foliage; 'Lanarth White' grows 3 feet high and wide with blue or pink fertile flowers and white ray florets in midsummer; 'Lilacina' has normally mauve ray florets that emerge deep blue in very acidic soils; 'Mariesii' usually bears pink flowers and sometimes variegated

Hydrangea quercifolia

green-and-silver foliage. *H. quercifolia* 'Snowflake' (oakleaf hydrangea)—6 feet tall and wide, with 12- to 15-inch-long panicles that have a double-flowered effect, changing from white to tan or pink in late summer, and very large oak-shaped leaves that turn reddish purple in fall; hardy to Zone 5; 'Snow Queen' grows 5 to 6 feet high and wide with large, upright flower clusters whose sterile florets are larger and more plentiful than the species and change to pink as they age; hardy to Zone 5.

Growing conditions and maintenance: In southern zones, plant hydrangeas where the hot afternoon sun will not wilt the foliage. Lacecaps do best out of full sun in any climate. Hydrangeas take well to pruning; cut back hills-of-snow hydrangea in early spring to encourage new growth, and prune oak-leaved forms after flowering, removing weak branches. Hydrangeas are intolerant of drought, even in winter. Propagate by soft cuttings taken in late spring.

Hypericum
(hy-PER-i-kum)
ST.-JOHN'S-WORT

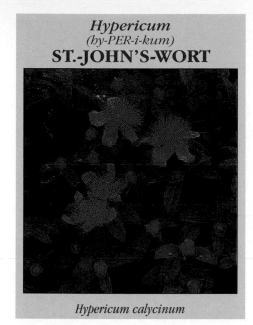

Hypericum calycinum

Hardiness: *Zones 3-9*

Plant type: *shrub or ground cover*

Height: *1 to 4 feet*

Interest: *flowers, fruit*

Soil: *poor, well-drained to dry*

Light: *bright full shade to full sun*

St.-John's-wort has bright yellow flowers over a long period in summer. Dry three-winged fruit capsules persist all winter.

Selected species and varieties: *H. calycinum* (creeping St.-John's-wort)—12 to 18 inches high, spreading by stolons to 2 feet wide, with very bright yellow, 3-inch-wide flowers all summer and semi-evergreen dark green leaves; Zones 5-8. *H. frondosum* (golden St.-John's-wort)—shrubby habit, 3 to 4 feet tall and wide, with reddish brown exfoliating bark, bluish green leaves 1 to 2 inches long and 1- to 2-inch-wide flowers from early to midsummer; Zones 5-8. *H.* 'Hidcote'—3 feet high and wide, blooming with 2½- to 3-inch-wide flowers in late spring to midsummer over dark green leaves; Zones 6-9. *H. prolificum* (shrubby St.-John's-wort, broombrush)—1 to 4 feet high and wide, with light brown exfoliating bark, dark to bluish green, narrow, oblong leaves up to 3 inches long and ¾- to 1-inch-wide flowers in summer; Zones 3-8.

Growing conditions and maintenance: A good plant for gravelly, limy soils; may be short-lived in poorly drained soils and high humidity. Prune in early spring.

Ilex
(EYE-lex)
HOLLY

Ilex 'Sparkleberry'

Hardiness: *Zones 3-9*

Plant type: *shrub or tree*

Height: *4 to 50 feet*

Interest: *foliage, fruit*

Soil: *moist, well-drained, moderately acid to neutral*

Light: *bright full shade to full sun*

Evergreen hollies have lustrous broad-leaved foliage and often showy berries; deciduous hollies are attractive in winter, when they produce red fruits. Female hollies of both types produce red, black, and sometimes yellow berries if a male is nearby. The smaller hollies are useful for edgings and rock gardens, the medium-sized varieties for foundation plantings and shrub borders, and the largest ones for screens and specimen trees.

Selected species and varieties: *I.* 'Apollo'—10 to 12 feet high and as wide, with reddish foliage aging to dark green. *I. crenata* (Japanese holly)—dense, rounded habit resembling boxwood with dark green, spineless leaves ½ to 1 inch long and black berries that are usually hidden under the leaves; Zones 5-8; 'Compacta' grows 5 to 6 feet tall and globular with leaves ¾ inch long; 'Convexa' is vase-shaped and dense, to 9 feet tall and broader than its height, with ½-inch leaves, one of the hardiest of the species; 'Dwarf Pagoda' has tiny leaves ¼ inch wide and up to ½ inch long; 'Helleri' is a dwarf mound growing very slowly to 4 feet tall by 5 feet wide, with small, fine-toothed leaves; 'Hetzii' grows 6 to 8 feet tall and round, with ½- to 1-inch leaves. *I. glabra* (inkberry, winterberry)—a multi-stemmed species 6 to 8 feet tall by 8 to 10 feet wide, becoming loose and open with age, with ¾- to 2-inch-long spineless leaves and black fruit; 'Compacta' grows 4 to 6 feet high with denser branching than the species; Zones 4-9. *I. opaca* (American holly)—15 to 30 feet high, conical when young but later spreading, with dark green, spiny evergreen leaves 1½ to 4 inches long and showy red or yellow fruit; 'Amy' has large lustrous leaves

Ilex crenata 'Compacta'

and large red berries; 'Cardinal', small, light red berries and small, dark green leaves; 'Goldie', yellow berries and non-glossy leaves; 'Old Heavy Berry', heavy yields of large red berries against large, dark green leaves; 'Jersey Knight' (male) has a dense upright habit and dark green leaves; Zones 5-9. *I. pedunculosa* (long-stalked holly)—large shrub or small tree 15 to 25 feet high, with wavy, shiny, smooth-margined leaves and berries on long stalks; Zones 5-7. *I.* 'Sparkleberry'—small red berries and nearly black bark. *I. verticillata* 'Winter Red' (winterberry, black alder)—a deciduous plant 6 to 10 feet tall and wide with 1½ to 3-inch spine-less leaves and a profusion of red fruit on bare branches in early winter; Zones 3-9.

Growing conditions and maintenance: Evergreen hollies suffer when exposed to harsh sun, severe winter winds, and drought, and some hollies languish in heat and humidity. If soil is either heavy or sandy, amend soil with organic matter such as leaf mold or peat moss. Water young hollies regularly.

Illicium
(ill-ISS-ee-um)
ANISE TREE

Illicium anisatum

Hardiness: *Zones 7-9*

Plant type: *evergreen shrub or tree*

Height: *6 to 25 feet*

Interest: *fragrance, flowers, fruit*

Soil: *moist, well-drained, fertile*

Light: *full shade to full sun*

The spicy aroma of the anise tree comes not from its flowers but from its broad, evergreen leaves. Small, star-shaped fruit clusters are decorative. *Note:* The species listed here may be poisonous.

Selected species and varieties: *I. anisatum* (star anise)—broad pyramidal shrub or small tree 8 to 25 feet high with fragrant, yellow-green to white flowers emerging in early spring; Zones 7-9. *I. floridanum* (Florida anise tree, purple anise)—multistemmed shrub 6 to 10 feet high, with dark green leaves 2 to 6 inches long and smelly but showy dark red flowers to 2 inches wide in spring. *I. parviflorum* (small anise tree)—8 to 20 feet tall, bearing 2- to 4-inch olive green leaves that emit some of the best anise odor of the genus. The yellow-green flowers appearing in late spring carry no odor.

Growing conditions and maintenance: Of these species, only *I. parviflorum* is adaptable to dry soil; it will succeed in very moist soil as well. Add peat moss or compost to the soil; maintain moisture. *I. anisatum* needs partial shade; *I. parviflorum,* partial shade to full sun; *I. floridanum* tolerates deep shade to full sun.

Impatiens
(im-PAY-shens)
BALSAM, JEWELWEED

Impatiens wallerana

Hardiness: *tender*

Plant type: *annual*

Height: *6 to 36 inches*

Interest: *flowers*

Soil: *moist, well-drained, fertile*

Light: *partial to bright full shade*

Easy-to-grow impatiens furnishes shady borders, edgings, or planters with a bevy of colors from spring until frost.

Selected species and varieties: *I. balsamina* (garden balsam)—10- to 36-inch mound, with usually double flowers in pink, salmon, red, purple, lavender, yellow, or white, borne along the stems or on top of the foliage, some very double; Camellia-Flowered Mixed 'Tom Thumb' has ruffled flowers at the top of 10- to 12-inch-high foliage. *I. wallerana* (busy Lizzy)—6- to 18-inch mounds with flat, five-petaled flowers 1 to 2 inches wide in salmon, orange, pink, white, red, rose, and violet, or bicolored with white borne directly over the foliage; Accent series grows 6 to 8 inches high with early-blooming single flowers; Dazzler series, 8-inch-high mounds with single flowers; Rosette mixture, 18 to 20 inches tall with single, semidouble, and double flowers.

Growing conditions and maintenance: Both species prefer loose, rich soil. Space according to eventual size and mulch to keep soil cool and moist; *I. wallerana* will grow taller with more water and fertilizer. Plants wilt in hot afternoon sun.

Jasminum
(JAZ-mi-num)
JASMINE, JESSAMINE

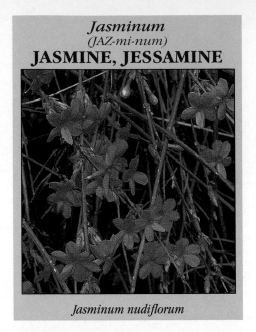

Jasminum nudiflorum

Hardiness: *Zones 6-10*

Plant type: *vine or shrub*

Height: *shrub to 15 feet, vine to 40 feet*

Interest: *form, stems, flowers*

Soil: *well-drained*

Light: *partial shade to full sun*

Jasmine forms a spreading mound of stiff, arching branches that remain green even in winter, sporadically producing yellow or white flowers. A good plant for slopes or for walls, jasmine can also be trained to climb a trellis or wall.

Selected species and varieties: *J. mesnyi* (Japanese jasmine)—spreading mound 5 to 6 feet high and greater in width with compound leaves of three leaflets and bright yellow tubular flowers that bloom periodically in early spring to midsummer; Zones 8-9. *J. nudiflorum* (winter jasmine)—3 to 4 feet high (to 15 feet on a trellis) and 4 to 7 feet wide with yellow flowers opening in winter; Zones 6-10. *J. officinale* 'Grandiflorum' (common white jasmine)—a deciduous or semi-evergreen shrub (10 to 15 feet tall) or climber (30 to 40 feet) with clusters of fragrant white star-shaped flowers blooming from summer to fall; Zones 8-10; reliably hardy to Zone 9 in the Southeast.

Growing conditions and maintenance: Jasmine grows well in poor soils and tolerates some drought. Flowers are produced on wood of the previous season; prune soon after flowering.

Kalmia
(KAL-mee-a)
AMERICAN LAUREL

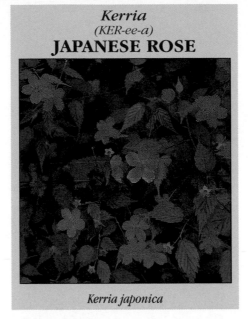

Kalmia latifolia 'Ostbo Red'

Hardiness: *Zones 4-9*

Plant type: *evergreen shrub*

Height: *2 to 15 feet*

Interest: *flowers, foliage*

Soil: *moist, well-drained, acid, fertile*

Light: *deep full shade to full sun*

With its lustrous foliage and sometimes star-shaped flowers, kalmia is an exquisite plant for shady areas.

Selected species and varieties: *K. latifolia* (mountain laurel)—round habit growing 5 to 15 feet high and wide, with 2- to 5-inch-long oval leaves, flowers in clusters 4 to 6 inches wide in late spring to early summer; 'Bullseye' has deep purplish buds that open to creamy white flowers with a purple band; 'Ostbo Red', bright red buds that open to deep pink flowers; 'Raspberry Glow', wine red buds opening to raspberry pink blooms; 'Richard Jaynes', red buds opening to pink blooms that are silvery white inside; 'Silver Dollar', pink buds and large white flowers; 'Tiddlywinks', a slow-growing dwarf 2 to 5 feet high with pink buds and lighter pink flowers.

Growing conditions and maintenance: Although kalmia adapts to deep shade, it flowers best in brighter light. In Zones 7-9, protect plants from hot afternoon sun. They do best in loose loam; add organic matter liberally to the soil when planting, and mulch to keep cool and preserve moisture. Remove flowers after they fade.

Kerria
(KER-ee-a)
JAPANESE ROSE

Kerria japonica

Hardiness: *Zones 4-9*

Plant type: *deciduous shrub*

Height: *3 to 8 feet*

Interest: *flowers, foliage, stems*

Soil: *well-drained*

Light: *partial to bright full shade*

Dense, airy mounds of foliage show off kerria's bright yellow flowers in spring. The medium green leaves turn yellow in autumn and drop, revealing bare green stems that hold their color all winter.

Selected species and varieties: *K. japonica*—3 to 6 feet tall with a greater spread of arching branches that bear glossy, heavily veined and coarse-toothed leaves 1½ to 4 inches long; 'Pleniflora' [also known as 'Flora Pleno'] (globeflower kerria) grows semierectly 5 to 8 feet tall with very double, pomponlike flowers 1 to 2 inches wide, more open in habit than the species; 'Picta' [also known as 'Variegata'] is a dwarf clone growing to 3 feet tall with gray-green leaves edged in white and single yellow flowers.

Growing conditions and maintenance: Kerria tolerates most soils and urban conditions but enjoys soil amended with organic matter. Excessive fertility produces reduced bloom. Remove winter-killed branches in early spring; other pruning should be done just after flowering. On 'Picta', remove any green shoots that emerge. Cut off old stems at the base every few years to maintain vigor.

Kirengeshoma
(ky-reng-esh-O-ma)
YELLOW WAXBELLS

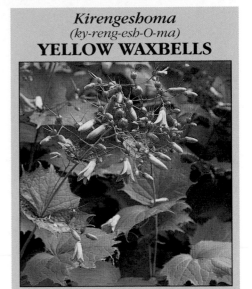

Kirengeshoma palmata

Hardiness: *Zones 5-8*

Plant type: *perennial*

Height: *3 to 4 feet*

Interest: *foliage, flowers*

Soil: *moist, well-drained, acid, fertile*

Light: *bright full shade*

Kirengeshoma is an unusual, semiexotic shade plant that is not often seen in the landscape. Shrubby but a bit spindly in habit, it produces handsome maple-like leaves on dark purple, semiarching stems and upright clusters of nodding yellow flowers in summer and fall. It makes an interesting specimen plant for edgings or borders.

Selected species and varieties: *K. palmata*—nearly round, toothed leaves, each with up to 10 lobes, arise from opposite sides of the stems and give an almost platelike appearance beneath clusters of 1½-inch-long butter yellow bell-shaped flowers whose buds last for months before opening.

Growing conditions and maintenance: Kirengeshoma needs soil that has been liberally supplemented with compost, leaf mold, or peat moss and is lime-free. Water during dry spells, and mulch to retain moisture. Propagate by dividing.

Lamium
(LAY-mee-um)
DEAD NETTLE

![Lamium maculatum 'White Nancy']

Lamium maculatum 'White Nancy'

Hardiness: *Zones 4-8*

Plant type: *perennial*

Height: *8 to 24 inches*

Interest: *foliage, flowers*

Soil: *moist, well-drained, average*

Light: *partial to full shade*

Dead nettle, so called because it does not sting like other nettles, is a vigorous, colorful ground cover with silvery foliage and flowers that bloom from late spring to summer. Several cultivars have been bred to be less weedy than the genus.

Selected species and varieties: *L. galeobdolon* [also listed as *Lamiastrum galeobdolon*] (yellow archangel)—to 2 feet tall with coarse-toothed 3-inch-long leaves and bright yellow blooms with brown marks; 'Herman's Pride' is 12 inches tall with green-and-silver leaves and yellow flowers; 'Variegata' has variegated green-and-silver leaves and yellow flowers. *L. maculatum* (spotted dead nettle)—a spreading ground cover to 18 inches high bearing small, crinkled leaves; 'Beacon Silver' has greenish silver leaves with green margins and pink flowers; 'Chequers' is a heat-tolerant cultivar with dark green leaves bearing a silver center stripe and violet flowers; 'White Nancy' has greenish silver leaves and white flowers.

Growing conditions and maintenance: Dead nettle needs little care. *L. galeobdolon* tolerates deep to bright shade. *L. maculatum* needs bright to partial shade.

Laurus
(LAR-us)
LAUREL, SWEET BAY

Laurus nobilis

Hardiness: *Zones 8-10*

Plant type: *large shrub or small tree*

Height: *30 to 40 feet*

Interest: *fragrance, form*

Soil: *well-drained*

Light: *partial shade to full sun*

Laurel is valued for its aromatic evergreen foliage, the same leaves that were used to fashion wreaths and crowns in ancient times and that are used for seasoning today. The berries yield an oil that is a perfume ingredient. Easily sheared, laurel is often kept in planters and trained into odd shapes. In the North, it can be brought inside to overwinter.

Selected species and varieties: *L. nobilis* (true laurel, bay laurel, bay tree)—grows very slowly with a pyramidal habit to 40 feet and has dark green elliptical or lance-shaped leaves to 4 inches long with small, inconspicuous yellowish green flowers in late spring or early summer followed by purple or black berries in the fall.

Growing conditions and maintenance: Laurel grows well in ordinary garden soil. A native of the Mediterranean region, it can endure dry spells once it is well established. In very hot regions, provide it with afternoon shade.

Leucojum
(loo-KO-jum)
SNOWFLAKE

![Leucojum vernum]

Leucojum vernum

Hardiness: *Zones 3-9*

Plant type: *bulb*

Height: *6 to 18 inches*

Interest: *flowers*

Soil: *moist, well-drained*

Light: *dappled shade to full sun*

A native of woodlands, the snowflake is at home in the dappled light of the shade garden. Dainty, bell-shaped white flowers bloom above dark green straplike leaves. Snowflakes look best when planted in masses and left undisturbed.

Selected species and varieties: *L. aestivum* (summer snowflake, Loddon lily)—12 to 18 inches tall with three to seven ¾-inch-long nodding flowers on each 12- to 18-inch stalk, blooming in the spring and early summer in the East but in the late fall and winter in warm areas of the West; 'Gravetye' [also known as 'Gravetye Giant'] produces 1½-inch flowers on 18-inch stems. *L. vernum* (spring snowflake)—10 inches tall with glossy green leaves and fragrant white flowers borne singly or in pairs on 6- to 12-inch stems in late winter or spring.

Growing conditions and maintenance: Although they grow in average garden soil, snowflakes prefer sandy loam to which leaf mold, peat moss, or dried compost has been added. Plant bulbs 4 inches deep. Bloom may not occur the first year. Propagate by dividing, but keep bulbs moist while moving.

Leucothoe
(loo-KO-tho-ee)
FETTERBUSH

Leucothoe fontanesiana 'Rainbow'

Hardiness: *Zones 4-9*

Plant type: *evergreen shrub*

Height: *2 to 6 feet*

Interest: *foliage, flowers, form*

Soil: *moist, well-drained, acid, fertile*

Light: *partial to bright full shade*

With its clusters of creamy, urn-shaped flowers, lustrous green leaves, arching branches, and spreading, broad-mounded habit, leucothoe looks stunning in the garden either as a specimen plant or planted in masses. The low forms make elegant ground covers.

Selected species and varieties: *L. davisiae* (Sierra laurel)—to 5 feet high with nodding upright panicles of flowers up to 6 inches long, borne above 1- to 3-inch leaves in late spring or early summer. *L. fontanesiana* (dog-hobble, drooping leucothoe)—3 to 6 feet high and wide, with arching branches of dark green, pointed, 2- to 5-inch-long leaves that turn red-bronze for fall and winter and fragrant 2- to 3-inch flower clusters protruding from beneath the foliage in spring; 'Rainbow' [also called 'Girard's Rainbow'] has leaves variegated in pink, yellow, cream, and green; 'Nana' is a dwarf 2 feet tall spreading to 6 feet; Zones 4-6.

Growing conditions and maintenance: Add peat moss, leaf mold, or dried compost liberally to soil when planting, and mulch to keep roots cool, particularly if exposed to sun. Prune after flowering.

Ligularia
(lig-yew-LAY-ree-a)
GOLDEN-RAY

Ligularia stenocephala 'The Rocket'

Hardiness: *Zones 4-10*

Plant type: *perennial*

Height: *2 to 6 feet*

Interest: *foliage, flowers*

Soil: *moist loam or bog*

Light: *bright full shade*

Large, often colorful leaves decorate clumps 4 to 6 feet tall topped with bold yellow to orange flowers in summer.

Selected species and varieties: *L. dentata* (bigleaf golden-ray)—20-inch-wide saucerlike leaves and daisylike flowers; 'Desdemona' has reddish leaves, with purple beneath, that turn bronze by summer on plants to 4 feet with reddish orange flowers; 'Othello' grows 3 feet tall with red-purple leaves and yellow-orange blooms; Zones 4-8. *L. stenocephala* [also listed as *L. przewalskii*] 'The Rocket'—clumps 4 to 6 feet tall with deeply cut leaves 8 to 12 inches wide and yellow flower spikes on black stems that emerge in summer and last longer than most blooms of the genus; Zones 5-8. *L. tussilaginea* [also listed as *Farfugium japonicum*]—leaves 12 inches wide on 2-foot-tall clumps with pale yellow flower clusters; 'Aureo-Maculata' leaves have yellow spots; Zones 7-10.

Growing conditions and maintenance: Because its enormous leaves lose large amounts of water, golden-ray does best in a cool spot where a continuous supply of moisture is assured. Propagate by division in spring or fall.

Ligustrum
(ly-GUS-trum)
PRIVET, HEDGE PLANT

Ligustrum japonicum

Hardiness: *Zones 7-10*

Plant type: *evergreen shrub*

Height: *6 to 12 feet*

Interest: *foliage, flowers, fruit*

Soil: *well-drained*

Light: *bright full shade to full sun*

A nearly foolproof staple in hedging, privet lends itself well to fast, easy foundation and screen plantings. Densely branched and upright, it takes extensive pruning well and can also be fashioned into a small tree. It is often sculpted into topiary designs. Panicles of creamy, somewhat odoriferous white flowers bloom at the ends of the twigs for a long period in spring. In fall, lustrous black berries mature and often linger into winter.

Selected species and varieties: *L. japonicum* (Japanese privet, wax-leaf privet)—very dark green, lustrous oval leaves, 1½ to 4 inches long and ¾ to 2 inches wide, with flower panicles up to 6 inches long appearing in mid- to late spring and ¼-inch blue-black berries.

Growing conditions and maintenance: Privet is extremely easy to grow and tolerant of almost all soils, including salty ones. It is also unthreatened by pests or diseases. Pruning constitutes the little maintenance this plant needs.

Liriodendron
(lir-ee-o-DEN-dron)
TULIP TREE

Liriodendron tulipifera

Hardiness: *Zones 4-9*

Plant type: *deciduous tree*

Height: *70 to 90 feet*

Interest: *form, foliage, flowers*

Soil: *moist, well-drained, slightly acid*

Light: *full sun*

A splendid tree for creating high, bright shade without competing for nutrients with its understory plantings, the tulip tree eventually forms a broad oval crown. Leaves are bright green, changing to rich yellow in fall. Showy greenish yellow cup-shaped flowers, with orange bands inside, appear in spring. Because of its great size, the tulip tree is not appropriate for small lots.

Selected species and varieties: *L. tulipifera* (yellow poplar, tulip poplar, tulip magnolia, whitewood)—70 to 90 feet high or more, beginning with a pyramidal habit, to 50 feet wide, the long petioles bearing 3- to 8-inch-wide leaves that are flat at the apex and show fine fall color.

Growing conditions and maintenance: Tulip trees need lots of root room; set the balled or container-grown plant in deep loam, then mulch and water adequately to prevent leaf yellowing. The tree is especially prone to attacks by aphids, whose honeydew secretions create fertile territory for an unsightly black fungus to develop on the leaves. Spared of drought stress and overcrowding from other large trees, the tree is usually long-lived.

Liriope
(li-RYE-o-pee)
LILYTURF

Liriope muscari 'Variegata'

Hardiness: *Zones 4-10*

Plant type: *ground cover*

Height: *8 to 18 inches*

Interest: *foliage, flowers, fruit*

Soil: *well-drained, fertile*

Light: *deep full shade to full sun*

The grasslike blades of liriope start out in tufts, gradually spreading until large clumps form. Ideal for use in edgings and rock gardens or as a ground cover, liriope also comes in variegated forms that provide textural accents. Flower spikes in purples or white bloom in late summer above the semi-evergreen foliage, followed by shiny black berries. In colder climates, the leaves look messy in winter.

Selected species and varieties: *L. muscari* (big blue lilyturf)—tufts of straplike leaves 18 inches tall and violet flowers; Zones 6-9; 'Gold Banded' is a compact form with wide, yellow-edged leaf blades; 'Monroe's White' grows 15 to 18 inches tall with narrower leaf blades than the species and white flowers; 'Variegata', 12 inches tall with creamy yellow leaf margins and lilac flowers; hardy to Zone 6. *L. spicata* (creeping lilyturf)—8 to 18 inches tall with leaves only ¼ inch wide and purplish white flowers; Zones 4-10.

Growing conditions and maintenance: Amend the soil with organic matter. Once established, liriope can tolerate dry shade. Shear or mow the old leaves before new growth begins in spring.

Lobelia
(lo-BEE-lee-a)
LOBELIA

Lobelia erinus 'Riviera Blue Splash'

Hardiness: *tender*

Plant type: *annual*

Height: *4 to 8 inches*

Interest: *flowers*

Soil: *moist, well-drained, fertile*

Light: *bright full shade to full sun*

The low, compact mounds of lobelia are covered with a profusion of flowers that bloom through summer and into fall. The mounding types make useful edging plants, while the trailing forms work well on retaining walls or in hanging planters.

Selected species and varieties: *L. erinus* (edging lobelia, trailing lobelia)—round, spreading compact habit to 8 inches tall with long, thin, serrated leaves; 'Crystal Palace' has cobalt blue flowers and bronzy green leaves; 'Cambridge Blue' is 6 inches tall with blue flowers; 'Riviera Blue Splash' produces white flowers with blue throats and petal margins; 'Cascade Mixed' is a trailing form with violet, blue, pink, or white flowers.

Growing conditions and maintenance: Lobelia needs protection from direct sun in hot climates. After all danger of frost has passed in spring, set plants 4 to 6 inches apart in soil that has been amended with leaf mold, peat moss, or finished compost. When the first blooming period has passed, cut plants back to half their height to encourage more flowers. Feed monthly with an all-purpose fertilizer.

Magnolia
(mag-NO-lee-a)
MAGNOLIA

Magnolia 'Elizabeth'

Hardiness: *Zones 4-9*

Plant type: *shrub or tree*

Height: *10 to 80 feet*

Interest: *flowers, foliage, fruit*

Soil: *moist, well-drained, acid, fertile*

Light: *partial shade to full sun*

This often coarse-textured genus produces some of the most conspicuous blooms of any tree in the landscape. The listed species include many hardy, deciduous varieties that do well in the North. Some magnolias make good understory specimens as large shrubs or small trees. Others are full-sized trees that are shade makers. The showy flowers bloom from early spring to midsummer, depending on the type. Long, often colorful fruits split, revealing the red seeds inside. Many species are now available that provide bloom when the plant is still young.

Selected species and varieties: *M. ashei* (Ashe magnolia)—a shrubby, multistemmed form 10 to 20 feet high with leaves 1 to 2 feet long and 6- to 10-inch-wide white flowers; Zones 6-9. *M. campbellii*—fragrant bright pink flowers shaped like cups and saucers on a tree that reaches 50 to 80 feet tall; Zones 7-9; ssp. *mollicomata* 'Charles Raffill' begins blooming in 7 to 8 years, yielding 6- to 7-inch-wide deep pink flowers touched with purple that open before the leaves, which are 6 to 10 inches long and 4 to 5 inches wide. *M.* 'Elizabeth'—a fast grow-

er to 30 feet tall with a profusion of fragrant, clear yellow flowers in midspring, beginning when very young; Zones 5-9. *M. fraseri* (ear-leaved umbrella tree, Fraser magnolia)—an understory tree for bright shade, 45 feet tall with fragrant 8- to 10-inch-wide white flowers blooming in late spring after the 8- to 15-inch leaves develop; Zones 5-8. *M.* x *loebneri* 'Ballerina' (Loebner magnolia)—15 to 20 feet tall and slightly wider, bearing fragrant white flowers with pinkish centers; Zone 4; 'Merrill' grows 25 to 30 feet tall, pro-

Magnolia campbellii

ducing 15-petaled white midspring blooms 3 to 3¼ inches wide; hardy to Zone 5. *M. tripetala* (umbrella tree, elkwood)—produces a tree form 15 to 35 feet tall, with creamy white, unpleasantly scented flowers up to 10 inches wide, 12- to 24-inch-long leaves on green branches like umbrella ribs and seed cones that turn pink in late summer; Zones 4-7. *M. virginiana* (sweet bay magnolia, swamp magnolia, swamp laurel)—shrublike plant to 20 feet tall in the North, 60 feet in the South, where it is evergreen, with fragrant waxy white flowers in early to midsummer and leaves 3 to 5 inches long with whitish undersides; Zones 5-9. *M. wilsonii*—shrubby habit to 24 feet tall with 4-inch fragrant, red-stamened, saucerlike flowers that first appear in late spring to early summer and often again in late summer; hardy to Zone 6.

Growing conditions and maintenance: Locate magnolias where ample moisture is assured, and fertilize in spring and midsummer (but not later) with an all-purpose acid fertilizer. Mulch to keep soil cool and moist. Do not cultivate or underplant; magnolias are surface rooters.

Mahonia
(ma-HO-nee-a)
HOLLY GRAPE

Mahonia bealei

Hardiness: *Zones 4-9*

Plant type: *shrub or ground cover*

Height: *10 inches to 12 feet*

Interest: *flowers, fruit, foliage*

Soil: *moist, well-drained, acid*

Light: *partial to bright full shade*

Mahonia's coarse texture and stiff habit are offset by fragrant flower clusters, berries that are enjoyed by birds, and spiny foliage that takes on winter color.

Selected species and varieties: *M. aquifolium* (mountain grape, holly barberry)—either broad and dense or upright and open, growing 3 to 6 feet and wider, with dark green leaves that turn red-purple in winter, 2- to 3-inch-long erect clusters of minute flowers that bloom in spring, and blue-black berries in late summer; Zones 4-8. *M. bealei* (leatherleaf mahonia)—an upright habit 6 to 12 feet high, with very spiny, dark blue-green leaves, fragrant yellow flowers in 3- to 6-inch clusters in late winter or spring, and blue berries in midsummer; Zones 6-9. *M. repens* (creeping mahonia)—a ground cover to 10 inches high with blue-green leaves that turn purple in winter, yellow flowers in April, and black berries in late summer; hardy to Zone 5.

Growing conditions and maintenance: Mahonias are intolerant of drought and drying winds. A mulch of pine needles or oak leaves helps maintain acidity in nearly neutral soils.

Matteuccia
(ma-TOO-chee-a)
OSTRICH FERN

Matteuccia struthiopteris

Hardiness: *Zones 4-7*

Plant type: *perennial*

Height: *2 to 6 feet*

Interest: *foliage*

Soil: *very moist, well-drained, fertile*

Light: *partial to bright full shade*

Under average garden conditions, these magnificently feathery, medium green, deciduous ferns easily tower to 4 feet—and even more in wet soil—making them excellent background plants. Vase-shaped, they spread vigorously by way of stolons and can soon cover large areas. Fertile fronds are useful in dried flower arrangements.

Selected species and varieties: *M. struthiopteris* (shuttlecock fern)—upright plumelike vegetative fronds with 30 to 50 pairs of feathery leaflets surround 12- to 18-inch-tall fertile fronds, which are olive green at first, then change to light brown.

Growing conditions and maintenance: Ostrich ferns appreciate consistently moist locations and can tolerate full sun only in moisture-retentive soil in cool climates. They also grow in wet, but not waterlogged, soil. Easy to maintain and very vigorous, they can become invasive. Divide by cutting the stolons and digging up the new plants.

Mazus
(MAY-zus)
MAZUS

Mazus reptans

Hardiness: *Zones 6-9*

Plant type: *ground cover*

Height: *2 inches*

Interest: *foliage, flowers, form*

Soil: *moist, well-drained, slightly acid, fertile*

Light: *partial shade to full sun*

A true ground hugger, mazus forms a dense, prostrate carpet with medium green oval leaves and one-sided clusters of charming flowers in late spring. It works well in rock gardens and borders, and since it tolerates occasional foot traffic, it makes an ideal plant for tucking between steppingstones.

Selected species and varieties: *M. reptans*—procumbent stems bearing inch-long coarsely toothed leaves that hold well into late fall or early winter and ½-inch-long flowers gathered into profuse lavender to purplish blue clusters, usually spotted with white or yellow in the center; 'Alba' has snowy white flowers.

Growing conditions and maintenance: Although mazus is sometimes listed as hardy in Zone 5, it is often killed back. Set plants 12 to 15 inches apart in moisture-retentive soil amended with organic matter such as compost or peat moss. Because mazus roots all along its stems, it competes well with weeds and grass. Propagate by dividing.

Mertensia
(mer-TEN-see-a)
BLUEBELLS, LUNGWORT

Mertensia virginica

Hardiness: *Zones 3-8*

Plant type: *perennial*

Height: *18 to 24 inches*

Interest: *flowers*

Soil: *moist to wet, well-drained, fertile*

Light: *partial to bright full shade*

A native wildflower of bushy habit, mertensia produces nodding clusters of trumpet-shaped flowers that weigh down the tops of stems in spring. Leaves open with a purplish sheen and mature to pale blue-green, gray-green, or lettuce green. Since the plant slips into dormancy shortly after flowering, it looks best in the company of plants like ferns that conceal its early-dying foliage. It also works well in rock gardens.

Selected species and varieties: *M. virginica* (Virginia bluebells, Virginia cowslip, Roanoke-bells)—stems 18 to 24 inches tall bear elongated-oval, thick-veined leaves, 2 to 5 inches long, and buds and new flowers that are pink, maturing to light blue or lavender; 'Alba' has white flowers.

Growing conditions and maintenance: Accustomed to woodland conditions, bluebell thrives in moist, peaty soil; streamside locations are ideal. In drier areas, mulch to retain moisture. Propagate by dividing the root mass after the plant becomes dormant, and reset 2 inches deep and 18 inches apart. Or start from seeds sown as soon as they are gathered.

Myrica
(mi-RYE-ka)
BAYBERRY

Myrica pensylvanica

Hardiness: *Zones 2-9*

Plant type: *shrub*

Height: *5 to 20 feet*

Interest: *form, fragrance, fruit*

Soil: *average to poor, well-drained*

Light: *bright full shade to full sun*

A medium- to fine-textured shrub with aromatic foliage and grayish white fruit in winter, bayberry makes a good border, massing, or foundation plant. In winter, northern bayberry, whose berries are used in candlemaking, shows off its attractive branching pattern. When limbed up to expose its grayish white bark, southern wax myrtle is a specimen tree.

Selected species and varieties: *M. cerifera* (southern wax myrtle, candleberry)—10 to 20 feet high and wide, with evergreen olive green leaves up to 3 inches long and ¾ inch wide and clusters of tiny berries; Zones 7-9. *M. pensylvanica* (northern bayberry)—5 to 12 feet high and wide, with lustrous oblong deciduous to semi-evergreen leaves, 4 inches long and 1 inch wide, and large yields of waxy fruit on female plants; Zones 2-6.

Growing conditions and maintenance: Apparently invulnerable to most adverse conditions including salt, northern bayberry does equally well in poor, sandy soil or heavy clay and suffers only when soil is too alkaline. Northern bayberry suckers freely to form large colonies. Both species take easily to pruning.

Nandina
(nan-DEE-na)
HEAVENLY BAMBOO

Nandina domestica

Hardiness: *Zones 6-9*

Plant type: *evergreen shrub*

Height: *2 to 8 feet*

Interest: *foliage, flowers, fruit, form*

Soil: *moist, well-drained*

Light: *bright full shade to full sun*

Heavenly bamboo forms clumps of upright canes from which narrow leaves come off at right angles. Erect panicles of creamy white flowers bloom in late spring, and huge clusters of brilliant red berries ripen in fall and persist all winter. It is lovely in groups and softens the effect of formal or coarse-textured shrubs. Despite its common name, it is not a true bamboo and does not spread invasively.

Selected species and varieties: *N. domestica* (sacred bamboo)—6 to 8 feet high and not nearly as wide, with leaves that emerge orange to purplish red and turn blue-green with age and flowers that open from pink buds; 'Harbor Dwarf' forms a compact mound 2 to 3 feet high with reddish purple leaves in winter; 'Moyer's Red' grows 6 feet high with vivid red coloration in foliage and fruit.

Growing conditions and maintenance: Tolerant of most soils, heavenly bamboo does best in fertile soil and is a long-lived, pest-free plant. To encourage denseness, cut a few canes back to different heights and thin out a few of the old ones every year. Winter color tends to get more intense under sun exposure.

Narcissus
(nar-SIS-us)
DAFFODIL

Narcissus 'Carleton'

Hardiness: *Zones 3-10*

Plant type: *bulb*

Height: *6 to 20 inches*

Interest: *flowers, fragrance*

Soil: *well-drained*

Light: *dappled shade to full sun*

Narcissus is a huge group of spring-blooming bulbs that vary greatly in size, shape, and color. Each bloom has an outer ring of six petals called the perianth and a raised center called a corona, which may be a small cup, a large cup of medium length, or, when it is very long, a trumpet. Hybrids number in the thousands, and the genus is grouped into 12 divisions. There are miniature cultivars within almost every division. Used in rock gardens or borders or naturalized, daffodils give years of carefree early color.

Selected species and varieties: *Division 1. Trumpet daffodils:* 10 to 18 inches tall with one flower per stem with a trumpet-shaped corona; 'Beersheba', white flowers on 15-inch stems; 'Lunar Sea', 18 to 20 inches tall with a yellow perianth and a white trumpet; 'Rijnveld's Early Sensation', yellow winter blooms on 13-inch stems. *Division 2. Large-cupped daffodils:* Solitary flowers with the corona more than one-third but less than the full length of the petals; 'Carbineer', bright yellow with an orange-red corona on 16-inch stems; 'Carleton', fragrant, soft yellow with a frilled corona and broad perianth, 18 to 20 inches tall; 'Ice Follies', 17 inches tall with white petals and a corona that turns from yellow to white. *Division 4. Double daffodils:* One or more flowers on each 12- to 16-inch stem, with the petals, corona, or both doubled; 'Cheerfulness', fragrant white with a corona flecked with yellow; 'Flower Drift', ivory white petals and a yellow-orange corona; 'Yellow Cheerfulness', fragrant yellow on yellow. *Division 6. Cyclamineus daffodils:* 8 to 14 inches tall with solitary yel-

Narcissus 'Lunar Sea'

low, white, or bicolored flowers having a long, wavy-rimmed corona and backward-flaring petals; hardy to Zone 4; 'February Gold', late-winter blooms with deep yellow petals and a yellow corona; 'Peeping Tom', all yellow, good for naturalizing; 'Tête-à-Tête', a miniature 6 to 8 inches tall, lemon yellow with a deeper yellow or orange corona; hardy to Zone 4. *Division 7. Jonquilla daffodils:* Delightfully fragrant flowers, as many as six to each 1-foot-tall stem; 'Pipit' has a fragrant white corona and pale yellow petals, to 15 inches; 'Sweetness' is 13 inches tall, very fragrant, all yellow; 'Trevithian', 17 inches with two to three very fragrant, deep yellow flowers per stem.

Growing conditions and maintenance: Plant large bulbs 6 to 8 inches deep, small ones 3 to 4 inches deep in well-prepared soil in fall, allowing time for the roots to become established before the ground freezes. Work peat moss or compost in for best results. After bloom, let foliage die down so the plant can build up nutrients for the next year's bloom. Propagate by dividing after foliage has died down. The chief pests are snails and slugs.

Nicotiana
(ni-ko-she-AN-a)
TOBACCO

Nicotiana alata

Hardiness:	*tender or Zones 9-10*
Plant type:	*annual or perennial*
Height:	*1 to 5 feet*
Interest:	*fragrance, flowers*
Soil:	*moist, well-drained*
Light:	*bright full shade to full sun*

The heavy, sweet fragrance of tobacco's trumpet-shaped flowers, clustered at the top of tall stems in summer, is most apparent at night. The flowers are pink, white, green, maroon, red, or purple. In the South, the listed species may overwinter. Leaves are narcotic or poisonous.

Selected species and varieties: *N. alata* (flowering tobacco)—up to 5 feet tall with low-growing clumps of large leaves and flower tubes up to 4 inches long, as well as dwarf forms that bloom during the day but are less fragrant; Nicki hybrids stand 10 to 16 inches tall with pink, red, white, yellow, or lime green flowers that do not close in the afternoon; annual. *N. langsdorffii*—3 to 5 feet tall with green flowers; annual. *N.* x *sanderae* 'Lime Green' (Sander tobacco)—a bushy annual with rose pink flowers 3 inches long and spoon-shaped leaves to 1 foot long.

Growing conditions and maintenance: Tobacco plants are easily grown from seed. Sow indoors 6 to 8 weeks before the last frost date and do not cover; they need light to germinate. Space plants 1 foot apart. Remove spent flowers to keep the plant blooming.

Ophiopogon
(o-fi-o-PO-gon)
LILYTURF

Ophiopogon japonicus 'Nana'

Hardiness:	*Zones 6-10*
Plant type:	*ground cover*
Height:	*2 to 14 inches*
Interest:	*foliage, flowers, fruit*
Soil:	*moist, well-drained*
Light:	*full shade to full sun*

Like liriope, with which it shares the common name lilyturf, *Ophiopogon* forms tufts of arching blades that spread to create a ground cover in any kind of light, including dense shade. Its flowers differ from those of liriope by appearing within the foliage, not above it. Clusters of small blue berries follow. Evergreen in the South, *Ophiopogon* is useful beneath trees and in borders and edgings.

Selected species and varieties: *O. japonicus* (dwarf lilyturf, dwarf mondo grass)—6 to 14 inches tall with dark green leaves ⅛ inch wide or less and up to several bluish violet flowers per stalk; 'Kyoto Dwarf' is only 2 inches tall with narrow, dark green leaves; 'Nana', roughly half as tall as the species; Zones 7-9. *O. planiscapus* 'Nigrescens' (black dragon)—purplish black foliage 6 inches tall, pink or lilac flowers and black berries; Zones 6-10.

Growing conditions and maintenance: Although lilyturf tolerates average garden soil, it grows best when peat moss or leaf mold has been added. In colder climates the foliage becomes shabby. Shear in early spring to promote new growth. Propagate by dividing in early spring.

Osmanthus
(oz-MAN-thus)
DEVILWOOD

Osmanthus fragrans

Hardiness: *Zones 7-10*

Plant type: *evergreen shrub*

Height: *8 to 30 feet*

Interest: *fragrance, foliage*

Soil: *moist, well-drained, acid, fertile*

Light: *bright full shade to full sun*

Devilwood's clusters of tiny white four-petaled fall flowers may be mostly hidden by its foliage, but its fragrance is spectacular. Some species have hollylike leaves with spines that are gradually lost as the plant ages; because of their density, these shrubs make good barrier plants. Others are useful as foundation plants, in borders, and as screens, but are especially valuable near walkways.

Selected species and varieties: *O.* x *fortunei* (Fortune's osmanthus)—oval habit, 15 to 20 feet tall, with white flowers in the fall; Zones 8-10. *O. fragrans* (fragrant olive, tea olive)—the most fragrant form, a 15- to 30-foot shrub or tree that sometimes produces a spring bloom as well, with lustrous dark green spineless leaves; reliably hardy only in Zones 9-10. *O. heterophyllus* 'Gulftide' (holly olive, Chinese holly, false holly)—dense, upright form 8 to 15 feet high with glossy green leaves and prominent spines; 'Variegatus' slowly grows to 8 feet or so, with white margins on the leaves; Zones 7-9.

Growing conditions and maintenance: Devilwood weathers pollution, is relatively pest free, and can be heavily pruned.

Osmunda
(oz-MUN-da)
FLOWERING FERN

Osmunda cinnamomea

Hardiness: *Zones 2-10*

Plant type: *perennial*

Height: *2 to 6 feet*

Interest: *foliage, form*

Soil: *moist to wet, acid, sandy loam*

Light: *bright full shade*

These stately, deciduous ferns grow wild mostly in marshes and swamps, where they reach even greater heights, but they also adapt to the home garden. Spreading slowly on rhizomes, they make excellent background plantings in borders and rock gardens or against a wall. Cinnamon fern can be used to hide leggy shrubs.

Selected species and varieties: *O. cinnamomea* (cinnamon fern, fiddleheads, buckhorn)—a 2- to 4-foot-tall sterile frond that looks like a cinnamon stick rising above light green foliage changing to gold in late summer before finally turning brown; Zones 3-9. *O. claytoniana* (interrupted fern)—2 to 4 feet tall with tierlike new spring growth; Zones 2-8. *O. regalis* (royal fern)—3- to 6-foot-tall fronds opening wine red then turning green, with 2- to 3-inch-long feathery leaflets that turn bright yellow in fall.

Growing conditions and maintenance: Flowering ferns thrive in soil consisting of 1 part loam, 1 part sand, and 2 parts leaf mold or peat moss. The interrupted fern needs highly acid conditions. Cinnamon and royal ferns can tolerate part sun if the soil remains wet, as by a stream or pond.

Pachysandra
(pak-i-SAN-dra)
SPURGE

Pachysandra terminalis

Hardiness: *Zones 4-9*

Plant type: *ground cover*

Height: *4 to 12 inches*

Interest: *foliage, flowers*

Soil: *moist, well-drained, acid, fertile*

Light: *partial to dense full shade*

Pachysandra forms an attractive, vigorous ground cover that thrives in shady areas where other plants may not. Japanese pachysandra tolerates dense shade and competes well with shallow-rooted trees.

Selected species and varieties: *P. procumbens* (Allegheny spurge)—flat gray-green or blue-green scalloped-edged deciduous to evergreen leaves, 2 to 4 inches long and 2 to 3 inches wide, sometimes mottled with brownish purple, that turn bronze in fall, and fragrant white or pinkish early-spring flower spikes 2 to 4 inches long. *P. terminalis* (Japanese pachysandra)—lustrous green toothed evergreen leaves, 2 to 4 inches long and 1 inch wide, in clusters at the end of unbranched stems 6 to 10 inches high, with 1- to 2-inch spikes of white flowers in spring and insignificant white berries in the fall; Zones 4-8; 'Green Carpet' has small, waxy green leaves and, at 4 inches, hugs the ground; Zones 4-9; 'Silver Edge' has green leaves edged with white.

Growing conditions and maintenance: Set the plants 12 inches apart in soil enriched with leaf mold or peat moss. Keep soil mulched until plants start to spread.

Parthenocissus
(par-then-o-SIS-us)
WOODBINE

Parthenocissus tricuspidata

Hardiness: *Zones 3-9*

Plant type: *vine*

Height: *50 feet or more*

Interest: *foliage*

Soil: *average to poor*

Light: *full shade to full sun*

A tough, extremely fast climber that can easily scale 10 feet and more in a season, woodbine can make short work of covering walls, trellises, and slopes. Fastening itself to a structure with tendrils, it needs no support. Its dark green compound leaves turn purplish red to crimson in fall.

Selected species and varieties: *P. henryana* (silver-vein creeper)—leaves with five leaflets up to 2½ inches long that are bluish green veined with white when young, with purple undersides, and turn red to reddish purple in fall; Zones 7-8. *P. quinquefolia* (Virginia creeper, American ivy, five-leaved ivy)—five leaflets up to 4 inches long, opening reddish bronze then turning dark green, then purplish to crimson in the fall, with greenish white early-summer flowers and small blue-black berries visible after the leaves have fallen. *P. tricuspidata* (Japanese creeper, Boston ivy)—leaves are three-lobed, simple, and lustrous; Zones 4-8.

Growing conditions and maintenance: Woodbine tolerates almost any soil, polluted conditions, winds, and salt. Although it is prey to a number of pests, it usually needs little care.

Phlox
(flox)
PHLOX

Phlox divaricata 'Fuller's White'

Hardiness: *Zones 3-9*

Plant type: *perennial*

Height: *5 to 14 inches*

Interest: *flowers*

Soil: *moist, well-drained, acid, fertile*

Light: *partial to bright full shade*

Phlox and its flat, five-petaled flowers come in a variety of plant forms suitable for rock gardens, borders, retaining walls, and perennial beds. The flowers, borne singly or in loose clusters, sometimes bear a noticeable eye at the center.

Selected species and varieties: *P.* 'Chattahoochee'—1-inch-wide, deep violet flowers with purple eyes on a spreading tuft of stems to 12 inches tall; Zones 4-9. *P. divaricata* (wild sweet William, blue phlox, woodland phlox)—semi-evergreen oval leaves hug the ground beneath 1-foot-tall scapes topped with blue, purple, or white flowers; Zones 3-9; 'Dirigo Ice' reaches 14 inches with fragrant pale lavender flowers; 'Fuller's White' has white flowers. *P. stolonifera* (creeping phlox)—creeping 5- to 10-inch stems with evergreen leaves forming a mat with blue, pink, or white flowers; Zones 3-8; 'Blue Ridge' has pale blue flowers and lustrous foliage, 'Pink Ridge', pink flowers.

Growing conditions and maintenance: These species of phlox like humus-rich soil. Plant 1 to 1½ feet apart in soil well supplemented with leaf mold, peat moss, or compost. Propagate by division.

Pieris
(PYE-er-is)
ANDROMEDA

Pieris japonica

Hardiness: *Zones 4-8*

Plant type: *evergreen shrub*

Height: *2 to 12 feet*

Interest: *foliage, flowers*

Soil: *moist, well-drained, acid, fertile*

Light: *bright full shade to full sun*

A broad-leaved evergreen offering four-season interest, andromeda has bronzy reddish new growth, early-spring flower panicles, and ornamental buds that form in summer for next year's bloom.

Selected species and varieties: *P. floribunda* (fetterbush, mountain andromeda)—rounded, bushy habit 2 to 6 feet high and wide, with erect panicles of white flowers 2 to 4 inches long that bloom for 2 to 4 weeks and leaves 1 to 3 inches long; Zones 4-6. *P. japonica* (lily-of-the-valley bush, Japanese pieris)—a dense form 9 to 12 feet tall and 6 to 8 feet wide with lustrous deep green leaves up to 3½ inches long and ¾ inch wide and drooping 5-inch-long flower panicles that last for 2 to 3 weeks; Zones 5-8; 'Flamingo' has deep rosy red flowers; 'Valley Fire' produces vivid red new growth with large white flowers; 'White Cascade' has white flower panicles lasting for 5 weeks.

Growing conditions and maintenance: Enrich soil with peat moss, leaf mold, or compost. Andromeda blooms best with spring sunshine. Remove faded flowers to keep the plant from producing seed. If pruning is needed, do it after flowering.

Pinus
(PYE-nus)
PINE

Pinus strobus

Hardiness: *Zones 3-8*

Plant type: *tree*

Height: *50 to 100 feet*

Interest: *form, bark*

Soil: *moist, well-drained*

Light: *bright full shade to full sun*

These majestic pines are shade makers rather than shade seekers. The finely textured and dense eastern white pine is also useful as a screen.

Selected species and varieties: *P. ponderosa* (ponderosa pine, western yellow pine)—growing 60 to 100 feet tall under landscape conditions and forming a narrow crown as it ages, it is void of branches for at least half of its height and has dark to yellowish green needles 5 to 10 inches long, brownish black furrowed bark when young, changing to yellowish brown to cinnamon red plates; Zones 3-7. *Pinus strobus* (eastern white pine, Weymouth pine)—fast-growing up to 80 feet tall and 20 to 40 feet wide, with grayish green smooth bark when young maturing to dark grayish brown, and producing 3- to 5-inch-long bluish green needles in groups of five; Zones 3-8.

Growing conditions and maintenance: Eastern white pine can tolerate bright shade as it is growing, but it does best when it receives full sun at maturity. Though both species prefer moist, deep loam, they tolerate a range of other soils. Ponderosa pine accepts alkaline soils.

Pittosporum
(pit-o-SPO-rum)
PITTOSPORUM

Pittosporum tobira

Hardiness: *Zones 8-10*

Plant type: *evergreen shrub*

Height: *10 to 12 feet*

Interest: *form, fragrance, foliage, flowers*

Soil: *well-drained to dry, sandy*

Light: *deep full shade to full sun*

A broad-spreading, extremely dense evergreen shrub with leathery, dark green rhododendron-like foliage, pittosporum is widely used in the South for hedges, screens, and foundation plantings. It also makes an excellent container plant. It produces clusters of five-petaled flowers in spring that are not showy but smell like orange blossoms.

Selected species and varieties: *P. tobira* (Japanese pittosporum, Australian laurel, mock orange)—10 to 12 feet or more and spreading up to twice its width, with fragrant ½-inch wide flowers that open creamy white and turn yellow with age and are borne in 2- to 3-inch wide clusters amid thick, very dark green leaves that are 1½ to 4 inches long and about 1 inch wide.

Growing conditions and maintenance: Pittosporum grows well in hot, dry climates and tolerates clay soil as long as it is well-drained. Mealy bugs may be a pest, but otherwise pittosporum requires little maintenance and takes well to heavy pruning.

Podophyllum
(po-doh-FIL-um)
MAY APPLE

Podophyllum peltatum

Hardiness: *Zones 3-9*

Plant type: *perennial*

Height: *12 to 18 inches*

Interest: *foliage, flowers, fruit*

Soil: *moist, well-drained, slightly acid, fertile*

Light: *full to dappled shade*

This woodland wildflower bears huge, deeply lobed leaves up to 1 foot wide and nodding six- to nine-petaled, 2-inch-wide white flowers that arise in spring at the joint between two leaves. Flowers mature into 1- to 2-inch berries. The common May apple quickly spreads to form large colonies that may be invasive. The foliage dies down in summer. The seeds, stem, and root are poisonous, but the fruits are said to be edible, though not palatable.

Selected species and varieties: *P. hexandrum* (Himalayan May apple)—clumped stems 12 to 18 inches tall, with six-petaled white to pink flowers that bloom before the three- to five-lobed 10-inch leaves unfurl. *P. peltatum* (common May apple, wild mandrake, raccoon berry)—leaves start developing before the flowers, which are often hidden by the foliage and are followed by yellow fruit.

Growing conditions and maintenance: Often found in boggy, low-lying areas near woodland streams, May apple thrives in constantly moist soil to which leaf mold has been added. Propagate by dividing in late summer or fall. Mulch with leaf litter in winter.

Polygonatum
(po-lig-o-NAY-tum)
SOLOMON'S-SEAL

Polygonatum odoratum 'Variegatum'

Polystichum
(po-LISS-ti-kum)
HOLLY FERN

Polystichum munitum

Primula
(PRIM-yew-la)
PRIMROSE

Primula sieboldii

Hardiness: *Zones 3-9*

Plant type: *perennial*

Height: *10 inches to 3 feet*

Interest: *flowers, fruit*

Soil: *moist, well-drained, fertile*

Light: *deep to bright full shade*

Arching stems arise from rootstocks to bear 1½-inch-long greenish white bell-shaped flowers that dangle from the axils of parallel-veined green leaves in late spring. Black or blue fruits mature in fall. The plant spreads slowly by rhizomes to form a good ground cover for shade.

Selected species and varieties: *P. biflorum* (small Solomon's-seal)—to 3 feet tall or more, greenish white flowers with greenish lobes usually hang in pairs below the stem in late spring to early summer, followed by blue berries. *P. humile*—10 to 12 inches tall with heavily veined leaves; Zones 4-7. *P. multiflorum*—3 feet tall, white flowers with greenish apexes, in clusters of two to six usually on the bottom half of the stem; blue-black berries. *P. odoratum* 'Variegatum' (variegated Solomon's-seal)—1- to 3-foot-tall stems bearing leaves with white margins and tips, topped with fragrant white flowers having green spots in the throat, followed by blue-black berries; Zones 3-9.

Growing conditions and maintenance: Supplement soil with leaf mold, peat moss, or compost before planting. Propagate by division.

Hardiness: *Zones 3-9*

Plant type: *perennial*

Height: *1 to 4 feet*

Interest: *foliage*

Soil: *moist, well-drained, fertile*

Light: *deep to bright full shade*

The lustrous foliage of the holly fern provides evergreen beauty to rock gardens, borders, and edgings.

Selected species and varieties: *P. acrostichoides* (Christmas fern, canker brake)—18 to 24 inches tall, with dark green, once-divided arching fronds that are widest at the base, developing multiple crowns. *P. braunii* (shield fern, tassel fern)—dark green twice-divided fronds to 24 inches long, tapering to the base and arranged in a vaselike circle; Zones 3-8. *P. munitum* (western sword fern, giant holly fern)—2 to 3½ feet tall with long, narrow, once-divided fronds; Zones 6-9. *P. setiferum* (soft shield fern, hedge fern, English hedge fern)—semi-evergreen, glossy, rich medium green, twice-divided fronds, 1½ to 4 feet long and soft to the touch; 'Divisilobum' has a very lacy habit with thrice-divided leaves; Zones 5-8.

Growing conditions and maintenance: Holly ferns grow well in cool, rich, moist soil, although Christmas fern is tolerant of dry periods. Crown rot can be a problem; take special care to make sure the soil is well drained. Propagate by dividing in spring.

Hardiness: *Zones 4-8*

Plant type: *perennial*

Height: *6 to 24 inches*

Interest: *flowers*

Soil: *moist to wet, well-drained, fertile*

Light: *partial to bright full shade*

Primroses produce neat, vivid flowers above basal rosettes of crinkled foliage in spring and early summer. Flowers have five petals and are borne in clusters atop naked stalks. Depending on the variety chosen, primroses are excellent for mass plantings and in borders, rock gardens, stream banks, or naturalized areas.

Selected species and varieties: *P. denticulata* (drumstick primrose, globe primrose, Himalayan primrose)—globe-shaped clusters of flowers in pink, lilac, violet, red, white, or other colors on 8- to 12-inch stems in spring; Zones 4-7. *P. japonica* (Japanese primrose, Japanese candelabra primrose)—2-foot stems bear several whorls of flowers, candelabra style, in pink, purple, white, crimson, or purplish red with yellow eyes from late spring to midsummer; Zones 5-7; 'Miller's Crimson' has crimson flowers in six to eight tiered whorls; 'Postford White' has white flowers. *P. sieboldii* (Siebold primrose)—9 inches tall with white, rose, or purple flowers, 1½ inches wide, in mid- to late spring and scalloped leaves 4 to 8 inches long that die down after flowering has stopped; hardy to Zone 5. *P. veris* (cowslip)—8 inches tall, with nodding clusters of fragrant yellow flowers in spring. *P. vulgaris* (English primrose, common primrose)—solitary spring flowers in yellow, lavender, blue, and other colors on 6- to 9-inch stems amid scalloped, wrinkled leaves 10 or more inches long; ssp. *sibthorpii* usually has purplish pink, sometimes red, flowers.

Primula denticulata

Growing conditions and maintenance: Most of these primroses need very moist to wet, deep loam that is extremely well drained. English primroses and cowslips prefer drier, but still moist, soils. Cowslips grow best in slightly alkaline soil; the rest like slightly acid to acid soils. Primroses are also intolerant of hot, dry climates, although Siebold primrose is more heat hardy than the rest. In the South, find a cool spot completely out of the sun, perhaps by a brook. In the North, protect from winter winds. Mix peat moss, leaf mold, or compost with soil before planting, and add a scattering of bone meal. If the soil is heavy clay, add 1 part of sharp sand to 1 part each of clay and humus. Place the crown at, or slightly above, the soil level. Space plants about 1 foot apart. Tamp soil carefully to eliminate air pockets. Water deeply during dry periods. In colder climates, mulch with evergreen boughs in winter. Divide colonies every 3 or 4 years to increase vigor if they become crowded. Propagate by sowing in a cold frame so that the seeds receive alternate freezing and thawing.

Prunus
(PROO-nus)
PLUM, CHERRY

Prunus caroliniana

Hardiness: *Zones 5-10*

Plant type: *shrub or tree*

Height: *3 to 30 feet*

Interest: *foliage, form, flowers*

Soil: *moist, well-drained*

Light: *bright full shade to full sun*

Popular for hedges and screens, this broad-leaved evergreen has dark green foliage, a dense habit, and, depending on the species, a very broad-spreading form. Small white flowers appear in spring. Its stems, which smell like cherries when bruised, are poisonous to livestock.

Selected species and varieties: *P. caroliniana* (Carolina cherry laurel)—shrub or oval-form tree 20 to 30 feet tall and 15 to 25 feet wide, leaves 2 to 3 inches long and early-spring white flower racemes, 1½ to 3 inches long and ¾ inch wide; Zones 7-10. *P. laurocerasus* (common cherry laurel, English laurel)—shrub, 10 to 18 feet high and 25 feet wide, leaves 2 to 6 inches long and ¼-inch flowers in 2- to 5-inch racemes; Zones 6-8; 'Otto Luyken' blooms on a mound 3 to 4 feet high and 6 to 8 feet wide, leaves 4 inches long and 1 inch wide; 'Schipkaensis' grows to 4 to 5 feet; Zones 5-8; 'Zabeliana', 3 to 5 feet and up to three times as wide, willowy leaves; Zones 5-8.

Growing conditions and maintenance: Prunus tolerates most soils but prefers the addition of organic matter. Can be pruned freely.

Pulmonaria
(pul-mo-NAY-ree-a)
LUNGWORT

Pulmonaria saccharata 'Sissinghurst White'

Hardiness: *Zones 4-8*

Plant type: *perennial*

Height: *6 to 18 inches*

Interest: *foliage, flowers*

Soil: *moist, well-drained*

Light: *bright full shade*

Small mounds or clumps of oval leaves follow bell-shaped flowers that nod on arching stems in spring.

Selected species and varieties: *P. longifolia* (long-leaved lungwort, Joseph and Mary, spotted dog)—tight clump with leaves more than a foot long; 'Ankum' has blue flowers; 'Roy Davidson' has silver-and-green foliage. *P. montana* [also known as *P. rubra*] (red lungwort)—1 to 2 feet tall with bright red spring flowers; 'Barfield Pink' has pale green leaves and pink flowers; 'Bowles' Red', medium green leaves, often slightly spotted, and red flowers. *P. officinalis* 'Rubra' (blue lungwort, Jerusalem sage, Jerusalem cowslip)—white-spotted leaves and flowers that turn mottled violet. *P. saccharata* (Bethlehem sage)—white-spotted 6-inch leaves and funnel-shaped flowers on stems to 18 inches; 'Janet Fisk' has silver-splotched foliage and lavender-pink flowers in spring; 'Sissinghurst White' has large white flowers and spotted foliage.

Growing conditions and maintenance: Plant 12 to 18 inches apart. Cut foliage back severely after flowering and feed with an all-purpose fertilizer.

Quercus
(KWER-kus)
OAK

Quercus alba

Hardiness: *Zones 3-10*

Plant type: *tree*

Height: *35 to 100 feet*

Interest: *form*

Soil: *wide variety of preferences*

Light: *partial shade to full sun*

The king of shade makers, the oak tree has a wide canopy and a deep root system that allows underplanting. Most species retain their dead leaves well into winter.

Selected species and varieties: *Q. acutissima* (sawtooth oak, sawthorn oak)—35 to 45 feet tall, with bristly-toothed leaves that turn yellow in fall; Zones 5-9. *Q. alba* (white oak)—75 to 100 feet tall with a wide canopy of leaves that turn brown to dark red in fall; Zones 3-9. *Q. rubra* (red oak, northern red oak)—60 to 75 feet high and up to 50 feet wide, with sharp-lobed leaves that are bright red in fall; Zones 4-8. *Q. shumardii* (Shumard oak, Shumard's red oak)—40 to 75 feet tall with sharp-pointed leaves that turn red in fall; Zones 5-9. *Q. virginiana* (live oak, southern live oak)—to 80 feet tall and 100 feet wide, evergreen; Zones 7-10.

Growing conditions and maintenance: Select a site with deep loam and no hardpan, preferably in full sun. White oaks like heavy clay. Sawtooth oaks prefer acid, well-drained soils but tolerate other types. Red oaks prefer acid, sandy loams. Shumard oaks accept both dry and wet, poorly drained soils.

Rhododendron
(roh-doh-DEN-dron)
AZALEA

Rhododendron occidentale

Hardiness: *Zones 3-8*

Plant type: *shrub*

Height: *2 to 12 feet*

Interest: *flowers, foliage*

Soil: *moist, well-drained, acid, fertile*

Light: *partial to bright full shade*

Members of the genus *Rhododendron,* azaleas differ from rhododendrons in a number of ways, some of them rather technical. Among the visible differences, azaleas are more likely to be deciduous (though there are many exceptions), while rhododendrons are mostly evergreen; azalea flowers are usually funnel shaped, rhododendrons bell shaped; azaleas have five stamens, rhododendrons 10. Azalea is one of the most popular blooming shrubs for shade and offers a range of colors, sizes, and hardiness.

Selected species and varieties: Deciduous: Exbury and Knap Hill azaleas—upright-growing, 8 to 12 feet tall and nearly as wide, with medium green leaves that turn yellow, orange, or red in fall, and flowers in pink, yellow, orange, rose, red, cream, and off-white; Zones 5-7; 'Gibraltar' has extra large, brilliant orange, ruffled flowers and orangish fall foliage; Zones 4-8. Ghent azaleas (*R.* x *gandavense*)—shrubby habit 6 to 10 feet tall, with single or double flowers in yellow, white, pink, orange, red, and combination colors; generally hardy to Zone 5; 'Daviesi' has fragrant white flowers with yellow cen-

ters on a wide-growing, multistemmed plant; 'Narcissiflora', fragrant, double yellow, hose-in-hose blooms. Northern Lights azaleas—6 to 7 feet high and wide, with showy 1½-inch-long flowers in clusters of up to 12 that open before the leaves appear; hardy to Zone 3; 'Golden Lights' has fragrant yellow flowers; 'Rosy Lights', fragrant dark pink blooms brushed with rosy red; 'White Lights', pale pink buds that open to fragrant off-

Rhododendron schlippenbachii

white flowers with yellow centers. *R. atlanticum* (coast azalea, dwarf azalea)—3 to 6 feet high and wide, producing pinkish white flowers opening with or before blue-green leaves; hardy to Zone 6. *R. calendulaceum* (flame azalea, yellow azalea)—open habit, 4 to 8 feet tall and wide, with flowers in a multitude of yellows, pinks, oranges, peach, and red, and medium green leaves changing to a quiet yellow or red in fall; Zones 5-7. *R. occidentale* (western azalea)—a native of the West Coast, with white or pinkish flowers, 1½ to 2 inches wide, in late spring and red or yellow fall foliage; Zones 6-7. *R. prinophyllum* [also known as *R. roseum*] (rose-shell azalea, early azalea)—2 to 8 feet tall with densely branched, spreading habit, bright green foliage that turns bronze in fall, and bright pink flowers that smell like cloves; Zones 3-8. *R. schlippenbachii* (royal azalea)—6 feet tall with equal spread in a rounded upright habit, bearing large, fragrant, light to rose pink flowers that open with bronze foliage that turns yellow, orange, or red in fall; Zones 4-7. *R. vaseyi* (pink-shell azalea)—upright form to 8 feet with rose-colored, bell-shaped flowers appearing before medium green summer foliage that turns red in fall; Zones 5-8. Evergreen: Gable Hybrids—2 to 4 feet high and wide with glossy dark green 1-inch-long leaves and pink, red, lavender, and other colors; Zone 5; 'Caroline Gable' has large wavy-

Rhododendron Gumpo Group

edged leaves and large lavender flowers; 'Louise Gable', a round, dense form to 4 feet tall with deep salmon pink double flowers with dark blotches; 'Purple Splendor', purple hose-in-hose flowers; 'Rosebud', 4 feet high and wide with hose-in-hose double flowers similar to miniature roses in silvery deep pink. Girard Evergreen Hybrids—very showy plants with large flowers and profuse bloom, good for colder climates, with buds hardy to Zone 6; 'Girard Border Gem' has deep rose pink flowers that blanket the dwarf plant, hiding the ½-inch glossy dark green leaves, which turn red in winter; 'Girard Crimson', 2½-inch-wide bright red flowers and large, glossy green leaves; 'Girard Fuchsia', ruffled reddish purple flowers and dark green glossy leaves; hardy to Zone 6. Glenn Dale Hybrids—developed for the mid-Atlantic region, with large flowers whose buds are reliably hardy to Zone 7; 'Martha Hitchcock' has white flowers with purple edges. Kurume Hybrid azaleas—single or double flowers, usually pinks and reds, on a compact plant with small leaves; hardy to Zone 7; 'Coral Bells' bears 1½-inch-wide coral pink hose-in-hose flowers on a 3-by-4-foot plant; 'Hershey's Red', bright red flowers 2 inches wide, blooming early and hardy to Zone 6; 'Sherwoodii' [also known as 'Sherwood Orchid'], single reddish violet blooms with a darker blotch. North Tisbury Hybrids—'Joseph Hill' bears bright red flowers, 2 inches wide, in

a dense, large mound; hardy to Zone 6. Satsuki Hybrids—dwarf, spreading, evergreen shrubs with many flower types and color combinations; 'Amagasa' has deep pink flowers, 3½ inches wide; 'Beni-Kirishima' has double orange-red flowers; Gumpos come in a rainbow of colors on small, compact plants, including pink, rose, salmon, lavender, coral, white, and bicolors. *R. kaempferi* (torch azalea)—upright habit to 10 feet with deciduous or semi-evergreen foliage and orange-red to pink flowers; hardy to Zone 6. *R. ob-*

Rhododendron 'Purple Splendor'

tusum 'Amoenum' (Hiryu azalea, Kirishima azalea)—double magenta flowers on a semi-evergreen shrub to 3 feet; hardy to Zone 6. *R. yedoense* (Yodogawa azalea)—5 feet tall with double purple flowers and deciduous to semi-evergreen leaves, 1 to 3 inches long, that turn reddish purple in fall; hardy to Zone 6; var. *poukhanense* (Korean azalea) grows to 6 feet tall, with 1⅞-inch-wide, clear light to medium lavender flowers, and loses most of its leaves in winter; hardy to Zone 4.

Growing conditions and maintenance: Find a site protected from hot afternoon suns and cold winter winds. Add peat moss, leaf mold, or compost to soil. Unlike other azaleas, the royal and rose-shell types tolerate near neutral soils. For the acid-loving majority, be sure to maintain the soil's acidity if planting near a foundation; lime can leach out of building materials and raise the soil's pH. Keep soil moist and water deeply in dry periods, including before the onset of winter. Mulch to keep soil cool and conserve moisture; azaleas root close to the surface. Prune in early spring after blooming, cutting back to a bud or shoot.

Rhododendron
(roh-doh-DEN-dron)
RHODODENDRON

Rhododendron 'Yaku Princess'

Hardiness:	*Zones 4-9*
Plant type:	*shrub or tree*
Height:	*3 to 30 feet*
Interest:	*flowers, foliage*
Soil:	*moist, well-drained, acid, fertile*
Light:	*bright full shade to full sun*

If ever there was a magnificent flowering shrub for the shade garden, it is the rhododendron. Its showy bell-shaped flowers are usually borne in clusters at the end of branches in spring or early summer. Its large, dark green leaves and rotund nature accentuate the lavish displays of white, pink, lavender, purple, or red.

Selected species and varieties: Catawbiense cultivars and hybrids—6 to 10 feet tall and slightly less in spread, with flower colors ranging from lilac to purplish rose with touches of yellowish brown or green and leaves 3 to 6 inches long; Zones 4-8; 'Album Elegans' has white flowers; hardy to Zone 6; 'Lee's Dark Purple', a broad, compact habit with dark purple buds opening to medium purple flowers and wavy leaves; hardy to Zone 5; 'Mrs. C. S. Sargent', red-rose flowers spotted yellow; 'Nova Zembla', red flowers, heat resistant and hardy to Zone 5. Dexter hybrids—large plants with mixed parentage, resembling *R. fortunei,* with dense foliage; hardy to Zone 6; 'Scintillation' is a heat-tolerant cultivar that grows to 6 feet tall with compact form and has lovely, luminous pink flowers with amber throats.

R. yakusimanum selections and hybrids —usually compact shrubs, 3 to 4 feet high; hardy to Zone 6; 'Anna H. Hall' has rich pink buds opening to white flowers on a semidwarf plant; Zones 5-9; 'Centennial Celebration', fragrant, deeply

Rhododendron 'Nova Zembla'

frilled white flowers brushed with lilac-pink on a 4-foot-high plant; Zones 5-8; 'Yaku Princess', 3 to 4 feet tall and slightly wider, with ball-shaped trusses of two-tone pink spotted with green; Zones 4-8. Other cultivars of various strains: 'Baden-Baden' is a broad semidwarf with rich red, waxy flowers and slightly twisted foliage; reliably hardy to Zone 6; 'Ben Mosely' is lightly frilled and yields bright pink flowers with darker margins and dark red throats on a 4- to 6-foot plant; hardy to Zone 6; 'Blue Peter' is of variable size to 8 feet tall with frilled blue-violet and purple flowers; Zones 6-8; 'Boule de Neige' has a compact, rounded form, 5 feet tall by 8 feet wide, with white flowers; hardy to Zone 5; 'Chionoides', white flowers on a 5-foot plant; hardy to Zone 6; 'Dolly Madison', white flowers blooming early on an 8- to 10-foot plant; hardy to Zone 5; 'Janet Blair', 4 to 6 feet high, producing lavender-pink flowers with greenish throats; hardy to Zone 6; 'Vulcan's Flame' is a sun-tolerant variety, 4 to 6 feet tall, producing red flowers on red stems; hardy to Zone 6. Other species: *R. augustinii*—compact, upright habit to 10 feet with large, light gray-blue, pink, or mauve flowers with green spots and long, narrow leaves; hardy to Zone 7. *R. carolinianum* (Carolina rhododendron)—3 to 6 feet tall and wide, with leaves 2 to 3 inches long on red to purplish red stems, which bear clusters of white, pink, or lilac

flowers; Zones 5-8; var. *album* has white flowers. *R. fortunei* (Fortune's rhododendron)—fragrant pale pink, lilac, or white flowers and large dark green leaves on a large shrub or small tree 20 to 30 feet tall; hardy to Zone 6. *R.williamsianum*—pale rose flowers 2¼ inches wide on a low and spreading shrub to 5 feet; hardy to Zone 7.

Growing conditions and maintenance: Catawbiense and Yakusimanum hybrids can tolerate full sun in cool areas, where they are also reliably hardy. The other species and cultivars listed here prefer partial shade and accept bright full shade. Apply liberal amounts of organic matter

Rhododendron 'Scintillation'

such as peat moss, leaf mold, or compost to the soil. Make sure the site is very well-drained and there is no hardpan; poor drainage is usually the chief reason for rhododendron failure. If soil is heavy clay, amend it with sharp sand and peat moss or leaf mold as required, position the plant so that the top of the rootball is several inches above the soil level, and mulch thickly around the base of the shrub. If the plant has been container grown and is potbound, make vertical slits down the outside of the root mass before planting. Water deeply during dry periods, and mulch to keep the root zone cool and moist. Pinching off faded flowers helps to improve bloom the next year.

Rodgersia
(ro-JER-zee-a)
RODGERSIA

Rodgersia pinnata

Hardiness:	*Zones 5-7*
Plant type:	*perennial*
Height:	*2 to 6 feet*
Interest:	*flowers, foliage*
Soil:	*moist to wet*
Light:	*partial to full shade*

The feathery plumes of rodgersia rise above huge, coarse-textured, compound leaves up to 20 inches across.

Selected species and varieties: *R. aesculifolia* (fingerleaf rodgersia)—bronzy green, coarsely toothed, horse-chestnut-like leaves that are arranged like fingers on a hand and arise from 3- to 6-foot stems topped with creamy white or pink flower plumes; Zones 5-6. *R. pinnata* (featherleaf rodgersia)—plumes of buff pink flowers emerge from late spring to midsummer above bronze-tinted, dark green leaves with finely serrated margins on 3- to 4-foot stems; 'Superba' has very large red flowers. *R. podophylla* (bronzeleaf rodgersia)—finger-shaped leaves are green at first before turning to metallic bronze in summer, borne on 3- to 5-foot stems with yellowish white 1-foot plumes; Zones 5-6.

Growing conditions and maintenance: Space rodgersia 3 feet apart in soil that is constantly wet, such as at the edge of streams and ponds. In colder climates, provide winter protection by mulching. Propagate by division in early spring, leaving the soil intact around each section.

Sarcococca
(sar-ko-KO-ka)
SWEET BOX

![Sarcococca hookerana var. humilis]

Sarcococca hookerana var. humilis

Hardiness: *Zones 5-8*

Plant type: *evergreen shrub*

Height: *18 inches to 5 feet*

Interest: *foliage, fragrance, fruit*

Soil: *moist, well-drained, fertile*

Light: *partial to bright full shade*

A handsome plant with year-round ornamental value, sarcococca has shiny, narrow leaves on its roundly mounded shape. In late winter to early spring, inconspicuous but fragrant white flowers bloom, to be replaced by shiny black or red berries that linger into fall. Sarcococca spreads slowly by suckers; the low form makes a good ground cover.

Selected species and varieties: *S. confusa*—leaves to 2 inches long and ¾ inch wide on a densely branched shrub growing 3 to 5 feet tall and wide; Zones 7-8. *S. hookerana* var. *humilis* (Himalayan sarcococca)—18 to 24 inches tall and wide, blooming in early spring under 2- to 3½-inch-long and ½-inch-wide leaves; Zones 5-8. *S. ruscifolia* (fragrant sarcococca, fragrant sweet box)—very fragrant flowers and red fruits on a 3-foot-high-and-wide mound; Zones 7-8.

Growing conditions and maintenance: Best grown in Zone 8 in the South and along the Pacific Coast, *S. confusa* and *S. ruscifolia* need shelter in Zone 7. Protect from winter winds. Add leaf mold or peat moss to the soil to improve drainage. Mulch to conserve moisture.

Sasa
(SASS-a)
BAMBOO

Sasa veitchii

Hardiness: *Zones 5-8*

Plant type: *ground cover*

Height: *2 to 8 feet*

Interest: *foliage, form*

Soil: *moist, fertile*

Light: *bright full shade to full sun*

Bamboo displays long, green leaves that jut out from tall, cylindrical canes. A woody grass that develops rhizomes, running bamboo spreads rapidly, functioning as both a ground cover and, for the taller species, as a screen. It is evergreen except in the coldest climates.

Selected species and varieties: *S. palmata* (palm-leaf bamboo, palmate bamboo)—leaves up to 15 inches long and 4 inches wide, medium green above and bluish green beneath, arise from narrow canes up to 8 feet tall and slightly more than ¼ inch in diameter; hardy to Zone 5. *S. veitchii* (Kuma bamboo grass, Kuma zasa)—purplish canes 2 to 4 feet tall bear leaves up to 8 inches long and 2 inches wide that are dark green above and bluish gray below, developing straw-colored, dry leaf margins in fall; Zones 7-8.

Growing conditions and maintenance: Bamboo that is healthy and vigorous can quickly take over an area; restraints are essential. If foliage looks unkempt at the end of winter, prune plants to the ground. Propagate by division.

Saxifraga
(saks-IF-ra-ga)
SAXIFRAGE, ROCKFOIL

Saxifraga umbrosa

Hardiness: *Zones 7-9*

Plant type: *perennial*

Height: *4 to 24 inches*

Interest: *flowers, foliage*

Soil: *moist, well-drained, neutral, fertile*

Light: *full to dappled shade*

An ideal plant for rock gardens, saxifrage's rosettes of leaves form a mat from which runners or stolons spread. The red threadlike runners of strawberry geranium, which is also grown as a houseplant, produce baby plants. Delicate flowers rise above the foliage in spring.

Selected species and varieties: *S. stolonifera* (strawberry geranium, beefsteak geranium)—18- to 24-inch branched stems bearing 1-inch-wide white flowers above 4-inch-tall clumps of round, hairy leaves with white veins and red undersides, up to 4 inches wide. *S. umbrosa* (London-pride)—18-inch-high clumps of 2-inch-long oval leaves, pea green above and red beneath, with white, pink, rose, or bicolored flower sprays on 6-inch stems from late spring to early summer.

Growing conditions and maintenance: Saxifrages grow best in neutral, rocky soil but will tolerate other soils as long as they are very well drained but evenly moist. Generously enrich the soil with leaf mold or peat moss. Plant 8 to 10 inches apart in spring, and mulch lightly to overwinter. Apply an all-purpose fertilizer in spring. Propagate by dividing after flowering.

Skimmia
(SKIM-ee-a)
SKIMMIA

![Skimmia japonica photo]

Skimmia japonica

Hardiness: *Zones 7-9*

Plant type: *evergreen shrub*

Height: *3 to 4 feet*

Interest: *flowers, fruit, foliage*

Soil: *moist, well-drained, acid*

Light: *partial to bright full shade*

Skimmia forms a low mound of leathery leaves decorated in spring with clusters of flowers and in fall with bright berries that remain into the next spring. In order for a female bush to produce berries, a male bush, which produces larger flowers that are also fragrant, has to be located within 100 feet. Skimmia is beautiful in foundation plantings and in masses.

Selected species and varieties: *S. japonica* (Japanese skimmia)—a rounded, densely branched habit, slow growing to 3 to 4 feet tall and slightly wider, bearing bright green leaves, 2½ to 5 inches long, that are tightly spaced at the end of branches, and producing 2- to 3-inch clusters of red buds that open to creamy white flowers on reddish purple stems.

Growing conditions and maintenance: Japanese skimmia may be planted in Zone 9 on the West Coast and north to Zone 7 on the East Coast if given a protected location. In hot climates, site it out of afternoon sun. Foliage may discolor in winter sun. Add 1 part peat moss or leaf mold to every 2 parts of soil to improve drainage. Fertilizing and pruning are not usually necessary.

Smilacina
(smy-la-SEE-na)
FALSE SOLOMON'S-SEAL

Smilacina racemosa

Hardiness: *Zones 3-7*

Plant type: *perennial*

Height: *2 to 3 feet*

Interest: *flowers, fruit*

Soil: *moist, well-drained, acid, fertile*

Light: *bright to medium full shade*

A member of the lily family, false Solomon's-seal bears pyramidal-shaped flower panicles on dense clumps of arching stems above oval leaves that have prominent parallel veins. Colorful berries that are a favorite of wildlife follow the flowers. Native to moist woodlands, false Solomon's-seal is best used for wildflower gardens and for naturalizing.

Selected species and varieties: *S. racemosa* (false spikenard, treacleberry, Solomon's zigzag)—6-inch-long creamy white flower clusters are borne in mid- to late spring on arching zigzag stems 2 to 3 feet tall that also have pointed, oval to lance-shaped leaves to 9 inches long and small white or green berries that turn red in fall.

Growing conditions and maintenance: False Solomon's-seal thrives best in deep soil in cool, moist, shady locations, such as along a stream or pond. Amend the soil with compost, leaf mold, or peat moss. Propagate by dividing the rhizomes in fall, allowing at least one bud per segment. Replant with the bud facing up. Mulch with leaf litter to overwinter.

Stewartia
(stew-AR-tee-a)
STEWARTIA

Stewartia pseudocamellia

Hardiness: *Zones 5-9*

Plant type: *shrub or tree*

Height: *10 to 40 feet*

Interest: *flowers, foliage, bark*

Soil: *moist, well-drained, acid, fertile*

Light: *partial shade to full sun*

Stewartias produce camellia-like white summer flowers and vivid fall foliage. Japanese and Korean stewartia have multicolored exfoliating bark.

Selected species and varieties: *S. koreana* (Korean stewartia)—dense, conical tree 20 to 30 feet tall bearing 3-inch-wide flowers with yellow stamens and red-purple fall foliage; Zones 5-7. *S. ovata* var. *grandiflora* (mountain stewartia, mountain camellia)—flowers up to 4 inches wide with purple stamens and up to eight petals bloom on a bushy shrub or tree 10 to 15 feet tall and wide bearing 2- to 5-inch dark green leaves that turn red or orange in fall. *S. pseudocamellia* (Japanese stewartia)—semioval tree 20 to 40 feet high or more, with 2- to 2½-inch flowers that have orange anthers and yellow, red, or reddish purple fall foliage; Zones 5-7.

Growing conditions and maintenance: Mountain stewartia tolerates bright full shade; the others do best in partial shade protected from afternoon sun. Plant as a container or balled-and-burlapped plant when young, adding peat moss or leaf mold to the soil. Prune if harsh winter winds have killed the tender twigs.

Styrax
(STY-racks)
SNOWBELL, STORAX

Styrax obassia

Hardiness: *Zones 5-8*

Plant type: *tree*

Height: *to 30 feet*

Interest: *flowers, form*

Soil: *moist, well-drained, acid, fertile*

Light: *partial shade to full sun*

White flowers appear in late spring or early summer on this lovely specimen tree for lawn or patio. The Japanese snowbell has zigzag stems and smooth gray-brown bark with irregular orange-brown fissures. Sinewy gray branches twist and turn on the fragrant snowbell. Both forms create an attractive winter effect. If the deciduous leaves escape an early fall freeze, they turn reddish or yellow.

Selected species and varieties: *S. japonicus* (Japanese snowbell, snowdrop tree)—20 to 30 feet high with wide-spreading branches to 30 feet or more, bearing fine leaves held aloft and clusters of ¾-inch wide, bell-shaped flowers with yellow stamens, and gray-brown smooth bark with irregular orange-brown fissures; 'Kusan' is more compact than the species, growing to about 12 feet. *S. obassia* (fragrant snowbell)—drooping, fragrant racemes up to 8 inches long on a 20- to 30-foot tree with ascending branches bearing large, heart-shaped leaves.

Growing conditions and maintenance: Snowbells need a soil rich in organic matter. Transplant into the garden while still young. Prune in the winter.

Taxus
(TAKS-us)
YEW

Taxus cuspidata 'Densa'

Hardiness: *Zones 4-7*

Plant type: *shrub or tree*

Height: *2 to 60 feet*

Interest: *foliage, fruit*

Soil: *moist, well-drained*

Light: *partial shade to full sun*

A dark green needled evergreen of many sizes and shapes, the yew is widely used in foundation plantings, borders, and hedges. Female plants bear poisonous, pea-sized red berries, open at one end to expose a hard seed.

Selected species and varieties: *T. baccata* (English yew)—highly variable in form, growing 30 to 60 feet high by 15 to 25 feet wide, with reddish brown furrowed bark and needles up to 1¼ inches long; Zones 5-7; 'Adpressa' has needles ½ inch or less long on a shrub or small tree to 30 feet tall. *T. cuspidata* (Japanese yew)—shrub or tree of variable form 10 to 40 feet high and wide with reddish brown bark that exfoliates with age and needles ½ to 1 inch long; 'Densa' slowly grows to 4 feet high and 8 feet wide with red berries that contrast with very dark green needles.

Growing conditions and maintenance: Yews grow best in partial sun, but they tolerate open shade. Although *T. cuspidata* adapts to most soils, all yews require excellent drainage. English yew does well in either acid or alkaline soils.

Tiarella
(ty-a-REL-a)
FALSE MITERWORT

Tiarella cordifolia 'Slick Rock'

Hardiness: *Zones 3-8*

Plant type: *perennial*

Height: *6 to 12 inches*

Interest: *flowers*

Soil: *moist, well-drained, slightly acid, fertile*

Light: *medium to bright full shade*

Sweeps of frothy tiarella plumes blooming above rich green heart-shaped foliage lend an airy texture to the woodland garden. Good for massings, rock gardens, and wildflower areas, tiarella also provides fall color when its long-lasting leaves turn reddish to dark purple. Foamflower makes a good ground cover.

Selected species and varieties: *T. cordifolia* (foamflower)—downy, bright green, lobed leaves arise from creeping stolons to form a 6-inch-high mat and stems up to 1 foot long that bear white 1- to 4-inch flower racemes in spring; 'Eco Red Heart' has medium green leaves with red hearts in the center and pinkish flowers; 'Slick Rock', deeply cut, maplelike leaves and pinkish flowers. *T. wherryi* (lakela, Wherry's foamflower)—very showy, fragrant, pinkish white flower plumes bloom from late spring to early summer on 1-foot-tall white stems above nonstoloniferous clumps of rich green heart-shaped leaves.

Growing conditions and maintenance: Plant 12 to 18 inches apart in soil amended with organic matter such as leaf mold or peat moss. Foamflowers do not tolerate drought. Propagate by division in fall.

Tricyrtis
(try-SER-tis)
TOAD LILY

Tricyrtis hirta

Hardiness: *Zones 4-8*

Plant type: *perennial*

Height: *2 to 3 feet*

Interest: *flowers*

Soil: *moist, well-drained, slightly acid, fertile*

Light: *bright full shade*

Toad lilies bloom in summer or fall, producing flared, trumpet-shaped, spotted flowers either in clusters or singly in the leaf axils on tall stems. The foliage is often hairy. They are best used in perennial borders and rock gardens.

Selected species and varieties: *T. hirta* (hairy toad lily)—1-inch-wide white, cream, or pale purple waxy flowers spotted with dark purple appear singly or clustered in leaf axils at the top of 2- to 3-foot stems in fall. *T. latifolia*—yellow flowers with purple or brown spots bloom in clusters in early summer on 3-foot stems with mottled foliage. *T. macrantha*—nodding, soft to deep yellow shuttlecock-style flowers with reddish brown spots blooming in fall on hairy 3-foot stems.

Growing conditions and maintenance: Space rhizomes 12 to 18 inches apart in peaty garden loam. Remove dead leaves in late fall. Propagate by dividing in spring or fall. Toad lilies are half-hardy perennials; in the northern limits of their hardiness, dig up the roots, dry them, and store over the winter, or mulch heavily to overwinter in the ground.

Tsuga
(TSOO-ga)
HEMLOCK

Tsuga canadensis

Hardiness: *Zones 3-8*

Plant type: *shrub or tree*

Height: *40 to 70 feet*

Interest: *foliage*

Soil: *moist, well-drained, acid*

Light: *deep full shade to full sun*

Hemlocks are softly pyramidal evergreens whose graceful, drooping branches and small needles lend a fine texture to the shade garden. Canadian hemlock makes a beautiful, fine-textured hedge, screen, or accent plant.

Selected species and varieties: *T. canadensis* (Canadian hemlock, eastern hemlock)—tapering trunk 65 feet or more tall, bearing medium green needles ¼ to ⅔ inch long and oval ½- to 1-inch cones. *T. caroliniana* (Carolina hemlock)—45 to 60 feet tall, a species more tolerant of urban conditions, with darker green needles than those of Canadian hemlock and a stiffer form.

Growing conditions and maintenance: Unlike many other conifers, hemlocks tolerate shade well. They are shallow-rooted plants that are intolerant of wind, drought, and heat; add organic matter to sandy soils to aid in moisture retention, and mulch to keep soil moist and cool. Sunscald occurs at 95°F and above. Canadian hemlocks can be kept at 3 to 5 feet with shearing. Host to a number of pests, the hemlock has been besieged in parts of the East by the woolly adelgid.

Viburnum
(vy-BUR-num)
ARROWWOOD

Viburnum dentatum

Hardiness: *Zones 4-8*

Plant type: *shrub*

Height: *6 to 20 feet*

Interest: *flowers, fruit, foliage*

Soil: *moist, well-drained*

Light: *bright full shade to full sun*

Bearing prolific spring flowers in flat-topped cymes, viburnums are suited for shrub borders, masses, and specimens. The small red berries—a favorite of birds—turn black in mid- to late summer.

Selected species and varieties: *V. dentatum* (southern arrowwood)—to 15 feet tall, with coarsely toothed deciduous leaves, cymes of white flowers, and blue-black berries. *V. plicatum* var. *tomentosum* (double file viburnum)—8 to 10 feet high and slightly wider, with horizontal branches bearing white flower cymes 2 to 4 inches wide in spring, the outer sterile flowers being showy, the inner fertile ones plain, and dark green leaves that turn reddish purple in fall; Zones 5-8; 'Shasta' grows to 6 feet and twice as wide with 4- to 6-inch flowers. *V. sieboldii* (Siebold viburnum)—15 to 20 feet tall and two-thirds as wide, with white flower cymes 3 to 6 inches wide that nearly mask the dark green leaves and berries persisting from late summer into fall; Zones 4-8.

Growing conditions and maintenance: Viburnums tolerate a wide range of soils, requiring only adequate moisture and good drainage. Water during dry periods.

Vinca
(VING-ka)
PERIWINKLE

Vinca major 'Variegata'

Hardiness: *Zones 4-8*

Plant type: *ground cover*

Height: *6 to 12 inches*

Interest: *foliage, flowers*

Soil: *average, well-drained*

Light: *deep full to partial shade*

A workhorse for difficult shady areas, *Vinca* provides a mat of glossy dark green evergreen foliage on interlaced vines that bear blue, lilac, or white five-petaled flowers, 1 to 2 inches across, in spring and sporadically throughout the summer. Useful on slopes and under trees.

Selected species and varieties: *V. major* (greater periwinkle)—creeping or trailing vines to 12 inches high bear leathery leaves to 2 inches long and blue flowers in spring; Zone 7; 'Variegata' has white-and-dark-green leaves. *V. minor* (common periwinkle)—glossy leaves to 1½ inches long on prostrate stems that crisscross to form a mat 8 inches high, flowering in spring; 'Alba' has white flowers; 'Bowles Variety' [also called 'La Grave'], a clump-forming habit with light blue flowers; 'Gertrude Jekyll' is a prolific bloomer with white flowers, smaller leaves, and dense but very slow growth.

Growing conditions and maintenance: Grows best in moist, rich garden soil but is widely tolerant. Once established, common periwinkle weathers drought, poor soil, and competing tree roots. Greater periwinkle is less drought tolerant.

Viola
(vy-O-la)
VIOLET

Viola cucullata 'Freckles'

Hardiness: *Zones 3-9*

Plant type: *perennial*

Height: *3 to 8 inches*

Interest: *flowers, fragrance*

Soil: *wet to dry, well-drained*

Light: *bright full to dappled shade*

Members of a huge genus, the violets below produce tufts of heart-shaped leaves and fall, winter, or spring flowers. Spreading quickly by surface runners or rhizomes, they are useful as ground covers or in rock gardens and edgings.

Selected species and varieties: *V. cucullata* [also listed as *V. obliqua*] (marsh blue violet)—6 inches tall with spring blooms; 'Freckles' has pale blue flowers with purple spots; 'White Czar', white flowers with a yellow eye. *V. labradorica* (Labrador violet)—blue to violet flowers in spring on 3-inch stems with purplish ¾-inch-wide green leaves; Zones 3-8. *V. odorata* (sweet violet)—8-inch stems rising in clumps from long runners, bearing 1- to 3-inch leaves; hybrids of the species offer fragrant single and double flowers in purple, blue, rose, or white, blooming in fall and winter in warm climates and in spring in colder areas; Zones 6-9.

Growing conditions and maintenance: Mix organic matter into the soil. Marsh blue violets do well in moist or wet sites; sweet violets need a moist soil; Labrador violets tolerate drier conditions. Marsh and Labrador violets self-seed freely.

Woodwardia
(wood-WAR-dee-a)
CHAIN FERN

Woodwardia fimbriata

Hardiness: *Zones 3-10*

Plant type: *perennial*

Height: *1 to 9 feet*

Interest: *foliage, form*

Soil: *moist to wet, well-drained, fertile*

Light: *bright full shade*

Chain ferns come in distinctly different forms. The netted chain fern spreads vigorously on branching rhizomes to form a ground cover. Arising in a clump, the giant chain fern's spray of large, arching fronds makes a dramatic statement in the shade garden.

Selected species and varieties: *W. areolata* (netted chain fern)—erect, deciduous fronds rise 1 to 2 feet high from creeping rhizomes, the sterile fronds reddish green when new, turning glossy dark green with maturity, and bearing netted veins; Zones 3-9. *W. fimbriata* (giant chain fern)—arching, evergreen fronds to 9 feet high arise upright in clumps from woody rhizomes; Zones 8-10.

Growing conditions and maintenance: One of the easiest ferns to grow, the netted chain fern does best in soil that mimics its native habitat, the bogs and swamps of the East, although it tolerates drier conditions. The giant chain fern prefers consistently moist, shady settings.

Acknowledgments and Picture Credits

The editors wish to thank the following for their valuable assistance in the preparation of this volume:

Jim R. Brooks, Director, The Lawn Institute, Marietta, Georgia; Ethel M. Dutky, Extension Plant Pathologist, University of Maryland, College Park, Maryland; Yunghi C. Epstein, Lawson-Miller Associates, Washington, D.C.; Stanton Gill, Central Maryland Research and Education Center, University of Maryland Cooperative Extension, Ellicott City, Maryland; Robert B. McCartney, Woodlanders, Aiken, South Carolina; Holly Shimizu, Chief Horticulturist, U.S. Botanic Gardens, Washington, D.C.

The sources for the illustrations in this book are listed below. Credits from left to right are separated by semicolons, from top to bottom by dashes.

Cover: © Michael S. Thompson/designed by Ernie and Marietta O'Byrne, Eugene, Ore. Back cover insets: Jerry Pavia—art by Fred Holz—Jerry Pavia/designed by Louise G. Smith. End papers: © Michael S. Thompson. 2, 3: Leonard G. Phillips/designed by JoAnna Palmer. 4: Courtesy Robert S. Hebb. 6, 7: Bernard Fallon/designed by Sandy Kennedy, Kennedy Landscape Design Associates. 8, 9: M. Catherine Davis/designed by Yunghi C. Epstein. 10: Art by Fred Holz. 11: Alan L. Detrick—art by Fred Holz. 12, 13: Joanne Pavia; © Walter Chandoha. 14: Roger Foley/designed by Donald K. Hylton, Landscape Designer. 15: © Roger Foley/designed by Gordon Riggle. 16: © Walter Chandoha—Catriona Tudor Erler. 17: © Roger Foley/designed by Osamu Shimizu. 18: © Jane Grushow/Grant Heilman Photography, Lititz, Pa. 19: Jerry Pavia. 20, 21: Joanne Pavia;

© Lefever/Grushow/Grant Heilman Photography, Lititz, Pa. 22: © Jane Grushow/Grant Heilman Photography, Lititz, Pa. 23: © Walter Chandoha. 24, 25: © Roger Foley/designed by Osamu Shimizu. 26: Alan L. Detrick. 27, 28: Jerry Pavia. 29: Jerry Pavia/ designed by Ryan Gainey. 30: Jerry Pavia. 31: © Carole Ottesen. 32: © Larry Lefever/ Grant Heilman Photography, Lititz, Pa. 33: Roger Foley, courtesy William P. Steele III. 34, 35: © Walter Chandoha; Alan L. Detrick. 36, 37: © R. Todd Davis (2); Alan L. Detrick—C. Colston Burrell. 38, 39: © judywhite (2)—© R. Todd Davis. 41: Dency Kane/designed by Carol Mercer. 42, 43: © Charles Mann/ designed by Diana Ballantyne, Oregon Trail Gardens. 44, 45: C. Colston Burrell/designed by C. Colston Burrell, President, Native Landscape Design and Restoration, Ltd.; Michael Bates/ designed by Michael Bates, English Country Gardens, Glen Ellen, Calif. 46, 47: Leonard Phillips/designed by Dr. and Mrs. Guy M. Harbert Jr. 48, 49: Jerry Pavia/designed by Louise G. Smith. 50, 51: © Michael S. Thompson/designed by Ernie and Marietta O'Byrne, Eugene, Ore.; Michael Bates/designed by Michael Bates, English Country Gardens, Glen Ellen, Calif. 52, 53: Robert Walch/designed by David E. Benner, Horticulturist. 54: © Charles Mann/designed by Diana Ballantyne, Oregon Trail Gardens (2)—C. Colston Burrell/designed by C. Colston Burrell, President, Native Landscape Design and Restoration, Ltd.(2). 55: Michael Bates/designed by Michael Bates, English Country Gardens, Glen Ellen, Calif. (2)—Leonard Phillips/ designed by Dr. and Mrs. Guy M. Harbert Jr. (2). 56: Jerry Pavia/designed by Louise G. Smith (2)—© Michael S. Thompson/designed by Ernie

and Marietta O'Byrne, Eugene, Ore. (2). 57: Michael Bates/ designed by Michael Bates, English Country Gardens, Glen Ellen, Calif. (2)—Robert Walch/ designed by David E. Benner, Horticulturist (2). 58, 59: Leonard Phillips/designed by Dr. and Mrs. Guy M. Harbert Jr. 60: © Michael S. Thompson. 61: Joanne Pavia. 62: © Jane Grushow/Grant Heilman Photography, Lititz, Pa. 63: © R. Todd Davis. 64, 65: Jerry Pavia. 66: Art by Fred Holz. 67: William L. Ackerman. 68, 69: © judywhite; C. Colston Burrell. 70: Dency Kane. 71: © Jane Grushow/Grant Heilman Photography, Lititz, Pa. 72, 73: Leonard Phillips/designed by Barbara and John Seidler. 74: © Walter Chandoha. 75, 76: Art by Fred Holz. 77: Alan L. Detrick. 78: Leonard Phillips, courtesy Mrs. G. S. Williams. 79: © Walter Chandoha. 81: © Michael S. Thompson. 82: Art by Fred Holz. 83: © Michael S. Thompson; Michael Bates—art by Fred Holz. 84, 85: Art by Fred Holz. 92: Art by Lorraine Mosley Epstein—art by Fred Holz. 93: Art by Lorraine Mosley Epstein (2)—art by Fred Holz. 94: Art by Lorraine Mosley Epstein (2)—art by Fred Holz. 95: Art by Nicholas Fasciano—art by Lorraine Mosley Epstein—art by Catherine Anderson—art by Fred Holz. 102: Map by John Drummond, Time-Life Books. 104: Richard Shiell; Joanne Pavia. 105: © Michael S. Thompson; Jerry Pavia; Joanne Pavia. 106: © Michael S. Thompson; Jerry Pavia (2). 107: Jerry Pavia. 108: Richard Shiell; © R. Todd Davis; Jerry Pavia. 109, 110: Jerry Pavia. 111: © R. Todd Davis; Joanne Pavia; © Michael S. Thompson. 112: Jerry Pavia; Richard Shiell (2). 113: Jerry Pavia; Joanne Pavia; Jerry Pavia. 114: Jerry Pavia (2); © R. Todd Davis. 115: Jerry Pavia (2);

© Michael S. Thompson. 116: Jerry Pavia; Joanne Pavia; Jerry Pavia. 117: Michael Dirr; Jerry Pavia (2). 118: Joanne Pavia; © Michael S. Thompson; © judywhite. 119: Michael Dirr; Jerry Pavia; Joanne Pavia. 120: Jerry Pavia. 121: Jerry Pavia; Joanne Pavia; Jerry Pavia. 122: Jerry Pavia (2); Thomas E. Eltzroth. 123: © Robert E. Lyons; Steven Still; © Robert E. Lyons. 124: © Robert E. Lyons; © Michael S. Thompson; Jerry Pavia. 125: Jerry Pavia; Joanne Pavia; Jerry Pavia. 126: Jerry Pavia (2); © Robert E. Lyons. 127: Jerry Pavia. 128: C. Colston Burrell; Jerry Pavia (2). 129: © Robert E. Lyons; Jerry Pavia (2). 130: Michael Dirr; Jerry Pavia; © Michael S. Thompson. 131: Jerry Pavia; © judywhite; Jerry Pavia. 132: Jerry Pavia (2); Richard Shiell. 133: Jerry Pavia; © judywhite; Thomas E. Eltzroth. 134: Joanne Pavia; Jerry Pavia; Thomas E. Eltzroth. 135: Jerry Pavia; Joanne Pavia; Jerry Pavia. 136: Jerry Pavia; © Michael S. Thompson; Virginia R. Weiler. 137: C. Colston Burrell; © Robert E. Lyons; Thomas E. Eltzroth. 138: C. Colston Burrell; Jerry Pavia; Richard Shiell. 139: Jerry Pavia. 140: Jerry Pavia; Joanne Pavia; Jerry Pavia. 141: Jerry Pavia; Thomas E. Eltzroth; © Carole Ottesen. 142: Jerry Pavia; Joanne Pavia; © Michael S. Thompson. 143: Joanne Pavia; Thomas E. Eltzroth; C. Colston Burrell. 144: © Michael S. Thompson; Jerry Pavia; © Michael S. Thompson. 145: Jerry Pavia (2); © Michael S. Thompson. 146: © R. Todd Davis; Jerry Pavia; © R. Todd Davis. 147: Jerry Pavia; © Michael S. Thompson; Jerry Pavia. 148: Jerry Pavia. 149: Jerry Pavia (2); © R. Todd Davis. 150: © Michael S. Thompson; Jerry Pavia (2). 151: © judywhite; © Michael S. Thompson (2).

Books:

Arms, Karen. *Environmental Gardening.* Savannah: Half-moon Publishing, 1992.

Art, Henry W. *The Wildflower Gardener's Guide.* Pownal, Vt.: Storey Communications, 1987.

Atkinson, Robert E. *The Complete Book of Groundcovers.* New York: David McKay, 1970.

Austin, Richard L. *Wild Gardening.* New York: Simon & Schuster, 1986.

Bir, Richard E. *Growing and Propagating Showy Native Woody Plants.* Chapel Hill: University of North Carolina Press, 1992.

Bonnie, Fred. *Flowering Trees, Shrubs, and Vines.* New York: Galahad Books, 1976.

Brookes, John. *The Book of Garden Design.* New York: Macmillan, 1991.

Brown, George E. *Shade Plants for Garden and Woodland.* London: Faber and Faber, 1980.

Damrosch, Barbara. *The Garden Primer.* New York: Workman Publishing, 1988.

Druse, Ken. *The Natural Shade Garden.* New York: Clarkson Potter, 1992.

Duddington, C. L. *Evolution and Design in the Plant Kingdom.* New York: Thomas Y. Crowell, 1969.

Ellis, Barbara W., and Fern Marshall Bradley (Eds.). *The Organic Gardener's Handbook of Natural Insect and Disease Control.* Emmaus, Pa.: Rodale Press, 1992.

Erler, Catriona Tudor:
The Garden Problem Solver. New York: Simon & Schuster, 1994.
Step-By-Step Successful Gardening: Trees and Shrubs. Des Moines: Meredith® Books, 1995.

Fish, Margery. *Gardening in the Shade.* London: Faber and Faber, 1983.

Fretwell, Barry. *Clematis.* Deer Park, Wis.: Capability's Books, 1989.

Glattstein, Judy. *Garden Design with Foliage* (Garden Way Publishing). Pownal, Vt.: Storey Communications, 1991.

Griffiths, Mark. *Index of Garden Plants.* Portland, Ore.: Timber Press, 1994.

Hofman, Jaroslav. *Ornamental Shrubs.* Translated by Joy Turner-Kadeckova, edited by Denis Hardwicke. New York: Spring Books, 1969.

Horticulture and Landscape Design (4th ed.). Boston: Houghton Mifflin, 1961.

Isaacson, Richard T. (Comp.). *The Andersen Horticultural Library's Source List of Plants and Seeds.* Chanhassen: Minnesota Landscape Arboretum, 1993.

Joyce, David. *The Complete Guide to Pruning and Training Plants.* New York: Simon & Schuster, 1992.

Keen, Mary. *Gardening with Color.* New York: Random House, 1991.

Loewer, Peter. *The New Small Garden.* Mechanicsburg, Pa.: Stackpole Books, 1994.

McHoy, Peter. *Pruning: A Practical Guide.* New York: Abbeville Press, 1993.

McHoy, Peter, Tim Miles, and Roy Cheek. *The Complete Book of Container Gardening.* North Pomfret, Vt.: Trafalgar Square Publishing, 1991.

Morse, Harriet K. *Gardening in the Shade* (rev. ed.). Portland, Ore.: Timber Press, 1982.

Northen, Henry, and Rebecca Northen. *Ingenious Kingdom.* London: Prentice-Hall International, 1970.

Ogden, Scott. *Garden Bulbs for the South.* Dallas: Taylor Publishing, 1994.

Oosting, Henry J. *The Study of Plant Communities* (2d ed.). San Francisco: W. H. Freeman, 1956.

Ottesen, Carole. *Ornamental Grasses.* New York: McGraw-Hill, 1989.

Parcher, Emily Seaber. *Shady Gardens.* Boston: Branden Press, 1972.

Pearson, Robert, et al. *Courtyard and Terrace Gardens.* London: Cassell Educational/ Royal Horticultural Society, 1993.

Phillips, C. E. Lucas, and Peter N. Barber. *Ornamental Shrubs.* New York: Van Nostrand Reinhold, 1981.

Rose, Graham. *The Sunday Times Book of Woodland and Wildflower Gardening.* London: David & Charles, 1988.

Roth, Susan A. *The Four-Season Landscape.* Emmaus, Pa.: Rodale Press, 1994.

Schenk, George. *The Complete Shade Gardener.* Boston: Houghton Mifflin, 1984.

Shrubs and Trees (The Best of Fine Gardening series). Newtown, Ct.: Taunton Press, 1993.

Sinnes, A. Cort. *Shade Gardening.* San Francisco: Ortho Books, 1982.

Sperka, Marie. *Growing Wildflowers.* New York: Harper and Row, 1973.

Stevenson, Violet. *The Wild Garden.* New York: Viking Penguin, 1985.

Still, Steven M. *Manual of Herbaceous Ornamental Plants* (4th ed.). Champaign, Ill.: Stipes Publishing, 1994.

Taylor, Jane:
Climbing Plants (Kew Gardening Guides). Portland, Ore.: Timber Press, 1992.
The Shady Garden (The Wayside Gardens Collection). New York: Sterling Publishing, 1994.

Taylor, Patricia A. *Easy Care Shade Flowers.* New York: Simon & Schuster, 1993.

Taylor's Encyclopedia of Gardening (4th ed.). Edited by Norman Taylor. Boston: Houghton Mifflin, 1961.

Taylor's Guide to Shade Gardening. Edited by Frances Tenenbaum. New York: Houghton Mifflin, 1994.

Westcott, Cynthia. *Westcott's Plant Disease Handbook* (5th ed.). Revised by R. Kenneth Horst. New York: Van Nostrand Reinhold, 1990.

Western Garden Book (Sunset Books). Menlo Park, Calif.: Lane Publishing, 1989.

Wilson, Jim:
Landscaping with Container Plants. Boston: Houghton Mifflin, 1990.
Landscaping with Wildflowers. Boston: Houghton Mifflin, 1992.

Wyman, Donald. *Shrubs and Vines for American Gardens.* New York: Macmillan, 1969.

Yang, Linda. *The City Gardener's Handbook.* New York: Random House, 1990.

Zeman, Anne M. *Shade Gardening* (Burpee American Gardening series). New York: Prentice Hall Gardening, 1992.

Periodicals:

Bir, Richard E. "Native Azaleas." *Horticulture,* May 1992.

Bucks, Christine. "Impatiens: Made for the Shade." *Organic Gardening,* April 1995.

DiPaola, Joseph M. "Turfgrass Management in Shady Areas of Lawns." *Landscape Management,* February 1994.

Gilman, Arthur. "Hardy Ferns." *Horticulture,* October 1988.

Hallgren, Lee. "The Kinds of Sun and Shade." *Fine Gardening,* May/June 1993.

"Hostas That Brighten Shade." *Garden Gate,* April/May 1995.

Lovejoy, Ann. "Ferns for the Border." *Horticulture,* November 1993.

Maness, Thurman. "Jewel-Toned Flowers for the Shade." *Fine Gardening,* March/April 1995.

Meyer, William A., and Crystal Rose-Fricker. "Varieties for Shade." *Grounds Mainte-*

nance, August 1992.

Perry, Thomas O. "Gardening amid Tree Roots." *Fine Gardening,* July/August 1992.

Roth, Susan A. "Sure-Fire Flowers for Shady Spots." *Organic Gardening,* April 1992.

Shear, William A. "Wild Irises Extend the Bloom Season." *Fine Gardening,* March/April 1995.

Swell, Nancy. "Ferns!" *Gardening & Outdoor Living Ideas* (*Woman's Day* Better Living series), Vol. 5, no. 1, 1995.

Other Sources:

"Gardening with Wildflowers and Native Plants." Handbook #119. *Plants and Gardens, Brooklyn Botanic Garden Record,* 1989.

"How to Read a Seed Label to Determine Quality." Report. Marietta, Ga.: The Lawn Institute, n.d.

"Lawn Care Tips from the Pros." Report. Marietta, Ga.: The Lawn Institute, Spring 1995.

"Lawns across America." Report. Marietta, Ga.: Better Lawn and Turf Institute, n.d.

"Pruning Techniques." Handbook # 126. *Plants and Gardens, Brooklyn Botanic Garden Record,* 1991.

Index

Numerals in italics indicate an illustration of the subject mentioned.

A

Abelia: 31, 65, *chart* 66, *chart* 99, *104*

Acanthopanax: 54, 56

Acanthus: 69

Acer: chart 103, *104; palmatum,* 28, *54,* 104; species, 11, 14, 29, 30, *chart* 100, *104*

Achillea: 8-9

Achimenes: 61

Aconite: *105*

Aconitum: 87, 88, *charts* 97-98, *chart* 103, *105*

Adiantum: 21, 23, *36-37, chart* 98, *chart* 103, *105*

Aegopodium: 40

Aesculus: 14, 88

African lily: 17

Agapanthus: 17

Ageratum: 18, 61, 65

Air circulation: 10, 80, 82, 85, *charts* 93-95

Ajuga: 8, 13, 21, 26, 41, *64-65,* 69, 70, 89, *chart* 98, *chart* 103, *105*

Akebia: 24-25, 28, 33, 60, 65, *chart* 66, *chart* 101, *chart* 103, *106*

Alchemilla: 34, *54,* 87

Alder buckthorn: 32

Alexandrian laurel: *chart* 103, *117*

Algerian ivy: 125

Alumroot (*Geranium*): *chart* 103, 123

Alumroot (*Heuchera*): 18, 26, *36-37, chart* 103, *126*

Amelanchier: 20, 26, 28-29, *chart* 66

American ivy: 140

American laurel: *chart* 66, *chart* 103, *131*

Amethyst flower: *111*

Andromeda: 71

Andromeda (*Pieris*): 16, *chart* 66, *charts* 92-93, *chart* 103, *140*

Anemone: 65, 67, 69, 70, *chart* 103, *106;* x *hybrida,* 87, 91, *chart* 96; species, *61,* 91, *charts* 96-97, *106*

Angel-wings: *chart* 103, *112*

Anise (anise tree): 29, *chart* 103, *130*

Annuals: 37-38; shade-flowering, 8, 16, 17, 18, 21, 61, 65, 70, 71, 86, 87

Aphids: 86, *chart* 92

Apple: *chart* 66

Aquilegia: 34, *55, 56,* 57, 87, 90, *chart* 103, *107; canadensis,* 23, 39, *46-47, 55,* 70, *chart* 98, *107;* x *hybrida, chart* 96, 107; species, *6-7, 56,* 57, *72-73, 83, chart* 96, 107

Arborizing: 31

Arborvitae: 32

Ardisia: 65, *chart* 99, *chart* 101, *chart* 103, *107*

Arisaema: 61-62, *chart* 98, *chart* 103, *107*

Aristolochia: 60, 65, *chart* 101, *chart* 103, *108*

Aronia: 26

Arrowwood: 32, *chart* 66, *chart* 103, *150*

Artemisia: 54

Arum: 41, 67, *chart* 96, *108*

Aruncus: 34

Asarum: 13, 39, 41, *chart* 98, *chart* 103, *108*

Aspidistra: 21

Asplenium: 36-37

Astilbe: 8, 18, 21, 26, *31,* 34, *38,* 70, 87, *chart* 103, *109;* x *arendsii: 54,* 57, 88, *chart* 96, 109; care of, 86, 90; species, *24-25, 54, chart* 97, *109*

Athyrium: chart 103, *109; filix-femina,* 21, 35, *36,* 109; *goeringianum, chart* 98, *109; nipponicum,* 18, *24-25, 36-37, 54,* 88, *109*

Aucuba: 21, *32, chart* 99, *chart* 103, *110*

Australian laurel: *chart* 103, *141*

Autumn crocus: 65

Autumn fern: *119*

Azalea: 14, 15, 20, 23, 31, 32, 33, *46-47,* 60, 63, 65, *chart* 66, 70, 87, 88, *chart* 103, *144, 144-145, 145;* diseases of, *charts* 93-95; insect pests of, *chart* 92

Azalea leaf gall: *chart* 93

B

Baby's-tears: 8, 40-41

Bacterial diseases: *chart* 81

Bahia grass: 19, *chart* 40

Bald cypress: 11, 30

Balsam: *chart* 103, *130*

Bamboo: 32, 91, *chart* 103, *147*

Barberry: 27, 31-32, *chart* 103, *110*

Barrenwort: 27, *32,* 41, *chart* 103, *120*

Bay: *50-51*

Bayberry: 32, 33, 67, 70, *chart* 103, *137*

Bay laurel: *chart* 103

Bean tree: *61*

Bear's-breech: 69

Bear's foot (*Aconitum*): 105

Beautyberry: *chart* 66, 67

Beech: 11, 77

Beefsteak geranium: 147

Begonia: 16, 18, 61, 65, 69, 71, 88, *110;* diseases of, *chart* 95; species, 34, 90, *chart* 97, *110;* x *tuberhybrida:* 62

Berberis: 27, 31-32, *chart* 99, *chart* 103, *110*

Bergenia: 40, 69, 87

Bethlehem sage: 34, *143*

Biennials: 18

Bindweed: 22

Birch: *charts* 80-81

Bird's-nest fern: 36

Birthwort: *108*

Bishop's hat: 21, 62, *chart* 103, *120*

Bishop's-weed: 40

Black alder: *chart* 103, 129

Black cohosh: 88

Black dragon: *chart* 103, 138

Black haw: 67

Black tupelo: 11, 30

Black vine weevils: 80, *chart* 81, *chart* 92

Black widow: 123

Bleeding heart: 8, *26,* 34, 36, 39, 60, 63, *64,* 70, *chart* 103, *118*

Bletilla: chart 97, *chart* 103, *111*

Bloodroot: 39

Bluebell: *chart* 103, *128*

Bluebells: *63, chart* 103, *136. See also* Virginia bluebells

Blue poppy: *50*

Bog gardens: 20, 30, *69*

Bog rosemary: 71

Borders: 18-19, *27,* 32, 36

Boston ivy: 14-15, *16,* 33, *140*

Botrytis blight: *chart* 94

Bottlebrush buckeye: 88

Bougainvillea: 15
Boulder fern: *117*
Box (boxwood): *18*, 26, *29*, *30*, 31, 32, 33, *chart* 103, *112*
Boxwood decline: 31
Briza: 19
Broad buckler fern: 119
Broombrush: 129
Browallia: 18, *chart* 97, *chart* 103, *111*
Brunnera: 21, 87, *chart* 97, *chart* 103, *111*
Buckhorn: *139*
Bugbane: 8, 34, 88
Bugle: *105*
Bugleweed: 8, 18, 21, 26, 41, 69, 89, *chart* 103, *105*
Bulbs: 8, 17, 21, 26, 61-62, 64, 67, 68, 70
Bunchberry: 23, 41
Bush honeysuckle: 32, *69*
Bush violet: 18, *chart* 103, *111*
Busy Lizzy: *chart* 103, *130*
Buxus: 33, *chart* 99, *chart* 103, *112*

C

Caladium: 8, *14*, 37, 79, *chart* 103, *112*
Calla lily: *44-45*
Callicarpa: *chart* 66
Calycanthus: *chart* 66, 70
Camellia: 20, 31, 33, *chart* 66, *67*, 69, *112*; care of, 67, 91; diseases of, *charts* 93-94; insect pests of, *chart* 92; species, *chart* 66, 67, *chart* 99, *112*
Campanula: *6-7, 55*
Camptosorus: 37
Canary ivy: 125
Candleberry: 137
Candytuft: *62*
Canker brake: 142
Cardinal flower: *52-53*, 63
Carex: 39, *chart* 103, *113*; species, *24-25*, *44-45*, *54*, *55*, *chart* 98, *113*
Carolina allspice: *chart* 66, 70
Cast-iron plant: 21
Cedrus (cedar): *24-25*, *56*
Celandine poppy: *20-21*
Centipede grass: 19, *chart* 40
Centranthus: *50-51, 57*
Cercis: 8, 28, *56*, *chart* 66, *charts* 99-100, *chart* 103, *113*
Chain fern: 21, *chart* 103, *151*
Chamaecyparis: *57*, *62*, *chart* 103

Chasmanthium: *39*
Checkerberry: *chart* 103, 122
Chelone: 88
Cherry: 14, 16, 20, *chart* 66, *chart* 103, *143*
Cherry laurel: 20, 29, *chart* 103, *143*
Chestnut vine: 33
Chimonanthus: 63
Chinese holly (*Osmanthus*): 139
Chinese orchid: *chart* 103, *111*
Chionanthus: 60, 63, *chart* 66
Chocolate vine: *chart* 103, *106*
Choisya: 55
Chokeberry: 26, 67
Christmas berry: *chart* 103, *107*
Christmas fern: 21, 37, *chart* 103, 142
Christmas rose: 89, *chart* 103, *125*
Chrysanthemum: *6-7*, 65
Chrysogonum: 21, 88, *chart* 98, *chart* 103, *113*
Cimicifuga: 8, 34, 87, 88
Cinnamon fern: 36, *37*, *chart* 103, *139*
Cladrastis: 11, 30
Claytonia: 36
Clematis: 12, 65, *chart* 66, 70, 77, 82, *chart* 101, *chart* 103, *114*; species, 8, 15, *114*
Cleome: 8
Clethra: *chart* 66, 70
Clintonia: 39
Colchis ivy: 125
Coleus: 37-38, *38-39*
Columbine: *6-7*, 18, 21, *22*, 23, 34, 39, *46-47*, *50-51*, 70, *83*, 90, *chart* 103, *107*
Common names: *chart* 103
Container gardens: 16-17, *68-69*, 71, *charts* 80-81, 90
Convallaria: 69, *charts* 96-97, *chart* 103, *114*
Convolvulus: 22
Cooperative Extension Service: 81, 82
Coral bells: *chart* 103, *126*
Coralberry: *chart* 103, *107*
Cornel: *115*
Cornelian cherry: 29, *chart* 66, *chart* 103, 115
Corn lily: 39
Cornus: 8, 60, *chart* 66, *chart* 103, *115*; *florida*, 29, 57, *chart* 100, *115*; *mas*, 29, *chart* 66, *chart* 103, 115; *nuttallii*, 29, *chart* 100, 115; x *rutgersensis*, *chart* 99, 115;

species, 23, 32, 83-84, *115*
Corsican mint: 87
Corsican pearlwort: 87
Corydalis: 8, 71, *chart* 103, *115*; *lutea*, 34, 64, 88, *chart* 96, *chart* 103, 115; species, *54*, *81*, *chart* 97, *115*
Corylopsis: 8, *chart* 66, *chart* 99, *chart* 103, *116*
Cotinus: 56
Cotoneaster: *chart* 66
Cowslip: *chart* 103, *143*
Crab apple: 16
Cranesbill: *chart* 103, *123*
Creeping fig: 33
Creeping Jenny: 87
Crested fern: 119
Crocus: 21
Cucumber tree: 30
Cup fern: *117*
Cyclamen: 86, *chart* 95, *charts* 97-98, *chart* 103, *116*
Cymbalaria: 56
Cyrtomium: *chart* 98, *chart* 103, *116*
Cystopteris: 37

D

Daffodil: 21, 35, *46-47*, 69, *chart* 103, *137*, 137-138, *138*
Danae: *chart* 99, *chart* 103, *117*
Daphne: 21, 33, *44*, *54*, *chart* 66, 67, *chart* 99, *117*
Darmera: 28
Daylily: 18, 21, 26, 27, 70, 71, 78, 88, 89, *chart* 103, *126*
Deadheading: *83*, 84
Dead nettle: 8, 21, 41, *chart* 103, *132*
Deer: 80
Delphinium: *6-7*
Dennstaedtia: 21, 35-36, *chart* 98, *chart* 103, *117*
Deodar cedar: *50*
Deschampsia: 39
Design: 8, 17, 63; for city gardens, *14*, *15*, 15-17, *16*, *17*, 70-71; of herbaceous borders, 18-19, *27*, 32, 36; of woodland gardens, *20-21*, 20-23, *22*, *23*; *See also* Foliage; Garden rooms; Plant selection
Design zones: 14, 17; inner zone, *14*, 14-17, *15*, *16*, *17*; middle zone, 14, 17, *18*, 18-19, *19*; outer zone, 14, 17, *20-21*, 20-23, *22*, *23*
Devilwood: 14, *chart* 66, *chart* 103, *139*

Dianthus: 56
Dicentra: 8, 18, 21, 70, 71, 87, *chart* 103, *118*; species, *26*, 36, 88, *chart* 96, 118; *spectabilis*, *54*, *57*, 64, *72-73*, 89, *chart* 96, *chart* 98, *118*
Dichondra: 40
Diervilla: 32
Digitalis: 87, *chart* 103, *118*; x *mertonensis*, 87, *chart* 97, *118*; species, *6-7*, *50-51*, 55, 57, 87, *chart* 96, *118*
Diphylleia: *chart* 103, *119*
Diseases: 31, 41, 79, 80, *charts* 80-81, 82, 83, 86, *charts* 93-95
Disporum: 54
Dog-hobble: *133*
Dogtooth violet: 61, 62
Dogwood: 8, 14, *15*, 17, *18*, 20, 28, 29, 32, 60, *63*, 64, *chart* 66, 68, 71, 83-84, *chart* 103, *115*
Doronicum: 89
Dragonroot: 62, *chart* 103, 107
Drainage: 68, 75, 77, 80
Drooping laurel: 32, *chart* 103
Dryopteris: 21, 36, *54*, *chart* 98, *chart* 103, *119*
Dudder grass: 105
Dutchman's-breeches: 36, 39, *chart* 103, *118*
Dutchman's-pipe: 60, *chart* 103, *108*

E

Elaeagnus: 8
Elephant's-ear: *chart* 103, *112*
Elkwood: 135
Elm: 11
Endymion: *128. See also Hyacinthoides*
English ivy: *50-51*, *125*
English laurel: *chart* 103, 143
Enkianthus: 70, *chart* 99, *119*
Environmental distress: 64, 81, 86, *chart* 92
Epimedium: 21, 27, 41, 62, 70, 71, *chart* 80, 90, *chart* 103, *120*; hybrids, *54*, 62, 89, *chart* 98, *120*; species, 62, 69, 89, 120
Eranthis: 67, *chart* 96, *chart* 103, *120*
Eremochloa: 19, *chart* 40
Espaliers: 29-30, *71*, 76
Eucalyptus: 19, 30
Eulalia: 39
Euonymus: 8, *chart* 103, *120*;

fortunei, 21, 33, 41, *chart* 99, *chart* 101, *chart* 103, *120*
Euphorbia: 21, *55, 56, chart* 103, *121*
Evening trumpet flower: *122*

F

Fagus: 11
False cypress: *62, chart* 103
False dragonhead: 88
False holly: *chart* 103, 139
False miterwort: 41, *chart* 103, *149*
False Solomon's-seal: 27, *chart* 103, *148*
False spikenard: *chart* 103, *148*
False spirea: *chart* 103, 109
Fancy fern: 36
Farfugium. 133. *See also Ligularia tussilaginea*
x *Fatshedera: lizei,* 60, 67, *chart* 101, 121
Fatsia: 67, 69, *chart* 99, *chart* 103, *121*
Ferns: 8, *15,* 17, 18, 21, 23, *24-25,* 26, 27, *35-37, 36-37,* 39, *52-53, chart* 80, 87, 88, 89, 90, *chart* 95; *See also Adiantum; Asplenium; Athyrium; Cyrtomium; Cystopteris; Dennstaedtia; Dryopteris; Gymnocarpium; Lygodium; Matteuccia; Osmunda; Polypodium; Polystichum; Polytrichum; Selaginella; Thelypteris; Thuidium; Woodwardia*
Fertilizing: 19, 32, 69, 78, 79-80, *charts* 80-81
Festuca (fescue): 19, *chart* 40
Fetterbush *(Leucothoe): chart* 103, *133*
Fetterbush *(Pieris): chart* 103, 140
Ficus: 33
Fiddleheads: *chart* 103, *139*
Filipendula: 55
Fire blight: *chart* 81
Fittonia: 21
Five-finger ferns: *36-37*
Five-leaved ivy: 140
Flower arranging: 87, 89
Flowering fern: *139*
Foamflower: 21, 39, 40, *44, chart* 103, *149*
Foliage: 8, 18, 87; color of and design, 17, 27; designing with perennial, 27, *34-35,* 34-39, *36-37, 38-39;* evergreen, 14,

16, 21, 23, 26, 28, 31, 32, 33; perennials with colorful, 8, 18, 21, 34, 35, 36, 37-38; shrubs with colorful, 8, 26, 27, 31, 32, 33; texturally interesting, 8, 18, 27, 33, 34, 35, 36, 37, 38; trees with colorful, 8, 28-29
Forget-me-not: 18, 21, *62,* 69, 70
Formosa rice tree: *121*
Forsythia: 83
Fothergilla: chart 66, 70, *chart* 99, *chart* 103, *121*
Foundation plantings: 32-33
Fountain grass: 19
Foxglove: *6-7,* 18, *44-45, 50-51,* 87, *chart* 103, *118*
Fox grape: 22
Fragile fern: 37
Fragrance: 33, 63, 86, 87
Fragrant ivy: 125
Friar's-cap: 105
Fringe tree: 63
Fuchsia: 16, 17, *56,* 61, *chart* 66, 69
Fumewort: *chart* 103, *115*
Fungal diseases: 41, 80, *charts* 93-95
Funkia: *chart* 103, 127

G

Galanthus: 8, 67, *chart* 96, *chart* 103, *122*
Galium: 39, 74
Garden rooms: *12-13;* inner zone, *14,* 14-17, *15, 16, 17;* middle zone, 14, 17, *18,* 18-19, *19;* outer zone, 14, 17, *20-21,* 20-23, *22, 23;* in woodlands, *20-21,* 20-23, *22, 23*
Gaultheria: 23, 70, *chart* 103, *122; procumbens,* 41, 67, *chart* 101, 122; *shallon,* 21, 60, 67, *chart* 99, *122*
Gelsemium: 15, 60, 65, *chart* 66, *chart* 101, *chart* 103, *122*
Gentiana: 57
Geranium: 54, *chart* 97, *chart* 103, *123;* hybrids, *54, chart* 97, 123; species, 21, *54, 56, 58-59, chart* 103, *123*
Geranium *(Pelargonium): 38-39*
Giant butterbur: *34-35*
Giant rhubarb: 8
Globeflower: *50*
Goatsbeard: 34
Golden-ray: *chart* 103, *133*
Goldenstar: 21, *chart* 103, *113*

Grass: ornamental, 18-19, *39;* turf, 19, *chart* 40, 41
Gray mold: *chart* 94
Green and gold: *chart* 103, *113*
Ground covers: 8, 13, 21, 26, 27, *chart* 40, 40-41, 87, 89; ferns as, 35-36; hostas as, 35; moss as, *41;* shade-blooming, 62, 65, 69, 70; turf grasses as, 19, *chart* 40, 41; weeds and, 40, 87; in woodland gardens, 21, 23, 37
Grubs: *chart* 92
Gunnera: 8
Gymnocarpium: 36

H

Haircap moss: *52-53*
Hakonechloa: 39, 41, *chart* 98, *123*
Halesia: 20, 28, 29, *chart* 66, *chart* 100, *chart* 103, *124*
Hamamelis: 8, 63, *chart* 66, *chart* 103, *124;* x *intermedia,* 87, 124; species, 26, 29, *30,* 67, 87, *chart* 99, *124*
Hardy geranium: *8-9*
Hardy orchid: *chart* 103, *111*
Hart's-tongue fern: *36-37*
Hawthorn: 20
Hay-scented fern: 21, 35-36, *chart* 103, *117*
Heavenly bamboo: *chart* 66, 67, *chart* 103, *137*
Hedera: 8, 41, 57, *chart* 101, *chart* 103, *125*
Hedge fern: *chart* 103, 142
Hedge plant: *133*
Hedges: *30,* 31-32
Helleborus (hellebore): *8-9,* 19, 21, 70, 87, *125;* species, 19, 89, *chart* 98, *chart* 103, *125*
Helmet flower: *chart* 103
Hemerocallis: 21, 55, 70, 86, *charts* 96-97, *chart* 103, *126*
Hemlock: *20-21,* 23, 29, *chart* 92, *chart* 103, *150*
Heuchera: 26, *36-37,* 54, 62, 70, 87, *chart* 103, *126;* species, 34, 38, *54, charts* 96-97, *126*
Hexastylis: 108
Holly: 8, 14, 16, 21, 23, 26, 28, 29, 31, 32, 33, 67, 69, 71, *chart* 103, *129*
Holly barberry: 135
Holly fern: 26, *chart* 103, 142
Holly grape: *135*
Honeysuckle *(Lonicera):* 32, 60, *chart* 66, 88

Horse chestnut: 14, 30
Hosta: 8-9, *11, 15,* 18, 21, 23, *26, 27, 31, 32,* 34-35, *35,* 38, *39,* 40, *54,* 57, *64-65,* 69, 70, *71, 78,* 86, 87, 88, 89, 90, *chart* 97, *chart* 103, *127;* diseases of, *chart* 95; *fortunei,* 34, 35, *35,* 127; insect pests of, *chart* 93; *plantaginea,* 86, 87, 127; *sieboldiana,* 17, *24-25,* 35, *35, 127;* species, *54,* 70, *72-73,* 127; x *tardiana, 35; undulata,* 24-25, 35, 127; *venusta, chart* 97, 127
Hummingbirds: 63, 88
Hyacinthoides: 62, chart 97, *chart* 103, *128*
Hyacinth orchid: *111*
Hydrangea: 8, 60, *64-65, chart* 66, 68, 71, *128; anomala, 16,* 33, 60, 70, *chart* 101, 128; climbing, *14,* 14-15, 33, 60, 70, 128; *quercifolia,* 32, *54,* 68, *chart* 99, *128;* species, *54, 56, chart* 99, 128
Hypericum: 65, *chart* 99, *chart* 101, *chart* 103, *129*

I

Ilex: 8, 29, *chart* 103, *129;* species, 31, 67, *charts* 100-101, *chart* 101, *chart* 103, *129*
Illicium: 29, *chart* 99, *chart* 101, *chart* 103, *130*
Impatiens: 6-7, 17, 18, 61, 65, *68-69,* 70, 71, 88, *chart* 103, *130*
Indian pink: 61
Indian turnip: *chart* 103, 107
Inkberry: *chart* 103, 129
Insects: 8, 31, 79, 80, *charts* 80-81, 82, 86, 90, *charts* 92-93
Interrupted fern: *chart* 103, 139
Ipomoea: 86
Iris: 52-53, 56, 57, *64-65,* 69, 70, *chart* 95
Ivy: 8, *33,* 35, 40, 41, 76, *chart* 103, *125*

J

Jack-in-the-pulpit: 61, *chart* 103, *107*
Japanese climbing fern: 88
Japanese creeper: *140*
Japanese holly fern: *chart* 103, *116*
Japanese laurel: *chart* 103, *110*

Japanese rose: *chart* 66, 71, *chart* 103, *131*
Jasmine *(Gelsemium):* 12, *chart* 66, 67, *chart* 103, *122*
Jasmine *(Jasminum):* 12, 65, *chart* 66, *chart* 103, *130*
Jasmine *(Trachelospermum): chart* 66
Jasminum: 65, *chart* 66, *chart* 99, *chart* 101, *chart* 103, *130*
Jerusalem cowslip: 143
Jerusalem sage: *44-45, chart* 103, 143
Jessamine *(Gelsemium):* 15, *chart* 103, *122*
Jessamine *(Jasminum): chart* 103, *130*
Jewelweed: *chart* 103, *130*
Joseph and Mary: 143
Judas tree: *chart* 103, *113*
Jupiter's-beard: *50-51*

K

Kalmia: 60, *chart* 66, 70, *chart* 99, *chart* 100, *chart* 103, *131*
Kentucky bluegrass: *chart* 40
Kerria: chart 66, 71, *chart* 100, *chart* 103, *131*
Kirengeshoma: 24-25, chart 96, *chart* 103, *131*
Kuma zasa: *147*

L

Laburnum: 61
Lacewings: *charts* 92-93
Lacing: *85*
Ladybugs: *charts* 92-93
Lady fern: 21, 35, *36*, 40, *chart* 103, *109*
Lady's-eardrops: *chart* 66
Lady's-mantle: 34, 40, 87
Lakela: 149
Lamiastrum: 132
Lamium: 8, 21, 41, *72-73, chart* 98, *chart* 103, *132*
Lath houses: 15
Laurel: 71
Laurus (laurel): 33, 65, *chart* 100, *chart* 103, *132*
Leaf miner: 31, 90
Leaf spot: 41
Leather flower: *chart* 103, *114*
Lenten rose: *chart* 103, *125*
Leopard plant: 8, 70
Leopard's-bane: 89
Leucojum: 67, *chart* 96, *chart* 103, *132*
Leucothoe: 32, *chart* 100, *chart*

103, *133*
Licorice fern: 36
Ligularia: 8-9, 69, 70, 87, 88, *chart* 96, *chart* 103, *133*; *tussilaginea, chart* 96, 133
Ligustrum: 14, 21, 32, 71, *chart* 100, *chart* 103, *133*
Lilium (lily): 21, 56, 63, 88, *chart* 95
Lily-of-the-field: *chart* 103, *106*
Lily-of-the-valley: 69, *chart* 103, *114*
Lily-of-the-valley bush: *81, chart* 103, *140*
Lilyturf *(Liriope):* 27, 39, 41, *chart* 103, *134*
Lilyturf *(Ophiopogon): chart* 103, *138*
Limbing up: 12, *83, 84*, 85
Lindera: 33
Linnaea: 36
Liriodendron: 14, 70, *chart* 101, *chart* 103, *134*
Liriope: 15, 27, 39, 40, 41, *chart* 98, *chart* 103, *134*, 138
Lobelia: 52-53, 57, 63, 70, 87, *charts* 97-98, *134*
Lobularia: 87
Loddon lily: *132*
Lolium: chart 40
London-pride: *147*
Lonicera: 32, *56*, 60, *chart* 66, 88
Lunaria: 21
Lungwort *(Mertensia):* 41, *chart* 103, *136*
Lungwort *(Pulmonaria):* 8, *38*, 70, *chart* 103, *143*
Lygodium: 88
Lysimachia: 87

M

Madeira ivy: 125
Magnolia: 14, 16, 20, *44*, 60, 65, *chart* 66, 68, 70, *chart* 101, *chart* 103, *135*; x *loebneri, chart* 101, 135; species, 29, 30, *54, 55, 56, chart* 100, *chart* 103, *135*
Mahonia: 8, 21, *31*, 60, 69, *chart* 103, *135*; species, 65, *chart* 66, *charts* 100-101, *chart* 103, *135*
Maiden grass: *8-9*
Maidenhair fern: 21, 23, *27*, *36-37, chart* 103, *105*
Maidenhair spleenwort: 37
Maintenance: timetable for, *charts* 80-81. *See also*

Diseases; Fertilizing; Insects; Mulching; Pruning; Watering; Weeds
Malus: 16, *chart* 66
Mandrake: *chart* 103, *141*
Maple: 11, 14, *15*, 17, *18*, 28, 29, 30, *41, 68-69*, 77, *charts* 80-81, 87, *chart* 103, *104*
Marlberry: 65, *chart* 103, 107
Mat spike moss: 37
Matteuccia: 32, 36, *54*, 88, *chart* 98, *chart* 103, *136*
May apple: 23, 39, *chart* 103, *141*
Mazus: 13, 26, 40, 41, 87, *chart* 98, *136*
Meadow rue: 21, 69, 88
Meconopsis: 50, *56*
Mentha: 87
Mertensia: 23, 27, *44, 54,* 87, 89, *chart* 98, *chart* 103, *136*
Mezereum: 117
Mildew: 41, 80, *chart* 94, *chart* 95
Mimulus: 28
Miracle plant: 60
Miscanthus: 39, 79
Mitchella: 23
Mites: *31, chart* 93
Mock orange: *141*
Moisture: 10, 22, 79. *See also* Drainage; Watering
Mold: 41
Mondo grass: *chart* 103, *138*
Money plant: 21
Monkey flower: *28*
Monkshood: *chart* 103
Moonflower: 86
Moss: *13*, 41, *52-53*, 78
Moss fern: *52-53*
Mountain camellia: 65, *chart* 103, 148
Mountain grape: *chart* 103, 135
Mountain laurel: 32, *38*, 60, *charts* 92-93, *chart* 103, *131*
Mountain tea: *122*
Mulching: 13, 23, 32, 70, 79, *charts* 80-81, 81
Myosotis: 69
Myrica: 21, 32, 70, *chart* 100, *chart* 103, *137*

N

Nandina: chart 66, *chart* 100, *chart* 103, *137*
Narcissus: 55, *72-73*, 87, *chart* 96, *chart* 103, *137*, 137-138, *138*

Nematodes: *chart* 92, *chart* 95
New York fern: 35
Nicotiana: 18, 21, 69, 86, 87, *chart* 98, *chart* 103, *138*
Ninebark: *44-45*
Northern sea oats: 39
Nursery beds: 90
Nyssa: 11, 30

O

Oak: 11, *13*, 14, 30, 77, *chart* 103, *144*
Oak fern: 36
Old-man's-beard: 60, *chart* 66
Olea: 11, 30, *chart* 103
Oleaster: 8
Olive *(Olea):* 11, 30, *chart* 103
Olive *(Osmanthus):* 67, 71, *chart* 103, *139*
Ophiopogon: chart 98, *chart* 103, *138*
Opossumwood: 124
Orchid pansy: 61
Oregon grape: 8, 21, *31*, 60
Oregon myrtle: *83*
Origanum: 55
Ornamental grasses: 18-19, *39*
Ornamental onion: *8-9*
Ornamental rhubarb: 21
Ornithogalum: 62
Osmanthus: 14, *chart* 66, 67, 71, *charts* 100-101, *chart* 103, *139*
Osmunda: 36, *37, chart* 98, *chart* 103, *139*
Ostrich fern: *32,* 36, *41, 44, chart* 103, *136*

P

Pachysandra: 26, 41, 65, *chart* 101, *chart* 103, *139*
Paeonia: 56
Painted lady fern: 18, *36-37*
Paper plant: 67, *chart* 103, *121*
Parthenocissus: 14-15, *16*, 33, *chart* 103, *140*
Partridgeberry: 23
Paspalum: 19, *chart* 40
Paths: *22, 27, 30*
Paulownia: 30
Peach: *chart* 66
Pelargonium: 38-39
Pennisetum: 19
Peony: *48-49*
Perennials: 8, 16, 17, 21, 23, 26, 27, *charts* 80-81, 84, 86, 87, 88, 89; foliage of in design, 27, *34-35,* 34-39, *36-37, 38-39*;

as ground covers, 35-36, 41; shade-flowering, 8, 18, 21, 39, 61-62, 63, 64-65, 67, 69, 70, 71; shade-fruiting, 67; for woodland gardens, 21, 23, 36-37, 38-39

Perennial spirea: *chart* 103, *109*

Periwinkle: 8, 13, 40, *41*, 62, 69, *chart* 103, *151*

Persian ivy: 125

Persian violet: *chart* 103, *116*

Petal blights: *chart* 94

Petasites: 34-35

pH: 33, 60, 74, 75, 78, 79, 80

Phlomis: 44-45, 55, chart 103

Phlox: 36, *chart* 97, *chart* 103, *140; divaricata,* 40, *46-47, 55, 56, 58-59,* 65, *chart* 97, *140; stolonifera,* 40, 41, *52-53,* 57, *chart* 97, 140; *subulata, 55*

Photinia: 32

Physocarpus: 44-45, 55

Physostegia: 88

Picea: 24-25

Pieris: 16, 26, 32, *chart* 66, 69, *81, chart* 100, *chart* 103, *140*

Piggyback plant: 40

Pinus (pine): 11, 14, *31, chart* 101, *141*

Pipe vine: *108*

Pittosporum: 14, 21, *chart* 100, *chart* 103, *141*

Plantain lily: 8, 21, 34, 70, *chart* 103, *127*

Planting: 32, 78; among tree roots, 75; timetable for, *charts* 80-81

Plant selection: 86-89; for evening interest, 86, 87; for evergreen foliage, 14, 16, 21, 23, 26, 28, 31, 32, 33; for fall bloom, 65, *chart* 66, 67; for flower arranging, 87, 89; for fragrance, 33, 63, 86, 87; of healthy trees, 29; for problem sites, 21, 34, 35, 37, 40, *68,* 68-71; for site environment, 68, 74, 81; for soil pH, 74; for spring bloom, 21, 39, 60, 61, 63, 64-65, *chart* 66; for summer bloom, 21, 39, 60, 61, 65, *chart* 66; for winter bloom, *chart* 66, 67. *See also* Annuals; Foliage; Perennials; Shade-flowering plants; Shrubs; Trees; Vines

Plum: *chart* 66, 143

Poa: chart 40

Podophyllum: 23, 39, *chart* 96, *chart* 103, *141*

Poison ivy: 22, 91

Polemonium: 56

Polygonatum: 24-25, 27, 87, *chart* 96, *chart* 103, *142*

Polypodium: 36, 37

Polystichum: chart 103, *142;* species, 21, *24-25,* 26, *36-37,* 57, *chart* 98, *142*

Polytrichum: 52-53, 57

Populus (poplar): *50,* 55

Primula (primrose): 8, 18, *22,* 23, 36, *44, 46-47, 50, 56,* 70, *chart* 103, *142,* 142-143, *143;* diseases of, *chart* 95; species, *22,* 23, *44, 50, 54, 55, 56, 83, charts* 96-97, *142, 143*

Privacy screens: 31, 32

Privet: 14, 21, 32, 71, *chart* 103, *133*

Problem sites: 21, 34, 35, 37, 40, *68,* 68-71

Pruning: 8, 12, 16, *82,* 82-85, *83, 84, 85,* 91; for disease control, *charts* 94-95; for insect control, 90, *charts* 92-93, *chart* 93; for shrub renewal, 82-84; for special effects, 28, 29-30, 31, *71, 76;* timing of, *charts* 80-81, 82; of tree roots, 11, 75, 78; of trees, 12, 14, 16, 20, 22, 75, 78, *82, 83, 84,* 84-85, *85*

Prunus: chart 66, *chart* 103, *143;* species, 20, 29, *charts* 100-101, *chart* 103, *143*

Pulmonaria: 8, 18, 34, 70, *charts* 97-98, *chart* 103, *143*

Pyracantha: 55

Q

Quaking grass: 19

Quercus: 11, *chart* 101, *chart* 103, *144*

R

Rabbits: 80

Rabbit's-foot fern: 36

Raccoon berry: *141*

Ragwort: *chart* 103, 133

Raised beds: *72-73,* 77

Redbud: 8, 14, 20, 28, *chart* 66, *chart* 103, *113*

Red spider: 86

Redwood: *44-45, 83*

Rhamnus: 32

Rheum: 21

Rhododendron: 8, 16, 20, 26, 31, 32, 60, 62, 67, 69, 71, 91, *charts* 92-94

Rhododendron: 55, 56, 58-59, 83, chart 100, *145,* 145-146, *146;* species, *19, 20, 56, 61, 83,* 145, 146

Rhododendron (azalea): *chart* 66, *chart* 103, *144,* 144-145, *145;* species, *20,* 70, 87, 88, *chart* 100, *144,* 145

Rhus: 22

River birch: 78

Roanoke-bells: *chart* 103, *136*

Rockfoil: *chart* 103, *147*

Rock gardens: 23, 34, 37

Rock geranium: 34, *chart* 103, 126

Rock polypody: 37

Rodgersia: 8, *chart* 97, *146*

Rohdea: 24-25

Root pruning: 75, 78, *82*

Rose: *8-9,* 12, *charts* 80-81

Royal fern: 36, *chart* 103, 139

Rust: 41, *chart* 95

Ruta: 54

Ryegrass: *chart* 40

S

Sacred bamboo: *137*

Sagina: 87

Salal: 21, 60, *122*

Sanguinaria: 39, *54*

Sapphire flower: *111*

Sarcococca: chart 66, 67, 70, *chart* 100, *chart* 103, *147*

Sasa: 32, *chart* 101, *chart* 103, *147*

Saxifraga (saxifrage): 18, 23, 41, 69, 70, *chart* 103, *147;* species, *24-25, 56, chart* 96, *147*

Scilla: 8, 70; *campanulata, 128. See also Hyacinthoides*

Scutellaria: 57

Sedge: *24-25,* 39, *44-45, chart* 103, *113*

Sedum: 56

Selaginella: 37

Serviceberry: 20, 26, 28-29, *chart* 66

Sevenbark: 128

Shade: altering, 11, 12-13; analyzing, 9-11, *10-11;* benefits of, 8; characteristics of plants for, 62-63; gardens in dappled, 10, *46-47, 48-49, 55, 56;* gardens in full, 10, *50-51, 52-53, 56,* 57; gardens in partial, 10, *42-43, 44-45, 54, 55;* prob-

lems with, 10, 68-71; structures and, 10, 11, 12, 15

Shade-flowering plants: annuals, 8, 16, 17, 18, 21, 61, 65, 70, 71, 86, 87; biennials, 18; bulbs, 8, 17, 21, 26, 61-62, 64, 67, 68, 70; for fall flowers, 65, *chart* 66, 67; ground covers, 62, 65, 69, 70; perennials, 8, 18, 21, 61-62, 63, 69, 70, 71; shrubs, 8, 12, 20, 31, 32, 33, 60, 63, 65, *chart* 66, 67, 68, 69, 70, 71; for spring flowers, 21, 39, 64-65, *chart* 66; for summer flowers, 21, 39, 65, *chart* 66; trees, 8, 16, 20, 28-29, 60, 63, 64, 65, *chart* 66, 67, 68, 70; vines, 8, 12, 60, 65, *chart* 66, 67, 70; for winter flowers, *chart* 66, 67

Shade-fruiting plants: 60, 67

Shade-making plants: 11, 14-15, 20, 28, 30

Shallon: *122*

Shearing: *charts* 80-81, 84

Sheepberry: 32

Shield fern: 21, 26, 37, *chart* 103, *119,* 142

Shortia: 23

Shrubs: 8, 12-13, 14, 21, 23, 26, 27, 31-33, 87, 88; with colorful foliage, 26, 27, 31, 32, 33; for containers, 16, 17; designing with, 31-33; espaliered, 76; evergreen, 14, 16, 21, 23, 26, 31, 32, 33; maintenance timetable for, *charts* 80-81; pruning of, *82,* 82-84; shade-flowering, 8, 12, 20, 31, 32, 33, 60, 63, 65, *chart* 66, 67, 68, 69, 70, 71; shade-fruiting, 67; for special purposes, 31-33; for woodland gardens, 20, 21, 23

Shuttlecock fern: *136*

Siberian bugloss: 21, *chart* 103, *111*

Siberian tea: 40

Sierra laurel: 133

Silver bell: 20, 28, 29, *chart* 66, *chart* 103, *124*

Silver-vein creeper: 140

Skimmia: chart 66, 69, 70, *chart* 100, *148*

Slugs: 80, *chart* 80, *chart* 93

Smilacina: 27, *chart* 96, *chart* 103, *148*

Snails: 80, *chart* 80, *chart* 93

Snakeroot: *chart* 103, 108

Snowbell: 29, 65, *chart* 103, *149*

Snowdrop: 8, 67, *chart* 103, *122*

Snowdrop tree: *chart* 103, *124*, 149

Snowflake: 67, *chart* 103, *132*

Soil: 22, 68, 80, *charts* 92-93; amendments and, 70, 71, 75, 79; pH of, 33, 60, 74, 75, 78, 79, 80; preparing, 19, 74-75

Soleirolia: 8, 40-41

Solomon's-seal: *17*, 21, *27*, 39, 61, *chart* 103, *142*

Solomon's zigzag: *148*

Spiceberry: *107*

Spicebush: 33

Spider plant: 8

Spigelia: 61

Spindle tree: 8, *chart* 103, 120

Spotted dog: 143

Spotted laurel: 21, *chart* 103, *110*

Spring beauty: 36

Spruce: *12-13, 17, 24-25, 39*, 74

Spurge *(Euphorbia):* 21, *chart* 103, *121*

Spurge *(Pachysandra): chart* 103, *139*

Squill: 8, 21

Star-of-Bethlehem: 62

St. Augustine grass: *chart* 40

St.-John's-wort: 65, *chart* 103, *129*

Stenotaphrum: chart 40

Stewartia: 28, 29, 60, 65, *charts* 100-101, *chart* 103, *148*

Stokes' aster: 88

Stokesia: 88

Storax: *chart* 103, *149*

Strawberry geranium: 147

Styrax: 29, 65, *chart* 101, *chart* 103, *149*

Sumac: 20

Sunburn: 81

Sunscald: 64, 86

Swamp fern: 119

Swamp laurel: *chart* 103, 135

Sweet alyssum: 87

Sweet bay: *chart* 103, *132*

Sweet box: *chart* 66, 67, *chart* 103, *147*

Sweet pepperbush: *chart* 66, 70

Sweet woodruff: *38*, 39, *74*

Sword fern: *36-37*

Sycamore: 30, 77

T

Tanacetum: 6-7

Tassel fern: 142

Taxodium: 11, 30

Taxus: 21, *24-25, 29, charts* 100-101, *chart* 103, *149*

Teaberry: 122

Terraces: 16, *23*

Tetrastigma: 33

Thalictrum: 6-7, 21, 69, 88

Thelypteris: 35

Thinning: 14, 78, 84, *85. See also* Pruning

Thrips: 86

Thuidium: 52-53, 57

Thuja: 32

Thunbergia: 69

Tiarella: 21, 41, *chart* 103, *149; cordifolia,* 39, *44, 54*, 57, *58-59, chart* 97, *149; wherryi, chart* 96, 149

Toad lily: *chart* 103, *150*

Toadshade: *20*

Tobacco: 69, *chart* 103, *138*

Tolmiea: 40

Trachelospermum: chart 66

Tradescantia: 70

Treacleberry: *148*

Trees: 12, 14, 16, 20, 23, 28-30; with colorful foliage, 8, 28-29; for containers, 16; designing with, 28-30; evergreen, 14, 21, 23, 28; maintenance timetable for, *charts* 80-81; planting under, 10, *75*, 77-78; pruning of, 12, 14, 16, 20, 22, 75, 78, *82, 83, 84*, 84-85; removal of, 14, 20, 22, 85; root feeding of, 79-80; root pruning of, 11, 75, 78; selecting healthy, 29; shade-flowering, 8, 16, 20, 28-30, 60, 63, 64, 65, *chart* 66, 67, 68, 70; shade-fruiting, 67; as shade makers, 11, 12, 14, 20, 28, 30; on small lots, 16, 17; sunscald of, 64, 86; thinning, 14, 78, 84, *85*; troublesome, 11, 30

Trellis: *76*

Tricyrtis: chart 98, *chart* 103, *150*

Trillium: 20, 27, 36, 39, *60*

Trollius: 50, 56

Troubleshooting: animal pests, 80, 86; diseases, 31, 41, 80, 82, 86, *charts* 93-95; environmental distress, 81, 86, *chart* 92; insect pests, 8, 31, 80, 82, 86, 90, *charts* 92-93

Trout lily: 68

Tsuga: 29, *54*, *chart* 101, *chart*

103, 150, *150*

Tufted hair grass: 39

Tulip: 21, *62*, 64, *65*

Tulip magnolia: *134*

Tulip poplar: *70, 134*

Tulip tree: 14, *chart* 103, *134*

Turf grass: 19, *chart* 40, 41

Turk's-cap: 105

Turtlehead: 88

Twinflower: 36

U

Ulmus: 11

Umbellularia: 83

Umbrella leaf: *chart* 103, *119*

Umbrella plant: *28*

Umbrella tree: 29, 30, *chart* 103, 135

United States: USDA hardiness zones, *map* 102

V

Veronica: 55, 56

Viburnum: 29, 32, *62, chart* 66, 70, *chart* 103, *150*; insect pests of, *chart* 92; species, 32, 67, 87, *chart* 100, *150*

Vinca: 8, 41, 62, 70, *chart* 103, *151*; species, 65, *72-73*, 89, *chart* 101, *151*

Vines: 14-15, 28, 33, 86, 87, 88; maintenance of, *chart* 80, 84; shade-flowering, 8, 12, 60, 65, *chart* 66, 67, 70; as shade makers, 14-15; training, 76

Viola (violet): *6-7, 17*, 18, 23, 39, 67, 69, *151*; species, *6-7*, 67, *chart* 97, *chart* 98, *151*; x *wittrockiana, 24-25*

Virginia bluebells: 23, 27, 38-39, *44*, 64, *136*

Virginia cowslip: *136*

Virginia creeper: 14-15, 33, *chart* 103, 140

Virgin's-bower: *chart* 66, *chart* 103, *114*

Vitis: 22

Voles: 80, 86

W

Wake-robin: 27

Walking fern: 37

Walnut: 19

Watering: 8, 19, 32, 69, 70, 80, *charts* 80-81, *charts* 93-95

Wavy-leaf shade lily: 127

Wax myrtle: 21, 70, *chart* 103

Weeds: 22, 40, 79, 82, 87

Weigela: 54

Western sword fern: *142*

White flies: 86

Whitewood: *134*

Wildflowers: 63

Wild geranium: 21

Wild ginger: 13, 23, *38*, 39, 41, *chart* 103, *108*

Wild sweet William: 40, *65*, *chart* 103, *140*

Windbreaks: 31, 32

Windflower: *chart* 103, *106*

Winter aconite: 67, *chart* 103, *120*

Winterberry: 67, 70, *chart* 103, 129

Winter creeper: 21, 33, 41, *chart* 103, *120*

Wintergreen: 41, 67, *chart* 103, 122

Winter hazel: 8, *chart* 66, *chart* 103, *116*

Wintersweet: 63

Wisteria: 15

Witch alder: *chart* 103, 121

Witch hazel: 8, 20, 23, 26, 29, *30*, 32, 63, *chart* 66, 67, 71, *chart* 103, *124*

Wolfsbane: *chart* 103

Woodbine: *chart* 66, *chart* 103, *140*

Wood fern: *chart* 103, *119*

Woodland gardens: 27, 36-37, 38-39; design of, *20-23*

Woodwardia: 21, *chart* 98, *chart* 103, *151*

Y

Yellow archangel: *chart* 103, 132

Yellow bleeding heart: *chart* 103, 115

Yellow poplar: *chart* 103, *134*

Yellow waxbells: *chart* 103, *131*

Yellowwood: 11, 30, *charts* 80-81

Yew: *12-13*, 16, 21, *26*, 28, *29*, 31, *chart* 92, *chart* 103, *149*

Yucca: 8-9, 70

Z

Zantedeschia: 55

Zebra grass: 79

Zoysia: chart 40

Other Publications:
NEW HOME REPAIR AND IMPROVEMENT
JOURNEY THROUGH THE MIND AND BODY
WEIGHT WATCHERS® SMART CHOICE RECIPE COLLECTION
TRUE CRIME
THE AMERICAN INDIANS
THE ART OF WOODWORKING
LOST CIVILIZATIONS
ECHOES OF GLORY
THE NEW FACE OF WAR
HOW THINGS WORK
WINGS OF WAR
CREATIVE EVERYDAY COOKING
COLLECTOR'S LIBRARY OF THE UNKNOWN
CLASSICS OF WORLD WAR II
TIME-LIFE LIBRARY OF CURIOUS AND UNUSUAL FACTS
AMERICAN COUNTRY
VOYAGE THROUGH THE UNIVERSE
THE THIRD REICH
MYSTERIES OF THE UNKNOWN
TIME FRAME
FIX IT YOURSELF
FITNESS, HEALTH & NUTRITION
SUCCESSFUL PARENTING
HEALTHY HOME COOKING
UNDERSTANDING COMPUTERS
LIBRARY OF NATIONS
THE ENCHANTED WORLD
THE KODAK LIBRARY OF CREATIVE PHOTOGRAPHY
GREAT MEALS IN MINUTES
THE CIVIL WAR
PLANET EARTH
COLLECTOR'S LIBRARY OF THE CIVIL WAR
THE EPIC OF FLIGHT
THE GOOD COOK
WORLD WAR II
THE OLD WEST

*For information on and a full description of any
of the Time-Life Books series listed above, please call
1-800-621-7026 or write:*
Reader Information
Time-Life Customer Service
P.O. Box C-32068
Richmond, Virginia 23261-2068